As you journey through the pages of this book of devotion to the Word of God. As you listen, you will be encouraged to deepen your relationship with Jesus Christ. Betty McCutchan has a counselor's heart and passion for the truth found in God's Word. She invites others to taste and see that the Lord is good. I am grateful to her for being a faithful servant of Christ and a true friend.

ADA FERGUSON, MA Liberty University; counselor, First Baptist Church, Texarkana, TX.

No matter where one may be in their walk with Christ, Betty McCutchan's devotional brings to all a daily word of encouragement, guidance and comfort from God's Word. Like an unexpected gift, her word for the day may be just what is needed at the time—a trustworthy aid for the journey.

JAYNE PEARSON FAULKNER, author of *The Place of Belonging*

It gives me great pleasure to recommend this devotional book from my dear and admired friend, Betty McCutchan. Betty is a radiant Christian woman who has experienced the fiery trials of life—and seen God sustain her and bring her through. I know you will be blessed as you read her words of encouragement and devotion.

JEFF SCHREVE, pastor of First Baptist Church Texarkana, TX; From His Heart Ministries

We have had the great pleasure of meeting Mrs. Betty McCutchan and personally experiencing her love for Jesus. The sweet peace and presence of God flows out of her; you want to listen to her every word. Now we have that opportunity, through her devotion, *Listen to the Silence: Be Still and Know That He is God.* So grab your coffee or tea, sit down, and be blessed as you enter the sweet silence of your Creator. Receive all He has for you today and know that Mrs. Betty's wisdom will help transform you into the creation you were meant to be.

SHEA WOOD and SUSAN MILLIGAN, Lock and Key Ministries; authors of *Moving Him In*

Betty's comments on each daily scripture are practical and thought provoking. They uplift me and give me a purpose for each day. The Lord is really using Betty to make the Lord real in our lives. I highly recommend this book.

LLOYD E. GARY MD, retired OB-Gyn physician, Texarkana, TX

LISTEN TO THE SILENCE

Be Still and Know That He Is God

BETTY McCUTCHAN

Deep River BOOKS

Unless otherwise noted, scripture taken from the Holy Bible, New International Version (), Copyright 1973, 1978, 1984, 2011 by International Bible Society, Used by permission of Zondervan. All rights reserved.

Scripture taken from The King James Open Bible Expanded Edition. Copyright 1985 by Thomas Nelson, Inc.

Scripture taken from the New King James Version. Copyright 1982 by Thomas Nelson, Inc. Used by permission. All rights reserved.

Words to "Count Your Blessings" by Johnson Oatman Jr, 1897 (January 26)

Words to the Doxology by Thomas Ken, 1695 (February 4)

Words and music to "Turn Your Eyes upon Jesus" by Helen Howarth Lemmen, 1922 (March 14)

Published by
Deep River Books
Sisters, Oregon
www.deepriverbooks.com

ISBN-13: 9781937756833
ISBN-10: 1937756831
Library of Congress: 2013935447
Printed in the USA
Design by Robin Black, www.blackbirdcreative.biz

Blessed are the people who know the joyful sound!
They walk, O LORD, in the light of Your countenance.
In Your name they rejoice all day long,
And in your righteousness they are exalted.
PSALM 89:15–16 NKJV

NTRODUCTION

What I tell you in the dark,
speak in the daylight;
what is whispered in your ear,
proclaim from the roofs.
MATTHEW 10:27

God continually speaks to us. Yet time and again, we do not hear His voice. He tells us: *"What I tell you in the dark, speak in the daylight; what is whispered in your ear, proclaim from the roofs."* Yet our minds are cluttered, filled with anything and everything—and, if we're honest with ourselves, nothing of real importance.

Far too often, we convince ourselves that we are clever enough and skilled enough to handle whatever life throws our way. Nothing could be further from the truth. Without God, we can do nothing—nothing at all. But *with God all things are possible* (Matthew 19:26), because we *can do all things through Christ who strengthens* us (Philippians 4:13 NKJV).

Join me this year as we embark on a journey into the land of God's silence. Listen to His still, small voice as He speaks, encouraging us to pick up the pieces of our shattered lives, and allow Him to put us back together again while trusting Him in everything that crosses our paths.

Our God is a mighty God. He's powerful and full of love and compassion for His children. As He reaches down to us, let us reach up to Him and listen as He speaks His words of truth, love, wisdom, understanding, and comfort. He *will never leave us nor forsake us* (Deuteronomy 31:6). We are never alone.

JANUARY

JANUARY 1

You have made known to me the path of life;
you will fill me with joy in your presence,
with eternal pleasures at your right hand.

PSALM 16:11

It may seem as if our Heavenly Father has placed the wrong path beneath our feet. We don't want to experience the excruciating pain and sorrow and the feelings of hopelessness and loneliness that tag our heels. Nevertheless, our Father's still, small voice is continually within us, directing us the way we should go. Whether we listen or not, God always makes known to us His path of life. Whether we agree or not, His path remains beneath our feet.

When we embrace His way, our Heavenly Father fills us with joy in His presence, for He has promised He *will never leave* us *nor forsake* us (Deuteronomy 31:6). *The LORD your God is with you, he is mighty to save. He will take great delight in you, he will quiet you with his love, he will rejoice over you with singing* (Zephaniah 3:17).

When the Lord's present path ends and He gives us a new one on which to walk, it is then we comprehend the *eternal pleasures* He has placed *at* our *right hand*. We rejoice with Him as we see in ourselves more of what He created us in Christ to become.

I will sing to the Lord all my life; I will sing praise to my God as long as I live.
PSALM 104:33

JANUARY 2

The LORD is close to the brokenhearted
and saves those who are crushed in spirit.

PSALM 34:18

There are times in all of our lives when we want to fall face down on the floor, screaming at the top of our lungs. The agony and pain within us is unbearable. No one seems to understand that our spirits are crushed and our hearts are broken into trillions of pieces. We feel abandoned, and like David we cry aloud, "No man cares for my soul" (Psalm 142:4).

Even though we know God is close to the brokenhearted, we cannot seem to feel His presence in us, much less grasp that He stands beside us. Mankind might not understand us or reach out to us, but our Lord God always does. As our Heavenly Shepherd tucks His wounded ones in His arms, He busily picks up the pieces of our broken hearts and puts them back together again. He sings His sweet song of love as He heals our brokenness.

In God's time He always makes *everything beautiful.*
ECCLESIASTES 3:11

You, Lord, keep my lamp burning; my God turns my darkness into light.
With your help I can advance against a troop; with my God I can scale a wall.
PSALM 18:28–29

JANUARY 3

Therefore do not worry about tomorrow,
for tomorrow will worry about itself. Each day has enough trouble of its own.
MATTHEW 6:34

Many of us are worriers. It matters little if it is something that happened yesterday, is here already, or something that might come along tomorrow. We worry and agonize and then worry some more. Our Heavenly Father assures us that each and every day will bring its own trouble. What is the point of wasting our time and energy fretting about what was, what is, or what might be?

Far better for us to fall on our knees, raise our hands in praise to our Lord God, and cast all our burdens on His shoulders. In fact, God instructs us to toss all our cares on Him, and assures us He will never let us down because *He will never let the righteous fall* (Psalm 55:22).

Jesus Christ died so we could become God's righteous ones. It's far better to engage our Heavenly Father in conversation, talking with Him about our troubles while enjoying listening to Him speak His Words of love, wisdom, and assurance.

JANUARY 4

Delight yourself also in the LORD,
And he shall give you
the desires of your heart.
PSALM 37:4 NKJV

Nothing is more delightful than to talk with our Lord. We can tell Him anything and everything. We can pour out our hearts to Him, knowing He is not judging us but listening intently, waiting for us to complete our words before speaking His.

He knows the desires of our hearts before we even express them. The absolutely wonderful thing about this is He also knows that over time the desires of our hearts will change from what we want to what He wants for us.

He is ever patient in our conversations with Him. His silence speaks volumes, for we know He hears us clearly and wants the best for us. The sound of His voice is what calms our spirits and fully opens our eyes to His will for us.

It is then we know the deepest desire of our heart is to be in His will.

For with you is the fountain of life; in your light we see light.
PSALM 36:9

JANUARY 5

Do you not know that your body is the temple of the Holy Spirit,
who is in you, whom you have received from God?
You are not your own; you were bought at a price.
Therefore honor God with your body.
1 CORINTHIANS 6:19–20

God asks us a very important question through the apostle Paul, one that probably confuses many of us. Once we take Jesus Christ as our Lord and Savior, God implants His Holy Spirit in us. God's Spirit is there for a purpose: to lead us, to guide us, and to direct our paths. God owns us. He adopted us into His family—we have become children of God. The blood of His precious Son, Jesus Christ, paid for our sins, guaranteeing us eternal life.

Think about it. God in us, God with us, God completely around us. God clearly tells us that we are no longer our own. All of God's children have a mission: to glorify our Father with our bodies and our spirits because we no longer belong to ourselves.

Yes, we can do what we want to do, when we want to do it, and how we do it. God never takes away our free will—He always leaves the choice up to us. God's Spirit continually sings His love songs to us, reminding us He *will never leave* us *nor forsake* us (Deuteronomy 31:6). Our job is to listen to His Spirit in us. The more we listen and the more we obey what He tells us, the more joy and peace saturate our lives. Glorifying God means to obey Him—with our bodies and with our spirits, for they belong to our Heavenly Father, who redeemed us and brought us unto Himself.

> For none of us lives to himself alone and none of us dies to himself alone.
> If we live, we live to the Lord; and if we die, we die to the Lord.
> So whether we live or die, we belong to the Lord.
> ROMANS 14:7

JANUARY 6

I will instruct you and teach you
in the way you should go;
I will counsel you
and watch over you.
PSALM 32:8

When God makes a promise, He always keeps it. It is we, God's children, who often hear what He says but ignore it, much preferring to go our way instead of His way. We are never without His help. He is always there, and He always shows us the road to take and what to say, what to do, and how to behave while we're on it. Not only this, but as we walk with Him along His way, He continually whispers comforting words into our ears that we need to hear as He either allows or sends stumbling blocks to help us grow into what He desires we become.

The path we are on is called sanctification, which means growing in Christ and more fully understanding God's blueprint for our lives. If our paths were smooth and clear without pain, suffering, and anguish, we would never grow into what our Heavenly Father created us in Christ to become. It is through life's darkness that His light radiates through us, scattering His light along the paths we have trod, enabling others to grow in Christ as we have grown. Our Heavenly Father is not only our Teacher, but our Counselor as well.

> And we, who with unveiled faces all reflect the Lord's glory,
> are being transformed into his likeness with ever-increasing glory,
> which comes from the Lord, who is the Spirit.
> 2 CORINTHIANS 3:18

JANUARY 7

> *We live by faith,*
> *not by sight.*
> 2 CORINTHIANS 5:7

Faith believes what we do not see. Faith trusts what we cannot fathom. Trusting our Heavenly Father requires removing our hands from anything that God either sends or allows into our lives. To trust God means to turn our lives over to Him, believing He will calm our fears, soothe our pains, dry our tears, and fight our battles, while never abandoning us or forsaking us.

It is only when we release ourselves completely to His love for us, removing our hands from overseeing our lives and keeping our focus steadily on His watch-care over us, that it matters not what road is beneath our feet. *The Sovereign LORD is my strength; he makes my feet like the feet of a deer, he enables me to go on the heights* (Habakkuk 3:19).

If God is for us, who can be against us? (Romans 8:31). We *can do all things through Christ who strengthens* us (Philippians 4:13 NKJV). Our Heavenly Father assures us He will always *meet all* our *needs according to the riches of his glory in Christ Jesus* (Philippians 4:19).

> To our God and Father be glory for ever and ever. Amen.
> PHILIPPIANS 4:20

JANUARY 8

Therefore I tell you,
whatever you ask for in prayer,
believe that you have received it,
and it will be yours.
MARK 11:24

J esus Christ tells us that *whatever* we *ask in prayer,* if we *believe* we will receive it then it will come to us. Knowing that we so frequently ask amiss, God clarified His Words even further, as Jesus prayed at Gethsemane before His arrest while His disciples fell asleep instead of doing what He requested: *"Stay here and keep watch"* (Mark 14:34). Jesus' soul was deeply troubled and distressed. He fell on His knees and prayed that if it were possible, He might be spared the coming suffering of the cross. Then He said, *"Abba, Father, everything is possible for You. Take this cup from me. Yet not what I will, but what You will"* (Mark 14:35–36).

Too often we are like the three disciples, Peter, James, and John, whom Jesus awakened three times as He prayed before His arrest. They were to be watching and praying; but instead they fell asleep. Do we not hear Jesus' words either, as they probably could have if they had remained alert? *All things are possible with God.* We know this, but do we pray how Jesus prayed? He wanted God to take away His cup of suffering from Him. But, more than that, He wanted to accomplish God's will in Him, not His will for himself.

Do we, like Jesus, pour our hearts out to God, confessing to Him what it is we want, and then pray, "But, Lord, not my will for myself, but Your will for me"? Let us all remember Jesus' words as He prayed in the Garden of Gethsemane, *"Everything is possible for you. Take this cup from me. Yet, not what I will, but what You will"* (Mark 14:36).

JANUARY 9

You have made known to me the path of life;
you will fill me with joy in your presence,
with eternal pleasures at your right hand.
PSALM 16:11

As we listen carefully to God's directions for our lives, it does not completely astound us when the highway we are on is filled with pain, anguish, hurt, and sorrow. Even though we know we are on the path our Heavenly Father has placed beneath our feet, we do not want to be where He instructed us to go. We think it would be much better in the sunshine rather than in a valley of darkness.

Yet, if we are attentive as our feet sink into the slimy mud that threatens to completely engulf us, we sense His presence with us. It is then His joy fills our souls. It saturates us with the peaceful knowledge that what now seems so agonizing is empowering us to grow more into what our Heavenly Father created us in Christ to become.

Then we can pray as Jesus prayed: *"Not as I will, but as you will"* (Matthew 26:39).

Those who know your name will trust in you, for you, LORD,
have never forsaken those who seek you.
PSALM 9:10

JANUARY 10

Rejoice in the Lord always.
I will way it again: Rejoice!
PHILIPPIANS 4:4

As we all know, life can be hard—extremely demanding. It seems we no sooner come to the end of one soul-searching road that another challenging one bounces on its heels. And our Lord God tells us to rejoice always? In fact, He says it twice to emphasize His command. *Rejoice!*

When we feel as if the bottom has fallen from beneath our feet or that we're sinking in quicksand, this is the time to look heavenward and begin counting the blessings God has poured out on us during our travels with Him. Try it, for as we bring to remembrance even the smallest blessings in our lives, our hearts erupt with joyous words of thankfulness bursting from our lips. We cannot keep rejoicing at bay. It is spontaneous.

So, my brothers and sisters in Christ, let us rejoice in the Lord always by falling to our knees and praising Him for all the magnificent, mighty, and awesome people, places, and events He sends our way.

Glorious and majestic are his deeds,
and his righteousness endues forever.
PSALM 111:3

JANUARY 11

With your help
I can advance against a troop;
with my God
I can scale a wall.
PSALM 18:29

We all have times that we want to do nothing but throw our hands skyward and shout, "I give up. I just quit. It's impossible!"

It matters not what lies at our feet, commanding us to get up and move on. We feel helpless, unable to breathe, much less do what needs to be done or say the words God puts into our mouths other than, "Why me, Lord? Why me?"

Unless we remember what God tells each one of us: *"I can do all this through Him who gives me strength"* (Philippians 4:13), we cannot acknowledge that with His help we can *advance against a troop* and *scale a wall*. Nothing is impossible with God.

Do we hear this? Nothing is impossible with God. Absolutely nothing! We can accomplish anything and everything through our Lord God, who is always with us, encouraging us to keep on keeping on.

And my God will meet all your needs according to the riches of his glory in Christ Jesus.
PHILIPPIANS 4:19

JANUARY 12

They left and found things
just as Jesus had told them.
So they prepared the Passover.
LUKE 22:13

When the time came for Jesus' last Passover meal before His crucifixion, He told Peter and John to *"Go and make preparations for us to eat the Passover"* (Luke 22:7). As they left to complete this mission, they asked Jesus where He wanted them to go and prepare it. Jesus gave them explicit instructions, which they obeyed.

As Peter and John entered the city they met a man carrying a jar of water, just as Jesus said they would. They followed the man, and at the house they asked the owner the question Jesus told them to ask, *"The Teacher asks: 'Where is the guest room, where I may eat the Passover with my disciples?'"* (Luke 22:11). Just as Jesus predicted, the disciples were shown a large upper room, already furnished. All Peter and John had to do was make preparations there.

It is the same for all of God's children. God has specific instructions for each of us, and they are plain and clear. Whatever He tells us to do and how and when, our job is to obey. It is then we gleefully discover what Peter and John learned—we always find the answers to all questions when we ask the Heavenly Father exactly the way He says to ask.

Our task is to trust and obey Him, just as Peter and John did. The timeframe in which things happen is up to God, not to us. All that is ever required of us is to trust our Lord and obey His instructions.

Trust in the LORD with all your heart and lean not on your own understanding;
in all your ways submit to him, and he will make your paths straight.
PROVERBS 3:5–6

JANUARY 13

I say to myself,
"The LORD is my portion;
therefore I will wait for him."
LAMENTATIONS 3:24

Most of us have experienced standing in a cafeteria line waiting for those behind the counter to place a portion of food we select on a plate and hand it to us. We've also been behind someone who is indecisive, seemingly unable to make their preferences known. This is when many of us begin to become impatient, wanting to get on with our mission of getting our food and sitting down to eat.

Unfortunately, many of us act the same way when waiting for God's portion. He is always giving out His will for us. Wise children of God wait for Him to act, for in His time He places in our lives what we need to experience in order to grow into what He created us in Christ to become. But this is not what we want. This is not what we ordered. It's too agonizing, heartbreaking, and unbearable. We don't want what He puts on our plates.

At such times, we don't understand it is far better to sit at table with Him, talking with Him and opening up our hearts to Him about His path for us. No matter how hard we try, if we try at all, it seems impossible to comprehend the sweet aroma of His food of sorrow, excruciating pain, and brokenness. All we know is that the food of agony is atrocious. It isn't sweet at all. It's rotten to the core—and we want none of it. It seems all we can do is sit at His feet and scream, "Why, Lord? Please take it away. I can't stand it!"

It is then our Heavenly Father reaches across His table, places His Hand over ours, and whispers, "Wait, My child. Remember, I never put more on your shoulders than you can bear." He then begins humming familiar words, one we've heard many times before. *He has made everything beautiful in its time* (Ecclesiastes 3:11).

It is then we fall to our knees whispering, *"To everything there is a season. A time for every purpose under heaven"* (Ecclesiastes 3:1 NKJV).

JANUARY 14

We have this hope
as an anchor for the soul,
firm and secure.
It enters the inner sanctuary
behind the curtain,
where Jesus, who went before us,
has entered on our behalf.
HEBREWS 6:19–20

Everyone needs something to hold on to in order to keep from straying off course or sinking. Everyone needs an anchor. Our anchor is hope, placed in our hearts along with God's Holy Spirit when we become a child of God. Our *anchor* is *firm and secure*. It never fails. It is we who fail ourselves as we toss hope aside, depending on our own strength or abilities to sustain us, instead of trusting Jesus' anchor in us.

King Solomon tells us, *"Hope deferred makes the heart sick, but a longing fulfilled is a tree of life"* (Proverbs 13:12).

I can do all things through Christ who strengthens me.
PHILIPPIANS 4:13 NKJV

JANUARY 15

Yet, O LORD, you are our Father.
We are the clay, you are the potter;
we are all the work of your hand.
ISAIAH 64:8

Before a potter sits down at his wheel, he has a pattern in mind of what he wants to create. He will sit at his treadle, working over and over again to perfect the lump of clay in his hands. It is the same with our Lord God, the Great Potter. Once we accept Jesus Christ as our Lord and Savior, we become our Heavenly Father's clay. He has a specific design in mind as He lovingly works on our lump of clay.

He is willing and working out His good pleasure to bring His clay into what He desires each lump to be—the image of His Son, Jesus Christ. As we know, some clay is rigid and stiff, seemingly resistant to the Potter's touch. Others are soft and malleable, as if comprehending what the Workman endeavors to accomplish.

It matters not the texture of the original clay. The Potter knows the length of time and the work required to mold each clump into a beautiful piece of art. It takes longer for some than for others, but the end result is the same for all.

It is when the Potter beholds these works He places in His eternal room that rejoicing bursts forth as each artistic piece praises the Potter for His wonderful work in them.

> **I beseech you therefore, brethren, by the mercies of God,**
> **that you present your bodies a living sacrifice, holy, acceptable to God,**
> **which is your reasonable service.**
> ROMANS 12:1 NKJV

JANUARY 16

I consider that our present sufferings
are not worth comparing with the glory
that will be revealed in us.
ROMANS 8:18

Life is challenging, filled with all kinds of sorrows, burdens, and grief. But life is also imbedded with deep and nurturing pleasures. It is during those thought-provoking times when we believe that the puzzle pieces we experience cannot bring rest for our souls that we want to hang our heads in despair, believing we cannot endure what comes our way.

But, as children of God, we can and we will go on. Not only that, but we will reach God's goal for us—what He created us in Christ to become. It is then that we joyfully raise our hands in praise to Him, glorifying Him for His majestic work in us, knowing without Him we can do nothing, but in Him and with Him through Christ we can do anything.

> **But He said, "The things which are impossible with men are possible with God."**
> LUKE 18:37 NKJV

JANUARY 17

When you pass through the waters,
I will be with you;
and when you pass through the rivers,
they will not sweep over you.
When you walk through the fire,
you will not be burned;
the flames will not set you ablaze.

ISAIAH 43:2

We all have times when the murky waters of distress and sorrow press in so hard that we believe we cannot survive. We also cringe when rushing waters of troubles threaten to sweep us away. It is when the raging fire of agony absolutely engulfs us that we believe it's over—we're done for. But we are wrong. Nothing is impossible with God. God tells us to *put on* His *armor* He has provided for us so that we can stand firm in Him and resist anything and everything that life sends our way (Ephesians 6:11). We are God's Christian soldiers.

At such times, all that is required is to reach out and put on God's armor that He provides: *the belt of truth buckled around your waist, with the breastplate of righteousness in place, and with your feet fitted with the readiness that comes from the gospel of peace. In addition to all this take up the shield of faith, with which you can extinguish all the flaming arrows of the evil one. Take the helmet of salvation and the sword of the Spirit, which is the word of God* (Ephesians 6:14–17).

And pray in the Spirit on all occasions with all kinds of prayers and requests.

EPHESIANS 6:18

JANUARY 18

My soul clings to you;
your right hand upholds me.
PSALM 63:8

As we stroll down the streets of our towns, we often see many children walking beside an adult—a parent, grandparent, aunt or uncle or cousin or friend—clinging to their hand. This gives security. Children know that the hand they grip is their confidence, which empowers them to feel safe and secure. If someone approaches them or a strange dog growls at them or a car blows its horn, they do nothing more than tighten their hold on the hand woven around theirs.

We, who are children of the King, can do likewise. As we walk with Him each and every day, we are secure in Him. Yes, countless events parade before us and around us, seeking to grab us away from our Father's protection, injure us, and perhaps even destroy us. As trusting children learn and grow through life experiences, so too do God's children. We have nothing to fear, for no matter what comes our way God is always with us. The trials, tribulations, and hard times mature us, enabling us to be more than we ever thought we could be.

So let us learn from the child in us—trust in the hand that holds us close to Him, for it will uphold us.

Trust in the LORD with all your heart and lean not on your own understanding;
in all your ways submit to him, and he will make your paths straight.
PROVERBS 3:5–6

JANUARY 19

*The LORD is close to the brokenhearted
and saves those who are crushed in spirit.*
PSALM 34:18

Sometimes when the broken pieces of our hearts lay crumbled at our feet, we cannot seem to comprehend that our Lord God is hovering over us, whispering sweet words of reassurance into our ears. As hard as we try to do otherwise, we seem to be able to do nothing but wobble with the emptiness in us, feeling the agonizing pain and wretchedness seeping into our souls. It gives us the impression it's impossible to zero in on that which engulfs us. We want nothing to do with it.

When we remember that the Lord is our Shepherd our eyes begin to fully open so that we see Him more clearly—what He is doing in us and through us. Even though we can't comprehend that He is willing and working in us to become what He created us in Christ to be, we feel His hand clasp ours, sweetly telling us to *lie down in* His *green pastures*. We rejoice in His presence, knowing that after a time with Him in His meadowlands He will then lead us *beside still waters*, where He begins to restore our souls. It is then we once again feel His *paths of righteousness* beneath our feet (Psalm 23:1–3 NKJV).

As He anoints our heads with His oil, our cups overflow, knowing that surely His *goodness and love will follow us all the days* of our lives and we will live with Him in His house forever (Psalm 23:5–6).

The LORD is my shepherd, I shall not be in want.
PSALM 23:1

JANUARY 20

The angel of the LORD encamps around
those who fear him, and he delivers them.
PSALM 34:7

Isn't it electrifying and comforting to know that an angel of the Lord surrounds all who belong to our Lord God? Imagine God's angel positioned around us. Does this not mean that God's angel assigned to us is always there? That's what God tells us.

So with God's Holy Spirit indwelling us and His angel encamped around us, what more do we need in order to stay in constant communication with Him? We are never alone. We are never forsaken. Once we take Jesus Christ as our Lord and Savior, we belong to God—now and forevermore.

We have only one responsibility when this happens. Our assignment is to trust our Heavenly Father in all things. His Spirit indwells us. His *angel encamps around* us. Jesus Christ, His beloved Son, died for us on the cross so that we could be adopted into God's family. We are children of God. Fantastic!

How could we not fall on knees, raise our hands heavenward, and praise Him for all He has done for us, is doing for us, and will continue doing for us until we meet Him at heaven's gate.

There is therefore now no condemnation to those who are in Christ Jesus,
who do not walk according to the flesh, but according to the Spirit.
ROMANS 8:1 NKJV

JANUARY 21

Wherefore glorify ye the Lord in the fires,
even the name of the LORD God of Israel
in the isles of the sea.
ISAIAH 24:15 KJV

How pleasing it is to know God has placed us on a lovely highway. We revel in the sights we see and sing sweet songs of praise to Him. However, when that beneath our feet suddenly turns into searing pain, as if we're walking through a blazing fire of agony and suffering, we prefer a quick escape. Our fragrant melodies cease. Try as we will, we can do nothing but shout and scream and plead with our Father to release us from the misery scorching our souls and threatening to take us under. Our pleasant highway was short-lived; our fiery pathway seems unending and excruciating.

It is when we hear sweet songs of praise again springing from our souls—the same ones we once sang to our Lord—that we know beyond any shadow of doubt that, regardless of the highway we are on, Jesus is with us every step of the way. He holds us by His right hand, comforting us and encouraging us to keep on keeping on, for in His time God makes all things beautiful.

I can do all this through him who gives me strength.
PHILIPPIANS 4:13

JANUARY 22

If God is for us,
who can be against us?
ROMANS 8:31

At times, all of us will walk through the fires of adversity. We may even feel as if the world is against us, laughing at us, berating us, and pointing fingers of accusation toward us. At the same time, we know that the coals of fire burning our flesh and soul are there to enable us to grow into what He created us in Christ to become

Regardless of the flames of adversity consuming us and our inability even to toss the dirty waters at our feet to quench the fire seemingly eating us alive, it matters not that others are condemning us. *If God is for us,* (and He is) *who can be against us?*

Let us never throw in the towel with thoughts of giving up. *With God all things are possible* (Matthew 19:26). Hallelujah and amen!

JANUARY 23

Rejoice in the Lord always.
I will say it again: Rejoice!
PHILIPPIANS 4:4

The mail arrives. We receive an unexpected tax refund. Shouts of joy erupt. The phone rings. Our daughter informs us we are going to be grandparents. Our hearts burst forth in joy imagining holding that precious creature in our arms. When good news arrives no one has to tell us to *rejoice,* much less tell us to do it *again*; but when adversity comes calling it's another matter altogether.

When the train of sorrow beckons us to climb aboard, we want none of it. Why wrestle with the baggage already on it, much less toss more on top of it; far better to arrive at our destination another way. Fortunately, there is no other way. Fortunately? Absolutely! Eagerly get on board.

Think of it this way: God Almighty is our Great Teacher. We are His students. None of us are alike. We are all different, meaning our paths will not be the same. Just as earthly teachers use different techniques to reach each student with what is needed for each one to attain another level, so does our Great and Mighty One. Our diploma awaits us the moment we enter the gates of heaven. Then we will have attained God's goal for us. Finally, we will be totally and completely what He created us in Christ to become.

No matter the depths of despair along our roads, the sorrows that infiltrate our hearts, let us all *rejoice,* for we know what awaits us when we graduate from God's classroom. At all times on our earthly journey let us *rejoice* as we pray the prayer of Jesus:

Father, if you are willing, take this cup from me;
yet not my will, but yours be done.
LUKE 22:42

JANUARY 23

Then go inside and shut the door
behind you and your sons.
Pour oil into all the jars,
and as each is filled, put it to one side.
2 KINGS 4:4

The writer of 2 Kings relates the story of a widow who needed help. Her husband's creditor came to her house with the purpose of taking her two boys as his slaves for the debt her husband owed him. She called out for help from Elisha, God's prophet, and informed him of her plight.

Elisha asked her a question similar to what we are asked by our Lord God when we are in dire straits, not knowing which way to turn: *"How can I help you? Tell me what do you have in your house?"* (2 Kings 4:1–2). Jesus asks us the same question Elisha asked the widow, *"How can I help you?"* Our Lord then asks us, "How strong is your faith?"

The widow responded, telling Elisha she didn't have anything to help solve her problem *except a small jar of olive oil.*

During our troubled times, more than likely our response to our Lord is like hers. "I don't have anything to help myself, Lord. Even the faith I need for my circumstances has almost drained me of trusting You because in my weariness there is so little of it left."

It is then our Lord God reminds us of our need to bring prayer partners into the equation and then go inside and shut our door behind us. As others pray for us and we pray for ourselves, trusting God to respond in His time, our almost depleted faith that God will not abandon us or forsake us begins to fill us from head to toe. The more we trust God to intervene for us, the more our faith grows.

Just as the widow's son informed her there were no more jars left to fill and *the oil stopped flowing* (2 Kings 4:6), so too does God's Son tell us in Matthew 25:21, *"Well done, my good and faithful servant."* We have obeyed God's Spirit and done exactly what God instructed us to do. It is then we more fully understand our need to never let our faith run dry—for we are in need of it all the time, not only when circumstances appear to be swallowing us whole.

Surely God is my salvation; I will trust and not be afraid.
The Lord, the Lord himself, is my strength and my defense;
he has become my salvation.
ISAIAH 12:2

JANUARY 24

Who comforts us in all our troubles,
so that we can comfort those in any trouble
with the comfort we ourselves
have received from God.
2 CORINTHIANS 1:4

What would happen if we thought of ourselves as God's Christian soldiers marching into battle? Wouldn't we be less afraid and more confident of what lies ahead if the soldiers in front of us were more skilled warriors? Yes!

They are the ones who know how to encourage us. They are the ones who can teach us warfare skills. They are the ones who understand our trembling hearts and are willing to take time to walk alongside us, inspiring us and equipping us to walk through the same battles they have experienced. They are the ones who have been in dark, lonely, and despicable skirmishes themselves. They are the ones who believed they would never see daylight again, but they did!

And so will we. Why? Our experienced brothers and sisters in Christ were encouraged by our Lord God the same way He is now comforting us through them. Our present battles will enable us to reach out to those behind us just as those who are now ahead of us are doing for us.

Once we complete any battle the Lord lays beneath our feet, we know beyond any shadow of doubt His goal for us is to inspire others through what we ourselves have experienced. It was so dark, lonely, and despicable that we came to believe we would never see daylight again, but we did. Not only that, but the Lord continually whispers His sweet words of comfort into our ears, words that we once did not hear. In the dark, we had nothing to say, but in His light His words enable us now to comfort those traveling our previous highway.

In fact, we enthusiastically proclaim His learned words from rooftops, reaching out to others through the help of the hand that reached out to us.

What I tell you in the dark, speak in the daylight;
what is whispered in your ear, proclaim from the roofs.
MATTHEW 10:27

JANUARY 25

You are my lamp, O LORD;
the LORD turns my darkness into light.
2 SAMUEL 22:29

Nothing seems more pleasing than to light a candle in the darkness that surrounds us. But sometimes when our electricity suddenly goes out, no matter how much we search for a candle before nightfall descends, we can find nothing to light our way.

The same principle applies as we travel life's highways. All of us will eventually hit a black spot, one that completely engulfs us. Disliking darkness, we search for light—any kind of illumination that will keep us from going under because at the same time deep waters rise beneath our feet, terrifying us.

"Not fair, Lord!" we scream. "I don't need this! Bad enough to be in this when I can see clearly." We moan and groan. "Take it away, Lord!" we scream once again.

God never puts more on us than we can bear. He delights in us and in His time He will always light our paths. God reaches down from above and grabs our hands and in His light pulls us *out of deep waters* and darkness (2 Samuel 22:17).

It is then we know, we understand: *With your help I can advance against a troop; with my God I can scale a wall* (2 Samuel 22:30).

As for God, his way is perfect; the word of the LORD is flawless.
He is a shield for all who take refuge in him.
2 SAMUEL 22:31

JANUARY 26

The LORD is my strength and my defense;
he has become my salvation.
He is my God, and I will praise him,
my father's God, and I will exalt him.

EXODUS 15:2

After Moses led the Israelites through the Red Sea on dry ground, the Egyptian army pursued them. The Lord told Moses to stretch out his hand over the sea so that when the Egyptian army entered it they would be swallowed by the returning waters of the sea. The Lord saved the Israelites from the Egyptians. The Israelites saw God's great power, and the people put their trust in God and in His servant Moses. When they understood the Lord was their salvation and had become their strength, they began singing a song of praise to the Lord.

Whenever we become overwhelmed with that which is dogging at our heels, threatening to drag us under, we too must turn to our Lord God for His strength and trust Him to lead, guide, and direct us. If we still have trouble feeling overwhelmed with our circumstances, then let's open our mouths and sing and meditate on the words of this song:

Count your blessings, name them one by one.

Count your blessings, see what God has done.

Count your blessing, name them one by one.

Count your many blessings, see what God has done.

(See 1 Thessalonians 5:18.)

We cannot begin counting our blessings, naming each one, and reflecting on them, without raising our hands in praise and thankfulness to our Heavenly Father for blessing us so mightily and loving us with His everlasting love. Our hearts will overflow with His peace.

In your unfailing love you will lead the people you have redeemed.
In your strength you will guide them to your holy dwelling.
EXODUS 15:13

JANUARY 27

*I wait for the L*ORD*,*
my soul waits,
and in his word I put my hope.
PSALM 130:5

How do impatient people learn to wait? Through the writer of Psalm 130, God is explicit in informing us how it happens. We put our hope and trust in God's Word. We cannot completely trust that which we do not comprehend. Studying God's Word enables us to wait on Him because His instructions are clear and understandable. As we sit in His classroom, listen intently to His Words, and complete His assignments for us, we grow in Him, trusting Him and learning how to accomplish everything our Heavenly Father instructs us to do. He is our Teacher, and His Holy Spirit makes clear the words in our Textbook—His Holy Bible.

As we all know, it takes time to learn anything. King David of the Old Testament said: *"But I have stilled and quieted my soul; like a weaned child with its mother, like a weaned child is my soul within me"* (Psalm 131:2).

Over time and in His time, as God's children we learn everything necessary for us to grow in Christ. Our Heavenly Father weans us as we gradually mature in Christ, knowing His process in us is completed the moment He greets us in heaven.

Your word is a lamp to my feel and a light for my path.
PSALM119:105

JANUARY 28

Whatever you do,
work at it with all your heart,
as working the Lord,
not for men.
COLOSSIANS 3:23

Who wants to take the garbage out, much less walk the family dog or prepare for tomorrow's math exam? What about mowing the lawn in extreme heat or enduring the bitter cold while shoveling snow? Needless to say, these kinds of tasks can become annoying, not to mention wearying if we allow them. To avoid grumbling and exasperation, our Heavenly Father has a plan to get us through.

He instructs us to look to Him for encouragement. When we begin working—ignoring what is draining us of joyfully accomplishing our tasks, and, instead, concentrating on His work in us and the countless blessings He has bestowed on us—we begin rejoicing in Him with grateful hearts for His mercy and grace and love for us. Without the death of His Son, we would not know such an awesome Heavenly Father, one who loves us unconditionally.

No one can do for us what Jesus Christ did on the Cross. He redeemed us, enabling us to be adopted into God's family. Praise Him! Adore Him! Work for Him! *It is the Lord Christ you are serving* (Colossians 3:24).

And whatever you do, whether in word or deed,
do it all in the name of the Lord Jesus,
giving thanks to God the Father through him.
COLOSSIANS 3:17

JANUARY 29

Though the fig tree does not bud
and there are no grapes on the vines,
though the olive crop fails
and the fields produce no food,
though there are no sheep in the pen
and no cattle in the stalls,
yet I will rejoice in the LORD,
I will be joyful in God my Savior.
HABAKKUK 3:17–18

It doesn't matters what our Lord allows in our lives or sends into our lives. We may face times of scrounging around desperately searching for food, finding nothing whatsoever to nourish our bodies to stay alive. We may have lost our jobs, with no money to pay the rent or buy gasoline for a soon-to-be repossessed car. Our bank accounts are empty. We may receive word that a tornado ripped our house to shreds while we were away for the day; or our physician may inform us we have a terminal illness. We may even be tossed into the depths of despair as our beloved one breathes a last breath.

Habakkuk of Old Testament times became a prophet of God in 609 B.C. The Babylonian nation was close to destroying Jerusalem and taking the Israelites captive. Many of God's people rightly concluded they would be defeated and enslaved and dumped in a strange and ungodly land. They did not know what their future held. None of us do.

As Habakkuk warned what was to come for God's people, he inserted an important word not only to reassure and uplift them but to encourage us well. He penned the important word *yet* in his writings, one so often ignored during challenging times. Regardless of what comes into our lives, we must take hold of that key word. We must say from the depths of our beings, "No matter what looms ahead, *yet, I will rejoice in the LORD, I will be joyful in God my Savior.*" And then shout from the mountain tops, *"The Sovereign LORD is my strength; he makes my feet like the feet of a deer, he enables me to tread on the heights"* (Habakkuk 3:19). Thank You, Lord. Regardless of what happens, yet we will trust You and follow You, knowing You are with us and will never leave us.

Now the Lord is the Spirit; and where the Spirit of the Lord is, there is liberty.
But we all, with unveiled face, beholding as in a mirror the glory of the Lord, are being transformed
into the same image from glory to glory, just as by the Spirit of the Lord.
2 CORINTHIANS 3:17–18 NKJV

JANUARY 30

Above all else, guard your heart,
for everything you do flows from it.
PROVERBS 4:23

One definition of heart from the *Encarta Dictionary* says "the heart is the basis of emotional life, in fact the source and center of emotional life. It is where the deepest and sincerest feelings are located and a person is most vulnerable to pain."

Have you ever said, "My heart is broken"? Most of us have. This is why God tells us to *guard* our hearts—put a watch around them (Philippians 4:7). How do we accomplish this? Only when we comprehend that our hearts are the most vulnerable part of ourselves—the place where our emotional life, deepest yearnings, and state of mind reside—are we able through the strength of Christ in us to *guard* our hearts.

When we do so, we grasp the meaning of what God tells us when He says He is willing and working in us of His good pleasure to bring us into the image of His Son, Jesus Christ. Our Heavenly Father either sends or allows many hurtful situations to come into our lives. He does so to draw us closer to Him, knowing when we get on the other side of our broken hearts, we will fall to our knees and praise and thank Him for His work in us, which enables us to be what we could never have become had our hearts not been saturated with such agony.

It is then we know: *And the peace of God, which transcends all understanding, will guard your hearts and your minds in Christ Jesus* (Philippians 4:7).

JANUARY 31

I wait for the Lord, my whole being waits,
and in his word I put my hope.
PSALM 130:5

Many of us have difficulty waiting. It doesn't matter what we're waiting for. We want what we want, when we want it, and how we want it. Only as we fall to our knees petitioning our Heavenly Father and trusting Him in any and all things, do we learn the power of waiting for the Lord. Waiting for Him strengthens our hope in Him. Our Holy God never disappoints us—never.

A newborn baby doesn't immediately bloom into a teenager or a young adult or even a wise, old person. Growth takes time. No one signs up for any kind of class without waiting to comprehend what is being taught. It is waiting on the Lord that gives us hope—trusting that He knows not only what is best for us but also the time it will take us to digest it in His growing process in us.

Did not King Solomon tell us in Ecclesiastes 3:11, *He has made everything beautiful in its time*? God has put *eternity* in our hearts. We *cannot fathom what God has done* (and continues to do) *from beginning to end.*

Trust in the Lord with all your heart, And lean not on your own understanding.
In all your way acknowledge Him, And he will direct your paths.
PROVERBS 3:5–6 NKJV

FEBRUARY

FEBRUARY 1

You have made known to me the path of life;
you will fill me with joy in your presence,
with eternal pleasures at your right hand.

PSALM 16:11

When we accept Jesus Christ as our Lord and Savior, we become new creatures in Christ. We are born again. At this time, God places us on a new path called sanctification. The purpose is to grow us into what we could never be without being born again—into the image of His Son, Jesus Christ.

Our Heavenly Father also places other gifts into our hands—spiritual gifts. Our responsibility is to take what He has given us and use it to help others seek Him so they also will be gifted, helping all of us along His road of sanctification.

As we go, God fills us with joy in His presence, even during painful circumstances. We have nothing to fear for He is always with us. His *eternal pleasures* are *at* our *right hand* (Psalm 16:11).

I keep my eyes always on the LORD.
WITH HIM at my right hand, I will not be shaken.
PSALM 16:8

FEBRUARY 2

Reckless words pierce like a sword,
but the tongue of the wise brings healing.
PROVERBS 12:18

All of us have times when reckless words leak out of our mouths. It may be when we allow ourselves to become angry and speak before thinking, or it may happen when we're not even aware of the words that burst from our lips, or it could be we are inattentive to what is happening around us. It doesn't matter how or when it happens, we just know that if we don't place a guard around our lips before speaking, we often become guilty of uttering thoughtless comments—irresponsible words that can pierce the hearts of those to whom they are spoken.

King Solomon was wise when he said, *"The tongue of the wise brings healing."* So let us not rush in where angels fear to tread, but wait on the Lord to direct our paths. *He is faithful and just and will forgive us our sins and purify us from all unrighteousness* (1 John 1:9) and give us an ample supply of His God-glue to keep our mouths closed until He instructs us when to open them and what to say when we do.

Set a guard, O Lord, over my mouth; Keep watch over the door of my lips.
PSALM 141:3 NKJV

FEBRUARY 3

Consider it pure joy, my brothers and sisters,
whenever you face trials of many kinds,
because you know that the testing of your faith
produces perseverance.

JAMES 1:2–3

No one has ever ambled along life's highway without encountering roadblocks of troubles. It seems we no sooner bump into one problem that another and then yet another comes calling at our door. We want to do nothing but scream and hightail it in the opposite direction. It is then God's Spirit grabs our hand, drawing us closer to Him and whispering in our ears, "Trust Me, My child. Trust Me."

It is similar to sitting in front of our television engrossed in what we see and suddenly hearing a beeping sound, with words scrolling across the top of the screen saying, "Testing. Testing." It irritates us. We begin to mumble and complain, perhaps even shouting at the TV, "Why are you doing this now? You're interrupting my program." The TV doesn't respond, and the testing continues until completed.

If we're thinking clearly, what we see and hear can bring us joy. For by it and through it we grow to understand that the test is there for a reason: to make certain that what is presented can be seen clearly and heard correctly. It encourages us to trust the station to know what they are doing and why they are doing it when they're doing it. After all, it's only a trial, and our TV story continues through it.

Our Lord God's trials test our faith and trust in Him. They are there to encourage us to keep on keeping on the path beneath our feet, for by it and through it we are growing more and more into that which He created us to become. What joy!

Those who sow in tears will reap with songs of joy.
Those who go out weeping, carrying seed to sow, will return with songs of joy,
carrying sheaves with them.
PSALM 126:5–6

FEBRUARY 4

You have searched me, LORD, and you know me.
You know when I sit and when I rise;
you perceive my thoughts from afar.
You discern my going out and my lying down;
you are familiar with all my ways.
Before a word is on my tongue you know it completely.
PSALM 139:1–4

No human on the face of the earth knows us like our Heavenly Father knows us. No matter how hard we try, if we try at all, we can withhold nothing from Him. He even knows the number of hairs on our heads. And yet, He loves us in a way that is beyond human love or comprehension. When Jesus Christ takes our hand and introduces us to His Father in heaven, we are reconciled to God by Christ's death, burial, and resurrection, and presented to our Father God, *holy in his sight, without blemish and free from accusation* (Colossians 1:22).

Think about it: No one knows us like God knows us. And yet, His love for us is so overwhelming that it is beyond our intellectual capacity. Sometimes we ask ourselves how God could love someone who at times speaks so carelessly, thinks so sinfully, and behaves in such an ungodly manner; but He does, and He always will.

An earthly parent cannot do for us what our Heavenly Parent does for us. A spouse cannot love us the way our Father loves us. Our children cannot bring us the kind of joy our Heavenly Father etches into our beings. God is the Way, the Truth and the Life, and He loves us and knows us in a way no one ever has or ever will.

Praise God from whom all blessings flow. Praise Him all creatures here below.
Praise Him above ye heavenly host. Praise Father, Son and Holy Ghost. Amen!

FEBRUARY 5

My dear brothers and sisters,
take note of this:
Everyone should be quick to listen,
slow to speak
and slow to become angry.
JAMES 1:19

No matter how skilled or insightful we may think we are, God does not assign us to solve our own problems or those of others in our own strength or wisdom. God uses that which He implants in us to accomplish His will—rather than what we have accumulated over the years, thinking we have the capacity to do God's will on our own, while neglecting to wait and listen to Him. This is one of the reasons why we need to take note of what our Heavenly Father tells us through Jesus Christ's brother James.

Instead of being so quick to act and speak and get things done, we need to be quicker about listening to God before acting or speaking a word. God has the answer for everything; we do not. No matter how long it takes, we must wait on God. Always! We can do nothing in and of ourselves. *In His time*, God makes all things *beautiful—His time*, not our time (Ecclesiastes 3:11).

The longer we wait on Him and if anger does spring up, its pace will be slow enough for us to know what to do with it when we see it. Listening to God before speaking, and slowing down our behavior before acting, cools any anger that might infiltrate us along the way. Regardless of whether the problem is ours or belongs to someone else, we have been called to help. We must *be quick to listen, slow to speak, and slow to become angry.*

Do not let any unwholesome talk come out of your mouths,
but only what is helpful for building others up according to their needs,
that it may benefit those who listen.
EPHESIANS 4:29

FEBRUARY 6

Reckless words pierce like a sword,
but the tongue of the wise brings healing.
PROVERBS 12:18

What is our objective when speaking to those who have hurt us? Do we want to hurl words of insult, overwhelming the hearts and minds of those we desire to wound? Or, instead, do we want to utter soothing words to those who have purposefully offended us? God always gives us a choice. We can look to Him before speaking or we can rush in where angels fear to tread, crying out hurtful words.

In Psalm 139:17–18 King David said, *"How precious to me are your thoughts, God! How vast is the sum of them! Were I to count them, they would outnumber the grains of sand—when I awake, I am still with you."* David understood that our loving Father knew him through and through. Whether he was resting or walking, God not only was familiar with all his ways, but He perceived David's thoughts as well. David confessed he was *fearfully and wonderfully made* (Psalm 139:2–3, 14).

David pleaded with God to *search* him—to *know* his *heart.* He asked God to *test* him and check out his *anxious thoughts*, making sure there was no *offensive way* in him (v. 23–24). David also said, *"Before a word is on my tongue you, LORD, know it completely"* (v. 4).

If David, a man after God's own heart, checked out his words before speaking them, what keeps us from doing likewise? Wise words bring healing. Reckless words pierce like a sword. Let us take to heart a *life-giving* rebuke spoken to us, and let us lovingly speak *life-giving* rebukes to others when needed as well.

Whoever heeds life-giving correction will be at home among the wise.
PROVERBS 15:31

FEBRUARY 7

Therefore, as God's chosen people,
holy and dearly loved,
clothe yourselves with compassion,
kindness, humility, gentleness and patience.
COLOSSIANS 3:12

As we awaken each morning and prepare for the day ahead of us, what do we choose to wear? God has laid out His clothing for us, consisting of compassion, kindness, humility, gentleness, and patience to name a few. Too often, probably in hastiness and wanting to get on with our day's schedule, we ignore the clothing our Father laid out and instead select our own attire of impatience, pride, abruptness, rudeness, and perhaps even our favorite cap of independence.

Our Lord God assures us through the writings of the apostle Paul that we are His *chosen people*. What a magnificent gift! Not only has He chosen us, but He tells us that we are *dearly loved* and we are *holy*. Holy means set apart—we are consecrated to God for His service and for godly living. He is our Heavenly Father.

Because we are each God's child, one whom He has chosen and loves dearly, would it not be wiser and more prudent of us to clothe ourselves in what our dear Parent has laid out for us to wear? Of course, it would. But as earthly parents, we know that our children often rebel at what we require of them. It is only as they begin maturing that they learn our ways and what we expect of them.

We are babes in Christ when we begin our journey with our Heavenly Father. As we mature in Him, we listen more attentively to what He instructs us to do and grow into what He has called us to be.

Bear with each other and forgive one another if any of you has a grievance against someone.
Forgive as the Lord forgave you. And over all these virtues put on love,
which binds them all together in perfect unity.
COLOSSIANS 3:13–14

FEBRUARY 8

But he said to me,
"My grace is sufficient for you,
for my power is made perfect in weakness."
2 CORINTHIANS 12:9

God's grace is His undeserved and unearned favor. When we take God's Son, Jesus Christ, as our Savior, God adopts us into His family. By God's grace, we become children of the King. As such, we lack for nothing. Our Father supplies all our needs—every one of them. We are never alone, for He is continually with us. No matter what enters our lives, our Father equips us with everything necessary to cope.

His power is made perfect in our weakness. Note that Almighty God did not tell us to depend on others or ourselves. We are to totally rest in His perfect power in us. We can do nothing in and of ourselves. *God will meet all* our *needs, according to the riches of his glory in Christ Jesus* (Philippians 4:19).

I can do all this through him who gives me strength.
PHILIPPIANS 4:13

FEBRUARY 9

The path of the righteous is level;
You, the Upright One,
make the way of the righteous smooth.
ISAIAH 26:7

Regardless of the rocks or debris beneath our feet as we travel the King's Highway, our Heavenly Father enables every one of His children to continue on the path He places us on. Regardless of the excruciating pain, feeling as if we are being ripped to shreds, we know through His Holy Spirit in us that we can wait for Him to lead us onward to His glorious pathways of sunshine and warmth. We can take in His glorious riches that in His time will soothe our sorrowful and throbbing hearts.

When we look backward at the debris behind us, we will fall to our knees and raise our hands in praise heavenward, for our Lord is growing us into something more than we ever could have become without traveling with Him on such roadways. Then we more fully understand how great His love for us is as He continues to grow us into the image of His Son.

You will keep in perfect peace those whose minds are steadfast, because they trust in you.

ISAIAH 26:3

FEBRUARY 10

Look to the LORD *and his strength;*
seek his face always.
PSALM 105:4

What do we do when we search for something we've misplaced or lost? We look for it, spending countless moments, days, or even years in our pursuit. We may even tell ourselves that, no matter how long it takes, we will find that for which we are searching.

As children of God we desperately need our Father's strength to withstand the howling winds of adversity and turmoil that dog our heels during our earthly journey. Completing a task or mission given us by our Father cannot be done in our own strength. Try as we might, we will always fail. If we are to succeed in fulfilling our God-given tasks, we must *seek His face always*—meaning just what says—always.

How do we accomplish this? The only way to know God in the way He wants us to know Him is to learn all we can about His ways, His plans, and His will for our lives. The only place we can find His answers is through immersing ourselves in His Word and through prayer and being in His presence. Far too many of us don't spend enough time this way. We believe our lives are too busy to take the time to achieve this.

Ask and it will be given to you; seek and you will find,
knock and the door will be opened to you. For everyone who asks receives;
the one who seeks finds; and to the one who knocks, the door will be opened.

MATTHEW 7:7–8

FEBRUARY 11

And we know that
all things work together for good
to those who love God,
to those who are the called
according to His purpose.
ROMANS 8:28 NKJV

No matter what enters the life of a child of God, God the Father takes it and works it into His child's life for His child's good. When Adam and Eve did that which God commanded them not to do, sin entered the world. As a result, everyone has *sinned and* fallen *short of the glory of God* (Romans 3:23). Every human being has a sin nature. Everyone is in need of a Savior—Jesus Christ, who took our sins and paid the penalty for them—to cleanse us and declare us righteous before the throne of God.

Our old sin nature remains in us, but as we walk God's pathways clutching our Heavenly Father's Hand, He enables us to recognize when we sin and forgives us as we confess sin to Him.

Not only this, but as we trust Him and wait on His guidance and leading, He takes even the most agonizing events that place a stumbling block beneath our feet and enables us to experience a joy we would never know had He not allowed us to walk such a path.

Nothing is sweeter for a child of God than to look back on such a passageway, as we are filled with praise and thanksgiving, knowing we could never be who God created us in Jesus Christ to become had such a stumbling block not hindered our path. We become more and more of who God predestined us to become.

Dear friends, now we are children of God,
and what we will be has not yet been made known. But we know that when Christ appears,
we shall be like him, for we shall see him as he is.

1 JOHN 3:2

FEBRUARY 12

Come to me,
all you who are weary
and burdened,
and I will give you rest.
MATTHEW 11:28

After saying these words, Jesus tells us to take His yoke He puts on us and learn from what He has allowed to come into our lives. A yoke is a harness placed on an ox's shoulders so that the animal can complete the task of its master. As a child of the King, we are to complete that which our Father has placed on our shoulders to accomplish His mission for us. In so doing, we know He is *gentle and humble in heart* because our Teacher has taught us this through multiple tasks He has given us. God is with us and nothing He sends our way can prevent us from discovering His *rest for our souls* through His work in us (Matthew 11:29).

So let us remember His words as we smile heavenward to Him, calling to mind what Jesus said, *"For my yoke is easy and my burden is light"* (v. 30). Praise God from whom all blessings flow.

FEBRUARY 13

But when he saw that the wind was boisterous,
he was afraid; and beginning to sink
he cried out, saying, "Lord, save me!"
MATTHEW 14:30 NKJV

No children of God have ever walked with the King without experiencing times of deep terror when the waters beneath our feet begin surging, threatening to boil over, seemingly wanting to drown us and leave nothing but a whisper of us behind. The only thing we can do and we know to do is scream out Peter's words, *"Lord, save me!"*

Peter and the disciples were in a boat out in the Sea of Galilee, *tossed by the waves, for the wind was contrary* (Matthew 14:24 NKJV). It was the middle of the night, and they saw Jesus' approaching them, walking on the water, which frightened them. Jesus called out, *"Take courage! It is I. Don't be afraid"* (v. 27).

Peter responded, "Okay, *if it's you, Lord*, just command *me to come*, and I will" (v. 28).

Jesus said, *"Come,"* and *Peter* immediately *got out of the boat* and began walking on water. It was then Peter apparently noticed the boisterous *wind* surrounding him, and he began *to sink* (v. 29–30).

Peter did exactly what we have done multiple times when walking toward our Lord Jesus Christ, obeying His order to come when He has a mission for us to accomplish. We immediately respond, but as we approach Him, we encounter the winds of fierce opposition pulling us downward and threatening to engulf us. Terror fills our hearts. We shout with Peter, "Help me, Jesus!" And of course, He does!

Jesus says to us as He did to Peter and His disciples afterwards, *"O you of little faith, why did you doubt?"* (v. 31). We fall to our knees as did His disciples and worship Him, articulating their very words, *"Truly you are the Son of God"* (v. 33).

Never fear. God enables us to do what He calls us to do, but if or when fear overtakes us, let us just cry out, "Help me, Jesus," knowing He will never let us sink. Never!

If God is for us, who can be against us?
ROMANS 8:31

FEBRUARY 14

*Always giving thanks
to God the Father for everything,
in the name of our Lord Jesus Christ.*
EPHESIANS 5:20

Our Lord God admonishes us through the apostle Paul to thank Him *for everything*. Everything? Yes, everything. No matter what comes into our lives, how long it lasts, or how disheartening it might be, we are to raise our voices in thanksgiving and praise to our Father. I have never known an earthly child to thank a parent for a scolding or a punishment, or for requiring regular attendance at school or good manners. When such thankful words do come from their mouths, it's usually when they have matured and reached a time when they are grateful for such. Then they rejoice that their parents loved them enough and enabled them to grow into what they could never have become without such parental love and discipline.

As children of God, we are growing and maturing in Christ. We may not feel like being grateful for all the circumstances God either allows or sends into our lives. Yet once they are completed, a deep joy that passes all understanding fills us as we begin to comprehend we could never be who we now are had our Heavenly Father not allowed us to walk with Him through our deep valleys of agony and distress.

For it is God who works in you to will and to act in order to fulfill his good purpose.
PHILIPPIANS 2:13

FEBRUARY 15

My flesh and my heart may fail;
but God is the strength of my heart
and my portion forever.
PSALM 73:26

If we're really honest with ourselves, none of us can claim we haven't tossed our hands into the air and shouted something like, "I give up, Lord. I just give up! I quit!" This doesn't mean we've turned away from God or His salvation. It just means we don't believe we can keep on doing what our Heavenly Father called us to do. It may be teaching a Sunday School class or singing in the choir or ministering to the elderly or taking care of a loved one or working for a mean boss or just being at home watching our kids mess up what we've just cleaned. We feel drained of every ounce of energy within us. Not only is our desire missing, but so is our strength.

When our hearts begin sinking, we're not aware that it is God's strength in us—not our strength in ourselves—that enables us to do the work. It is when we do not turn to Him for His strength to do what He has asked us to do that our flesh weakens and our hearts begin to fail.

This is a time to look Godward, remembering what He has so often said to us: "Rest in me, My child. Trust Me to renew your depleted strength and your weary heart. Do you not remember My portion is always there? It never runs dry. Trust Me, My child."

Then, looking heavenward, we thank Him for who He is and what He does for us—enabling us to keep on keeping on, for His strength in us is more than enough to do that which He calls us to do.

I can do all things through Christ who strengthens me.
PHILIPPIANS 4:13 NKJV

FEBRUARY 16

*You guide me with your counsel,
and afterward you will take me into glory.*
PSALM 73:24

I saiah writes that in God's time He would send His Son into the world *and the government will be on His shoulders. And He will be called Wonderful Counselor, Mighty God, Everlasting Father, Prince of Peace* (Isaiah 9:6). All of us have experienced Jesus as *Mighty God, Everlasting Father,* and *Prince of Peace,* but perhaps not all of us have gazed His way acknowledging He is also a *Wonderful Counselor.* Jesus is our holy Therapist—meaning He is available to us for healing—but unlike human counselors there is no need to schedule an appointment. All that is needed is to enter a quiet place, where He is waiting to talk with us about any and all things on our minds and in our hearts.

It matters not the questions we ask or the troubles we confess or the advice we seek. In the depths of our beings we know He already knows us as we truly are and loves us no matter what. We are free to open ourselves completely to Him, accepting His words of wisdom as He takes us by the hand and guides us to His light, which enables us to see that for which we seek.

Then we can continue on the day's adventures knowing He is with us and *will never leave us nor forsake* us (Deuteronomy 31:6). Praise God from whom all blessings flow!

**I will praise the Lord, who counsels me; . . . I keep my eyes always on the Lord.
With him at my right hand, I will not be shaken.**

PSALM 16:7–8

FEBRUARY 17

He put a new song in my mouth,
a hymn of praise to our God.
Many will see and fear the LORD
and put their trust in him.

PSALM 40:3

King David, whom God proclaimed was a man after His own heart, experienced count-less troubles in his lifetime. Knowing that God would always lift him out of a *slimy pit, out of the mud and mire* (Psalm 40:2) and give him a firm place to stand, he acknowl-edged his need to *wait patiently for the Lord* to act on his behalf (v. 1).

A man of God who could voice such words centuries before God revealed Himself through His Son, Jesus Christ, whom the apostle Paul preached about after Jesus' death and resurrec-tion, is awe-inspiring.

David never heard of Paul or read the words he wrote: *"Therefore we do not lose heart. Though outwardly we are wasting away, yet inwardly we are being renewed day by day. For our light and momentary troubles are achieving for us an eternal glory that far outweighs them all. So we fix our eyes not on what is seen, but on what is unseen, since what is seen is temporary, but what is unseen is eternal"* (2 Corinthians 4:16–18).

Yet David knew, as in our day we now know, *we have this treasure in jars of clay to show that this all-surpassing power is from God and not from us* (2 Corinthians 4:7).

Praise God that even though *we are hard pressed on every side,* we are not *crushed.* We may be *perplexed,* but we do not *despair.* Even if we are *persecuted,* we are never *abandoned.* Even if we are *struck down,* we will not be *destroyed* (2 Corinthians 4:8–9).

We always carry around in our body the death of Jesus,
so that the life of Jesus may also be revealed in our body.

2 CORINTHIANS 4:10

FEBRUARY 18

We do not want you to be uninformed,
brothers and sisters,
about the troubles we experienced
in the province of Asia.
We were under great pressure,
far beyond our ability to endure,
so that we despaired of life itself.
2 CORINTHIANS 1:8

Along God's road of redemption and the more we mature in Jesus Christ, the more we comprehend God's words through the apostle Paul—*troubles we experienced*. More than likely, our troubles won't be in the province of Asia, but nevertheless adversities will come. However, we will be *under great pressure, far beyond our ability to endure, so that we despair even of life*. Some of us may not yet have encountered pressures that have caused us to *despair even of life*, but the more mature we grow in Christ the nearer we are to being in this short-lived state, for that what's it is—brief.

It isn't until it is past us that we understand God allowed it in our lives for His purpose—to grow us into the image of His Son, Jesus Christ. When we comprehend this, we fall to our knees and thank Him for allowing us to travel such a road. We look at ourselves and grasp that we could never be what we now are had our Heavenly Father not allowed us to experience such troubles.

Come to me, all you who are weary and burdened, and I will give you rest.
Take my yoke upon you and learn from me, for I am gentle and humble in heart,
and you will find rest for your souls. For my yoke is easy and my burden is light.
MATTHEW 11:28–30

FEBRUARY 19

Everything is possible for one who believes.
MARK 9:23

One day when Jesus was walking with His disciples, a man approached Him with his son at his side. The man told Jesus that the boy was possessed by an evil spirit that had made his son unable to speak. His son also had seizures so fierce that they threw him to the ground and he foamed at the mouth and gnashed his teeth while his body became rigid. He then told Jesus that he had asked His disciples to rid his son of the evil spirit, but they were unable to do it (Mark 9:14–18).

Jesus responded by saying, *"You unbelieving generation. . . . How long shall I put up with you? Bring the boy to me"* (v. 19).

They brought the boy to Jesus, and the evil spirit *threw the boy into a convulsion. He fell to the ground and rolled around, foaming at the mouth* (v. 20)

Jesus then asked the man how long the boy had been like this (v. 21).

"From childhood," the father responded. He went on to tell Jesus that the spirit frequently threw his son into fire or water to kill him. Then the man said, *"If you can do anything, take pity on us and help us"* (v. 22).

"'If you can?'" said Jesus. "Everything is possible for one who believes" (v. 23).

The man then told Jesus, *"I do believe; help me overcome my unbelief!"* (v. 24).

Jesus rebuked the evil spirit, saying, *"I command you, come out of him and never enter him again"* (v. 25).

Shrieking, the evil spirit caused the boy to convulse violently again and then left the boy. Everyone around thought the boy was dead, but Jesus reached for the boy's hand and lifted him to his feet. Jesus and His disciples then left the scene, and the disciples asked him a question we so frequently voice: *"Why couldn't we drive* the evil spirit *out?"* (v. 28).

"This kind can come out only by prayer," Jesus replied (v. 29).

"Everything is possible for one who believes" (v. 23). Nothing, absolutely nothing is impossible for God.

Ask and it will be given to you; seek and you will find;
knock and the door will be opened to you. For everyone who asks receives; the one who seeks finds,
and to the one who knocks, the door will be opened.
LUKE 11:9–10

FEBRUARY 20

And my God will meet all your needs
according to the riches of his glory
in Christ Jesus.
PHILIPPIANS 4:19

Our Father never told us He would give us everything we want. He supplies *all* our *needs*—not all our wants. How grateful we are that He doesn't give us everything we want. Grateful? Absolutely! Think about it. If God supplied all our wants, what kind of people would we be?

Idolatrous, that's what! Do we not already grapple enough with idolatry? Even now it surrounds as we bow down to people, events, and things to which we're not even aware we are submitting. We somehow believe if we had a car like our friend's we would be happy, or if our house looked as grand and glorious as another's we would dance for joy. We even seek to belong to the "in" crowd and not the one we're already in. And what about cravings to go on fantastic, incredible vacations we hear others talk about, and also believing if we were the boss of our work life would be easier and simpler and so much better?

As parents, if we gave our children everything they wanted, what kind of adults would they become? Not the kind of people we enjoy being around. On the other hand, if we give our children the things needed for them to grow into responsible adults, usually they become exactly that—people who bring great joy to those who surround them.

Our Heavenly Father loves us and wants the very best for us. He wants us to mature and grow into what He created us in Christ to become. Nothing brings more joy into our lives as knowing, believing, and trusting that God supplies everything we *need* along our journey with Him.

For with you is the fountain of life; in your light we see light.
PSALM 36:9

FEBRUARY 21

For I am convinced that neither death nor life,
neither angels nor demons,
neither the present nor the future,
nor any powers,
neither height nor depth,
nor anything else in all creation,
will be able to separate us
from the love of God
that is in Christ Jesus our Lord.
ROMANS 8:38–39

The apostle Paul was committed to what His Heavenly Father called him to do—create churches by spreading the news of His Son, Jesus Christ, who died a sacrificial death so that those who come to the Father through His Son live eternally. Paul's mission wasn't easy; in fact it was filled to the brim with threats of death, imprisonment, and agonizing dilemmas and tribulations. Yet, no matter who or what crossed his path threatening to take him out, he never gave up. His mission was to complete what God called him to do.

Few are called to live the kind of life Paul lived, but all of us are called to be faithful to what God has enabled us to do. As we grow in Christ, we develop an awareness of His spiritual gift or gifts He placed in us when He adopted us into His family. God's mission for us is to use that which He gave us to help our church body grow in Christ and to spread the good news of salvation provided by the death and resurrection of His Son.

Some have a tendency to think of their spiritual gifts as inconsequential, not even meaningful enough to enable others to grow in Christ. Think again. One miniscule cell in a human body is essential to keep the whole body functioning correctly, effectively, and healthily. So let us keep on keeping on in that which our Heavenly Father has called us to do, trusting and thanking God for allowing us to be a part of His work, and assured our work is never insignificant or trivial.

I can do all this through him who gives me strength.
PHILIPPIANS 4:13

FEBRUARY 22

But Martha was distracted
by all the preparations
that had to be made.
She came to him and asked,
"Lord, don't you care
that my sister has left me
to do the work by myself?
Tell her to help me!"
LUKE 10:40

If we are attuned to God's Holy Spirit in us, we can hear His still, small voice calling out our name saying, *"You are worried and upset about many things"* (Luke 10:41).

"Yes, Lord, I am," we confess. "I have so much on my plate and so little time to get everything done. I don't even know where to begin."

Of course, we know where to begin—we just don't begin at the beginning. Instead, we spend far too much time ruminating about our problems and what is to be done rather than falling to our knees and petitioning our Heavenly Father, seeking His guidance. Mary, Martha's sister, understood her need to sit at the feet of Jesus and listen to Him (v. 39). On the other hand, Martha *was distracted by all the preparations that had to be made.* She wasted precious time flitting about here, there, and yonder, doing chores and allowing herself to become angry that Mary wasn't helping her accomplish these tasks.

Instead of sitting beside Mary at Jesus' feet, listening to Him talk and saturating her mind with His precious words, Martha chose to focus on what she believed was more important—getting a meal on the table. While doing so, she became irritated that Mary didn't help her but instead remained in Jesus' presence.

Do we not do the same each morning when we arise? Instead of opening our Bible and seeking a quiet and secluded place to commune with our Heavenly Father, we begin the day contemplating what our day holds and how to get it done rather than seeking God's will and direction first. It is imperative for us to first sit quietly in His presence and listen to Him, for if we do not we quickly become a "Martha."

Only one thing is *needed*—begin at the beginning, and God will take care of the rest.

"Martha, Martha," the Lord answered,
"you are worried and upset about many things, but few things are needed—or indeed only one.
Mary has chosen what is better, and it will not be taken away from her."

LUKE 10:41–42

FEBRUARY 23

Your word is a lamp for my feet
and a light on my path.
PSALM 119:105

Walking in total darkness is alarming. Not being able to see what is beneath our feet or in which direction we're proceeding takes away our breath. Even if our pathway is momentarily lighted and we have been given instructions how to reach our destination, we cannot be sure we are on the right road. Perhaps the light will go out in the middle of our journey or we make a wrong turn and cannot get back on track. Then what?

From time to time, feelings of being in darkness—not certain if we've made a correct choice or if we're walking in foolishness—creep up on us. This is why staying connected to our Heavenly Father and continually listening to Him is so vital. As we trust His words and the pathway on which He has placed us, we have no reason to fear. He will never abandon us. It is we who occasionally take detours or light our own candles that ignite anxiety and worry within us.

Remaining grounded in Him, trusting Him, continually listening to Him, and obeying His Holy Spirit keeps us safe and secure.

How sweet are your words to my taste, sweeter than honey to my mouth!
I gain understanding from your precepts; therefore I hate every wrong path.
PSALM 119:103–104

FEBRUARY 24

Whatever you do,
work at it with all your heart,
as working for the Lord,
not for human masters.
COLOSSIANS 3:23

It doesn't matter what we are in the process of working at or on. It doesn't matter if our task is simple and easy or powerful and strong. Regardless of what it is or who assigned it or if our job depends on it, if we do not *work at it with all* of our *heart* as if it is a mission from our Heavenly Father and not from our boss or teachers or parents or ourselves, we will not succeed at it—not in the way our Lord expects us to or we desire to.

Successful work requires putting our whole heart into it, *as working for the Lord* and not for others or ourselves.

And whatever you do, whether in word or deed,
do it all in the name of the Lord Jesus, giving thanks to God the Father through him.
COLOSSIANS 3:17

FEBRUARY 25

Come near to God
and he will come near to you.
JAMES 4:8

People love to receive invitations. It doesn't matter to what we're invited, for we have been asked by someone else to be in their company. The majority of times it delights us and causes us to feel special.

The Lord God has sent every human being on the face of earth an invitation to become a part of His family. All that is required is to positively respond to Him, thanking Him for inviting us to become His child, and accepting His invitation.

On arriving we meet His Son, the One who made it possible for us to be invited. Our brothers and sisters in Christ are rejoicing, encouraging us to become one with the Father as they now are. Our hearts rejoice!

It is then we realize we are different; we are no longer what we once were. We are new creatures in Christ. Our Heavenly Father's Holy Spirit indwells us, leading, guiding, and directing our lives. As we listen to Him, we begin to grow into what God created us in Christ to become—with all kinds of wonderful qualities we could never possess on our own. Deep within, we know there is no way we can accomplish anything without Him at our sides.

As we open His Holy Book in our hands and begin not only reading it daily and meeting with Him to talk about what we've read and experienced in our walk with Him, we frequently reach into our pockets and pull out an old invitation that He placed in our hands years ago. It says, "Draw near to me, and I will come near to you."

"Yes, Lord," we softly respond. "I know I can't do anything for myself or by myself, but I can do anything and all things through Your Son, Jesus Christ, who strengthens me."

At that moment we look heavenward with outstretched hands, reaching out for the hand that is reaching down to us.

> For God so loved the world that he gave his one and only Son,
> that whoever believes in him shall not perish but have eternal life.
> JOHN 3:16

FEBRUARY 26

For the revelation awaits
an appointed time;
it speaks of the end
and will not prove false.
Though it linger, wait for it;
it will certainly come
and will not delay.
HABAKKUK 2:3

God's prophet Habakkuk lived in a most difficult time during the reign of Jehoiakim, king of Judah. Habakkuk couldn't understand why his Lord did not put a stop to all the injustice, violence, strife, conflict, and destruction that surrounded him in his homeland. He complained to God saying, *"The law is paralyzed, and justice never prevails. The wicked hem in the righteous, so that justice is perverted"* (Habakkuk 1: 4). Habakkuk wanted God to respond to his call to Him for help and couldn't understand why God didn't immediately respond to his complaints.

God told Habakkuk to look at the nations around him because when he did, he would be utterly amazed at what God was going to allow to happen. He let his prophet know that even if He told him what He was in the process of doing, he wouldn't believe it. More than likely it stunned Habakkuk to hear God tell him the Babylonians, a ruthless and godless nation, would sweep over them and conquer Judah.

It was like the prophet was saying, "Lord, I know our nation is heading in an evil direction, but why would you allow *the wicked to swallow* us *up*—who are not as evil as they are?" (v. 13).

Habakkuk wanted an understandable response to his questions and, like us, wanted it right then.

If we listen to the words Habakkuk wrote and his stunning amazement about whom God would use to discipline his homeland, perhaps we will understand our own predicaments today. Our nation is not the nation it once was. We are turning from God and going our own way. We are admonished in 2 Chronicles 7:14 (NKJV): *"If My people who are called by My name will humble themselves, and pray and seek My face, and turn from their wicked ways, then I will hear from heaven, and forgive their sin and heal their land."*

Let us pray this prayer to our Lord God and sing the hymn of faith Habakkuk sang: *Though the fig tree may not blossom, Nor fruit be on the vines; Though the labor of the olive may fail, And the fields yield no food; Though the flock may be cut off from the fold, And there be no herd in the stalls—Yet I will rejoice in the LORD, I will joy in the God of my salvation. The LORD God is my strength; He will make my feet like deer's feet, And He will make me walk on my high hills* (Habakkuk 3:17–19 NKJV).

God holds America's future in His hands. In His time, He makes all things *beautiful* (Ecclesiastes 3:11). Let us turn from our wicked ways and turn back to God.

FEBRUARY 27

May your unfailing love be my comfort,
according to your promise to your servant.
PSALM 119:76

Our Lord God is trustworthy. He is dependable. His love for us never fails, regardless of what we say or do or think. No matter what comes along for us in life, no matter how disquieting or agonizing it might be, He will comfort us in it and through it. He is our Holy Shepherd. Even when or if we stray from His flock, He will leave His fold and come find us and rescue us, calling us by name, and putting us back in His sheep pen.

Once His sheep, always His sheep. Once we belong to Him, we will always belong to Him—no matter what.

I will praise God's name in song and glorify him with thanksgiving.
PSALM 69:30

FEBRUARY 28

Take delight in the LORD,
and he will give you
the desires of your heart.
PSALM 37:4

Children are enchanting little creatures, especially to their parents. We find great enjoyment to have one of them take delight sitting in our laps and engaging us in a heart-to-heart conversation. We love them to the depths of our beings. We take great pleasure in granting them that for which they ask—that is, if they ask wisely. Of course, as toddlers and young children they seem to want anything and everything that captures their attention. But as they mature, no longer sitting in our laps when in deep conversations with us, they seem instinctively to grasp what we will grant and what we will not.

The Lord God is our Heavenly Father. In our Christian childhood, it brings us great pleasure to sit in our Father's lap, asking Him for anything and everything that comes to mind. As we mature in Christ, however, growing in our knowledge of His love for us, we begin to want that which He wants for us more than what we want for ourselves. Delighting in His love for us changes the desires of our hearts.

Over time we learn to *be still before the* LORD, *and wait patiently for him* (Psalm 37:7).

The Lord makes firm the steps of the one who delights in him;
though he may stumble, he will not fall, for the Lord upholds him with his hand.
PSALM 37:23–24

FEBRUARY 29

Blessed are those who mourn,
For they shall be comforted.
MATTHEW 5:4 NKJV

On one occasion when crowds began gathering around Jesus and His disciples, Jesus left the crowds behind and took His disciples up to a mountain top and began teaching them about what it means to be *blessed*—what we call the Beatitudes (Matthew 5:1–11). The Greek word for *blessed* is *makarizo*, meaning happy or fortunate. Among the nine areas where Jesus used the word *blessed*, the theme of mourning was one of them. Have you ever wondered how *those who mourn* can be happy and fortunate?

A season of mourning enters everyone's life. When it happens, we are so distraught that we cannot help but look heavenward, pleading with our Lord God to take it away and asking Him over and over again why He allowed such to come into our lives. We feel forsaken by God, not blessed by Him. It seems we can do nothing but cry and wail, forgetting to eat, not able to sleep, or roaming around our house sinking into the depths of despair.

Because of our temperaments, personalities, life experiences, and many other factors, everyone will not experience the mourning process in the same way or for the same length of time. Regardless, we must walk with our Lord God, who is continually with us, not throw our hands in the air and run from our grief or dump it beneath our feet in an attempt to crush it and make it go away.

Why? God is with us every nanosecond of time, speaking His sweet words of comfort into our ears and rocking us in His arms. As time passes we begin to comprehend that in His time, God makes all things beautiful—including the process of mourning the loss of someone or something that has been ripped from our lives.

This is the time we fall to our knees, hands raised heavenward, and thank God for His work in us, as we now see ourselves more of what He created us in Christ to become. We are blessed by the *God of all comfort, who comforts us in all our tribulation, that we may be able to comfort those who are in any trouble, with the comfort with which we ourselves are comforted by God* (2 Corinthians 1:4 NKJV).

Have we not learned that few people seem to understand the path we are now on more than those who have walked the same paths themselves?

For just as we share abundantly in the sufferings of Christ,
so also our comfort abounds through Christ. If we are distressed, it is for your comfort and salvation;
if we are comforted, it is for your comfort, which produces in you patient endurance of the same
sufferings we suffer. And our hope for you is firm, because we know that just as you
share in our sufferings, so also you share in our comfort.
2 CORINTHIANS 1:5–7

MARCH

MARCH 1

*Cast all your anxiety on him
because he cares for you.*
I PETER 5:7

Before instructing us to cast our anxieties, burdens, and life struggles on Him, God tells us: *"Humble yourselves, therefore, under God's mighty hand, that he may lift you up in due time"* (1 Peter 5:6). Far too many of us believe we can fix anything that creeps into our lives, regardless of what it might be. If we're honest with ourselves, we know beyond any shadow of doubt that we cannot solve the puzzle pieces on our plate because we don't have the ability or the strength to do so. Instead we wallow in self-pride; convincing ourselves we can do it if we just keep trying.

When we take our troubled hearts before the throne of God and cast our burdens on Him, He assures us He will lift us up in His time. Until that time arrives, our Heavenly Father saturates our hearts with His *peace, which transcends all understanding* (Philippians 4:7) and His love that endures forever (Psalm 100:5).

He has made everything beautiful in its time.
He has also set eternity in the human heart; yet no one can
fathom what God has done from beginning to end.
ECCLESIASTES 3:11

MARCH 2

*The LORD replied,
"My Presence will go with you,
and I will give you rest."*
EXODUS 33:14

So often when our Heavenly Father gives us an assignment, we respond as Moses did when he said to God, *"You have been telling me, 'Lead these people,' but you have not let me know whom you will send with me"* (Exodus 33:12). Like Moses, many of us want detailed information before embarking on God's plans for us, and we want it laid out step by step. Even then, from time to time, we falter, perhaps seeking a knowledgeable person to assist us.

Unlike Moses, however, we always have God's Holy Spirit in us. He is not only at our sides but also within us, whispering in our ears and directing our paths. When we don't acknowledge His presence we quench the Holy Spirit, which causes Him grief. As our Heavenly Father, God loves us and wants the very best for us. He grants us free will, meaning He allows us a choice—to go His Way or to go our own way as we seek to fulfill His plans for our lives.

It is only when we obey God's Holy Spirit in us that we find God's rest, His heavenly reward for submission to His will in our lives.

Be very careful, then, how you live—not as unwise but as wise, making the most of every opportunity.
EPHESIANS 5:15–16

MARCH 3

"Bring them here to me," he said.
MATTHEW 14:18

Have you ever gone to the Lord and explained a seemingly impossible situation to Him? Jesus' disciples did. A crowd surrounded them in a solidary place while Jesus healed the sick among them. As evening approached, the disciples explained to Jesus that He needed to send the crowd into nearby villages so they could buy something to eat (Matthew 14:14–15).

Jesus replied, "They do not need to go away. You give them something to eat" (v. 16).

"All we have is *five loaves of bread and two fish*," the disciples replied, probably glancing around at the crowd of about five thousand men with hungry looks on their faces, not even figuring in the women and children (v. 17).

Although they had witnessed Jesus' miracles countless times, the disciples must have thought, *No way. This is impossible.*

How many times have we said such words to our Heavenly Father? "It's impossible, Lord," we mumble. "It'll never happen!"

"Bring them here to me," Jesus responded.

As we bring to Him the desires of our hearts and listen to Him as He tells us what to do with what little we have, Jesus not only grants our request but multiplies it, with buckets full of blessings left over. Let us never say something is impossible because *all things are possible with God.*

Jesus replied, "What is impossible with men is possible with God."
LUKE 18:27

MARCH 4

Therefore, as God's chosen people,
holy and dearly loved,
clothe yourselves with compassion,
kindness, humility, gentleness and patience.
COLOSSIANS 3:12

As God lays out His clothing for us to wear each day, sometimes we agree with His choices and sometimes we don't. In fact, there are times when we want nothing to do with what He selects for us to put on.

"How on earth can I wear compassion today when I will be in a group of friends who have betrayed me?" we protest. "And kindness and gentleness? No way!"

A ton of pride rises in our hearts, and we know beyond a doubt that we won't be gentle and patient today—especially not around them. It is only when we pick up God's scarf labeled *"Bear with each other and forgive one another if any of you has a grievance against someone"* (Colossians 3:13) that we gasp, fall to our knees with tears brimming in our eyes, and remember our own horrible behavior and sins of which He has forgiven us.

When we spy His beautiful coat of love, however, we quickly grab it, with excitement in our hearts. We know if we put it on it will blend in with His shoes of compassion, His stunning dress of kindness, His sweater of humbleness, His hat of gentleness, and His necklace of patience. His love continually binds us *in perfect unity* with our precious Lord and Savior (Colossians 3:14).

"Yes, Lord, thank You so much for clothing me today in Your apparel."

As we leave our house, a deep sense of peace and thankfulness fills our hearts.

Humble yourselves before the Lord, and he will lift you up.
JAMES 4:10

MARCH 5

For where your treasure is,
there your heart will be also.
MATTHEW 6:21

Our Heavenly Father allows His children to choose what they believe will comfort them or bring them peace. It takes time walking with Him, remaining close to Him, for us to choose wisely. Only by lingering in His presence in our present moments will His everlasting love fill our hearts. It is only when we step out of His presence to agonize over the past or become anxious about the future that we sink into gloom and doom.

When we know in our heart of hearts that He is first and foremost in our lives then we hold fast to His Treasure—Emmanuel, God with us. No person, thing, event, or place can do what our Heavenly Father can do for us as we walk with Him through His valleys of darkness or up on His mountains and down into His forests and desert plains saturated with heat and dryness.

You have made known to me the path of life; you will fill me with joy in your presence,
with eternal pleasures at your right hand.
PSALM 16:11

MARCH 6

The one who has knowledge uses words with restraint,
and whoever has understanding is even-tempered.
PROVERBS 17:27

The longer we walk with the Lord, the closer we grow to Him. The more we know about Him, the more we are willing to close our mouths, choosing our words wisely before uttering them. Far too often, however, we rush in where angels fear to tread. Somehow we convince ourselves we're wise enough, smart enough, and prepared enough to handle whatever life sends our way.

"Perhaps what I just said was rather harsh," we confess to God, "but they needed to hear it, didn't they, Lord? They are too full of themselves! Right?"

God whispers into our ear. "My dear child, it is not they who are full of themselves but you who of full of yourself."

We close our eyes, groaning, with tears pouring down our cheeks. Then we fall to our knees and lift our hands heavenward, whispering, "Forgive me, Lord! Forgive me. You are right. It is I who am too full of myself."

Perhaps if we pause and in our mind's eye dip into God's bottle of honey, relishing in its sweetness before speaking a word, its deliciousness would not only please our tongues but also cause us to be more even-tempered and understanding before we speak.

> Gracious words are a honeycomb, sweet to the soul and healing to the bones.
> PROVERBS 16:24

MARCH 7

My eyes are ever on the LORD,
for only he will release my feet from the snare.
PSALM 25:15

One day when evening approached, Jesus suggested He and the disciples get into a boat and go to the other side of the lake, leaving the crowd behind. *A furious squall came up, and the waves broke over the boat, so that it was nearly swamped* (Mark 4:35–37). Jesus must have been very tired for He had gone to the stern of the ship and fallen asleep. In fear, His disciples quickly rushed to His side and woke Him, screaming, *"Teacher, don't you care if we drown?"* (v. 38). They knew if He didn't do something and do it quickly, they would die. Only He could rescue them from disaster.

In like manner, King David admitted he was lonely and afflicted and the troubles of his heart were numerous (Psalm 25:17–18). He wanted God to look down on what was going on in his life. So then did His disciples, and so do we. We must do as Jesus instructed us to do: Keep our eyes ever on Him. God does for us exactly what He did for David and also for the disciples. He rebukes the fierce winds of our troubled lives and calms our storms saying, *"Quiet! Be still!"* (Mark 4:39).

As He releases us from the snare beneath our feet, we also hear Him say to us as He did to His disciples, *"Why are you so afraid? Do you still have no faith?"* (v. 40).

> Show me your ways, O LORD, teach me your paths; Guide me in your truth and teach me, for you are God my Savior, and my hope is in you all day long.
> PSALM 25:4–5

MARCH 8

And pray in the Spirit on all occasions
with all kinds of prayers and requests.
EPHESIANS 6:18

Our Lord God urges us to bring our requests to Him in prayer. Many of us think this means kneeling beside our beds with eyes closed, heads bowed, and hands folded beneath our chins, voicing words. This is a delightful way to approach the Lord, but we can't always do it this way nor does our Lord expect us to. We are to *pray in the Spirit on all occasions.*

Does this not mean no matter where we are or what is in our minds or on our hearts we are invited to pray? Absolutely! It doesn't matter if our requests are hasty or extremely short—perhaps only one word like, "Help!" We might even be walking around the mall and notice a child crying while clutching his mother's arm, knowing he needs God's comfort, and we can silently petition our Lord to give it.

We may be driving down the road on a beautiful fall morning and raise our hearts to Him in thanksgiving for His glorious colors before our eyes, or we might ask Him to forgive us for running through a yellow traffic light and thank Him for keeping us safe.

God not only is our Heavenly Father, but He is our dearest Friend. He never tires of listening to us. He enjoys communicating with us. It delights His heart. And the great thing about this is we can always be in His presence, regardless of the time of day or night or the circumstances surrounding us. He is always available to talk with us. We can sing King David's song, *"Evening, and morning, and at noon, will I pray, and cry aloud: and he shall hear my voice"* (Psalm 55:17 KJV).

Pray without ceasing.
1 THESSALONIANS 5:17 KJV

MARCH 9

My sheep listen to my voice;
I know them,
and they follow me.
JOHN 10:27

Sheep are precious animals, but they are not the wisest creatures—far from it. They require a lot of attention and care. They need a shepherd to lead them and guide them to their food and water and to keep them penned up at night so that no harm befalls them if they stray.

David of the Old Testament times was a shepherd before God anointed him to rule over Israel. Perhaps this is one of the reasons that God said David was a man after His own heart. It's obvious as we read about David in our Bibles that, even though he sinned, he remained faithful to God and to God's people by shepherding them, leading them in the way they should go.

David used an analogy when comparing our Heavenly Father to a shepherd in Psalm 23. The Lord is our Shepherd, and we shall not want for anything because, being the good and faithful Shepherd He is, His watch care over us is more than supreme—it is holy. No earthly shepherd can do for his sheep what our Shepherd does for His sheep.

Not only does He make us *lie down* and rest when needed, but He leads us to refresh ourselves in *quiet waters*. And when the going gets rough, he restores our souls. When the troubles and grief of the shadow of death surround us, we have no fear because we know He is constantly with us, comforting us. And to top it off, He anoints our heads with His precious *oil in the presence of our enemies* to the point of our cups running over with His peace.

With joyful voices, we lift our hands heavenward, thanking Him from the depths of our beings that He is our Shepherd whose goodness and love follows us all the days of our lives—and we *dwell in the house of the Lord forever.*

Always giving thanks to God the Father for everything, in the name of our Lord Jesus Christ.
EPHESIANS 5:20

MARCH 10

I rejoice in your promise
like one who finds great spoil.
PSALM 119:162

We make promises to others we don't always keep, and others don't always keep the promises they make to us. But, hallelujah, our Lord God always keeps the promises He makes! We can count on it! Even if we can't see the giant diamond field beneath our feet at the moment we search for His *great spoil,* we know that in His time and in His way it will become visible to us. When God whispers in our ears His words of reassurance, support, and aid, rest assured that it's a given—meaning God has never failed us and He never will!

Our problem, if one develops, is our failing to put our faith in Him—to trust Him to accomplish what He tells us He will do for us, in us, and through us. *We are more than conquerors through* Christ who loves us and always keeps the promises He makes us (Romans 8:37).

If God is for us, who can be against us?
ROMANS 8:31

MARCH 11

Let us then approach
God's throne of grace
with confidence,
so that we may receive mercy
and find grace to help us
in our time of need.
HEBREWS 4:16

Sometimes we goof up at work and find ourselves in our boss's office searching for the right words to redeem ourselves, hoping we won't get fired. Our confidence oozes beneath our feet as we gulp and hang our heads in shame, wanting what happened to evaporate.

Thank goodness, not so with our Heavenly Boss. Everyone makes a huge mess at some time or other as we walk with our Holy Redeemer, the One who always forgives us as we confess our sins to Him. We may have trouble forgiving ourselves, and others who are harmed by our blunders might not be willing to forgive us either, but, rest assured, when we *approach His throne of grace with confidence,* God's *mercy and grace* are always present *in our time of need.*

Besides this, on our walks with Him He teaches us how to forgive ourselves even if others refuse to do so.

We know that in all things God works for the good of those who love him,
who have been called according to his purpose.
ROMANS 8:28

MARCH 12

Do not conform
to the pattern of this world,
but be transformed
by the renewing of your mind.
Then you will be able to
test and approve what God's will is—
his good, pleasing and perfect will.
ROMANS 12:2

Far too many of us submit to the patterns of this world, seeking to go along just to get along. Our friends, as well we ourselves, sometimes engage in conduct that is considered approved for the times in which we live. Nothing could be further from the truth. God instructs us through the apostle Paul, to be transformed by the renewing of our minds—in other words, we are to heed what God tells us in His Word rather than what others tell us that is not compatible with His Word. This is why it is so necessary for us to get in His Word and stay in His Word.

It's sort of like living in a house that has existed for a long time—out of date and obsolete, or so we convince ourselves. We want to renew it, bring it up to date. This doesn't mean tearing down everything inside or outside it. It simply means taking note of its foundation and what its Master Planner designed it to be—sturdy and secure, meeting all His required standards. If done correctly, adhering to His original design, it will stand the test of time and remain firm and secure in life's storms.

The only way to test and approve God's will for us, regardless of how young or old we may be, is to stick to our Master Planner's original, perfect design laid out for us in His created foundation—one that endures forever.

For the word of God is alive and active. Sharper than any double-edged sword, it penetrates even to dividing soul and spirit, joints and marrow; it judges the thoughts and attitudes of the heart.
HEBREWS 4:12

MARCH 13

While he was in Bethany, reclining at the table
in the home of Simon the Leper,
a woman came with an alabaster jar
of very expensive perfume, made of pure nard.
She broke the jar and poured the perfume on his head.

MARK 14:3

Mary, the sister of Martha and Lazarus, is the woman who came to the house of Simon the Leper to anoint Jesus' head with expensive perfume. The alabaster jar in her hands contained perfume made of pure nard. Mary broke her jar and poured its contents on Jesus' head.

Judas Iscariot, the disciple who would soon betray Jesus, was also present. He kept the money for the disciples and, unknown to them, had pilfered some of their cash. He must have gasped, as other guests may have done also, saying, *"Why this waste of perfume? It could have been sold for more than a year's wages and the money given to the poor"* (Mark 14:4). They reprimanded Mary.

Jesus told them to leave her alone and quit bothering her because *she has done a beautiful thing.* After explaining they would always have the poor with them and they could help them anytime they wanted, He informed them that He wouldn't always be with them. He went on to say, *"She did what she could. She poured perfume on my body beforehand to prepare for my burial"* (v. 6–8).

May Jesus say of us on what He said of Mary: *"She did what she could."* No matter where we are or what is happening around us or to us, let us do for our Lord and Savior, Jesus Christ, all that we can by proclaiming Him as the Lord and Savior of all mankind—Emanuel.

Truly I tell you, wherever the gospel is preached throughout the world,
what she has done will also be told, in memory of her.

MARK 14:9

MARCH 14

*Come near to God
and he will come near to you.*
JAMES 4:8

Mary adored Jesus Christ. She could not listen enough to His words as she sat at His feet and absorbed everything He said, while her sister, Martha, busied herself with household chores. Mary also went to the house of Simon the leper to anoint Jesus' feet with precious perfume shortly before Jesus was arrested and crucified. As those who sat at table with Jesus at Simon's house chastised and mocked Mary for wasting expensive perfume instead of giving its cost to the poor, Jesus came to her rescue, reprimanding those who scorned her. He exclaimed that Mary did what she could.

Others might believe we don't do much for the Lord, but we do what we can when we draw near to Him, for when we do He is ever near us, exclaiming that we did what we could and that is sufficient for Him.

*"Turn your eyes upon Jesus.
Look full in His wonderful face.
And the things of earth will grow strangely dim
in the light of His glory and grace."*

MARCH 15

*But the one who
stands firm to the end
will be saved.*
MATTHEW 24:13

Helen Howarth Lemmen wrote the words and music to "Turn Your Eyes upon Jesus." When she became blind, her husband left her. She was all alone and lived on precious little, but it is obvious by the words of her songs that she continually sat at the feet of Jesus, listening to Him whisper in her ears His words and His music.

This dear lady stood firm to the end and, as a result, has encouraged and blessed the lives of countless others who endure harsh circumstances. As we look into our Lord's precious face, all of life's troubles and pains grow very dim, for we see in Him what He is creating us in Christ to become. So let us look heavenward, not only praising and thanking God for Helen, but thanking Helen that she stood firm to the very end, trusting her Lord and Savior, Jesus Christ, and blessing us while doing so.

Holy, holy, holy
is the Lord Almighty;
the whole earth
is full of his glory.
ISAIAH 6:3

MARCH 16

How priceless is your unfailing love, O God!
People take refuge in the shadow of your wings.
PSALM 36:7

Far too many of us roam about seeking a kind of love that will satisfy our emptiness, not realizing that earth's beautiful love that surrounds us cannot accomplish this. We are imperfect people living in an imperfect world. Even though our Lord and Savior sends us an imperfect mate, family, or friends who love us as we also love them—imperfectly—we cannot fill that emptiness in us until we look heavenward. Then we see our Master's outstretched hand bidding us to find refuge in the shadow of His wings—in Jesus Christ, our Lord and Savior.

It is then we comprehend His priceless and unfailing love for us. Even though we fail Him, sometimes even turning away from Him, His love for us never ends. Even when He calls home our loved ones, we know His unfailing, abiding love remains in us, and we find His precious *refuge in the shadow of* His *wings.*

And so we know and rely on the love God has for us. God is love.
Whoever lives in love lives in God, and God in them.
1 JOHN 4:16

MARCH 17

Fight the good fight of the faith.
Take hold of the eternal life
to which you were called
when you made your good confession
in the presence of many witnesses.
1TIMOTHY 6:12

In his letter to Timothy, Paul speaks about teachers of false doctrines whose words result in *envy, strife, malicious talk, evil suspicions and constant friction between people of corrupt mind, who have been robbed of the truth and who think that godliness is a means to financial gain* (1Timothy 6:4–5). Paul then urges Timothy and us to turn our backs on all of this and instead *pursue righteousness, godliness, faith, love, endurance and gentleness* (v. 11).

"No, no!" Paul cautions. "There is far more to life than being rich."

Fight the good fight of the faith.

God charges us through Paul to *keep this command without spot or blame until the appearing of our Lord Jesus Christ* (v. 14). Not only this, but our Heavenly Father lets us know that all events will happen in God's time. *"The blessed and only Ruler, the King of kings and Lord of lords, who alone is immortal and who lives in unapproachable light, whom no one has seen or can see* (v. 15). So let us carry His torch, admonishing ourselves and others to *fight the good fight of faith.*

To him be honor and might forever. Amen.
1 TIMOTHY 6:16

MARCH 18

But as for me,
I watch in hope for the Lord,
I wait for God my Savior;
my God will hear me.
MICAH 7:7

At times we can lose hope when we voice a request to God and it seems to us it isn't going to happen. We wait and we wait and we wait, and yet zero occurs. Then we feel as if we've asked amiss, wondering how we could be so off track. Our hope sinks to the bottom of the pit in which we find ourselves. Then all of a sudden, the sun rises in our hearts as God delivers to us an "ah-ha" moment.

"Yes, My child," we hear as we listen to God. "You have waited and waited and waited, and your behavior has shown that you know that I heard your request. But . . ."

"Oh, dear," we mumble, "what did I do wrong, Lord?"

"Did I not tell you that *hope* is *an anchor for the soul, firm and secure* (Hebrews 6:19)?"

"But . . . but," we stutter, shaking our heads back and forth and holding them shamefully in our hands.

A sweet smile crosses the Lord's face as He says: *"I did this so that by two unchangeable things in which it is impossible for God to lie,* you *who have fled to take hold of the hope set before* you *may be greatly encouraged"* (Hebrews 6:18).

And we reply, *"But now, Lord, what do I look for? My hope is in you"* (Psalm 39:7). Amen.

MARCH 19

Blessed are those who find wisdom,
those who gain understanding.
PROVERBS 3:13

It is the desire of God's heart that those whom He adopts into His family grow into wise and understanding people. This cannot happen without pain because such rough roads and patches of deep sorrow open our eyes to the need to submit to God's plan for our lives— growing us into the image of His Son, Jesus Christ.

It is only as we grow in Christ that we comprehend the necessity of suffering for Christ's sake. It is when we submit to whatever God either sends or allows into our lives that we gain from it. Submitting means learning and obtaining godly wisdom and understanding, and then reaching out to others who are on the same road, for every child of God must travel this highway.

Give thanks in all circumstances,
for this is God's will for you in Christ Jesus.
1 THESSALONIANS 5:18

MARCH 20

Blessed are those who mourn,
for they will be comforted.
MATTHEW 5:4

As Jesus gathered with His disciples on the Mount of Olive, He sat and taught them. His first lessons began with the Beatitudes, which each begin with the word *blessed.* When used here, it refers to receiving God's favor, regardless of our circumstances. The Beatitudes describe what God expects of us as followers of His Son.

Many of us, however, gasp when we hear that we are receiving God's favor when we mourn. In our suffering, wanting nothing to do with the excruciating pain that envelopes us, we look heavenward and seek something more than favor from our Heavenly Father. Rather than being comforted, we want what was and no longer is to return.

While on this highway of grief, we seem deaf to being taught. We're too preoccupied with what engulfs us—a broken heart crumbled into millions of pieces.

In the depths of our despair, we are unaware that our Heavenly Father is picking up those pieces and putting them back together again. It isn't until we reach the other side of this agonizing path that our ears and eyes are opened to what God's comfort has brought us—for as we now view ourselves in His mirror, we see more of what He created us in Jesus Christ to become.

Then we fall to our knees and thank Him for walking with us every step of the way, enabling us now to comfort those walking the path we once traveled.

> **The Lord is close to the brokenhearted and**
> **saves those who are crushed in spirit.**
> PSALM 34:18

MARCH 21

Humble yourselves
before the Lord,
and he will lift you up.
JAMES 4:10

Many of us find it difficult to ask for help. We're capable, knowledgeable, and able to do this or that or the other—or so we convince ourselves. We're not weaklings and we don't need assistance, or so we believe. Yes, we might be rather smart, accomplished, and skilled, knowing much, but unfortunately we lack what is most essential in God's eyes—humility. Pride is abhorrent to God. God tells us in Proverbs 16:18 that *Pride goes before destruction, a haughty spirit before a fall.*

All of us have at least a smidgen of pride nestling in our hearts. So let us not emulate the Edomites, whom God admonished through the writing of Obadiah: *"The pride of your heart has deceived you, you who live in the clefts of the rocks and make your home on the heights, you who say to yourself, 'Who can bring me down to the ground?'"* (1:3).

God's response to this is: *"Though you soar like the eagle and make your nest among the stars, from there I will bring you down"* (v. 4).

Let us *humble* ourselves *before* our *Lord* so that *He* can *lift* us *up.*

MARCH 22

Even to your old age and gray hairs
I am he, I am he who will sustain you.
I have made you and I will carry you;
I will sustain you and I will rescue you.

ISAIAH 46:4

Being physically able and mentally competent comes easily in our younger years for most of us. We relish this and hold on to it, often taking it for granted. It is not until we experience aging creeping up on us that we begin to look into our future and question what it might hold. People in their fifties, sixties, seventies, and even eighties don't look the way they did decades ago. It seems they now dress differently, appearing more casual, with many not showing gray in their hair, much less with many wrinkles on their skin. They frequent exercise gyms and are seen out and about engaging in many fascinating activities.

Yet we all grow old; it's a given. Just as our Heavenly Father has sustained His aging ones for centuries, so He continues to do exactly that for the "new" older generations, who need Him and His promises as much as their forefathers did before them.

Regardless of life changes and what they bring about, from time to time the elderly need to be sustained and rescued. God promises to do exactly that! We can always count on Him and rest in His promises! Praise the Lord!

Trust in the Lord with all your heart and lean not on your own understanding;
in all your ways submit to him, and he will make your paths straight.

PROVERBS 3:5–6

MARCH 23

Who of you by worrying
can add a single hour to your life?
Since you cannot do this very little thing,
why do you worry about the rest?
LUKE 12:25–26

As Jesus talked with His disciples, he warned them about worrying because it is a waste of time and energy. Yes, we may lose our jobs and find no food on the table. We could be terrorized by thoughts of the stock market crashing and our country going bankrupt. We could spend countless hours and minutes frightened of losing our loved ones in tragic circumstances; or we could grab hold of every immeasurable, disturbing thought racing through our minds and play them over and over again, determined to resolve things ourselves.

Everyone knows that death is inevitable; however, no one knows exactly when it will happen. We can witness the signs of death approaching, but we cannot predict the exact moment it will arrive. Not only can we not add a single hour to our life, we cannot even patch on a nanosecond to the time God grants us to live.

Jesus tells us, *"Do not worry about your life"* (Luke 12:22). Our Heavenly Father knows what we need. He is our Holy Shepherd. As we seek His Kingdom, He provides everything we need. What more could we possibly want?

For where your treasure is, there your heart will be also.
LUKE 12:34

MARCH 24

Anxiety weighs down the heart,
but a kind word cheers it up.
PROVERBS 12:25

Every word that comes from our mouths is extremely important. We all fall short of recognizing this because we often speak without first thinking. We live in a world filled with all kinds of people, many of whom are in desperate need of encouragement. All it takes to accomplish this is turn our minds and thoughts off ourselves and focus instead on those who cross our paths.

If we do this, it is not difficult to sense a sagging heart with a burden on its shoulders. We cannot take the load away, but we can always give a moment of respite with a gentle and kind word flowing from our mouths, which will sink into ears in profound need of compassion and understanding.

Praise be to the God and Father of our Lord Jesus Christ,
the Father of compassion and the God of all comfort, who comforts us in all our troubles,
so that we can comfort those in any trouble with the comfort we ourselves receive from God.
2 CORINTHIANS 1:3–4

MARCH 25

Show me your ways, O LORD,
teach me your paths;
Guide me in your truth and teach me,
for you are God my Savior,
and my hope is in you all day long.
PSALM 25:4–5

When attempting to teach anything to anyone, we must open eyes and guide others along the paths of the knowledge of truth—what we gained with our Lord at our sides through our own life experiences. We pass down to future generations information we learned along God's highway. This is why it is extremely critical that we stay attentive and attuned to what our Lord God is teaching us as we walk with Him. We want to emulate Him faithfully, following in His footsteps.

King David followed God, but that did not mean from time to time he did not stray from His Shepherd's way. David lifted his hands in troubling times and petitioned God to uplift his soul and guide him in the direction he should go, forsaking the temptations that sometimes engulfed him. Even though God tells us David was a man after His own heart, it doesn't mean David was perfect, continually staying on God's straight and narrow path. Thankfully, David learned from the Master Teacher, who taught him to say, *"My eyes are ever on the LORD, for only he will release my feet from the snare"* (Psalm 25:15).

May our eyes also remain fixed on our Teacher so that we, like David, will keep our eyes forever on our Lord God, knowing he will also release our feet from the snares that come our way.

May these words of my mouth and this meditation of my heart be pleasing in your sight,
O LORD, my Rock and my Redeemer.
PSALM 19:14

MARCH 26

When Jacob awoke from his sleep, he thought,
"Surely the LORD is in this place,
and I was not aware of it."
GENESIS 28:16

After Jacob's twin brother, Esau, married a Hittite woman, their mother, Rebekah, overheard Esau say that after their father died he would kill Jacob for stealing his birthright and blessing. Isaac, Esau's father, knew nothing of Esau's threat against Jacob, but when Rebekah approached Isaac and let him know how disgusted she was living among *these Hittite women,* she said, *"If Jacob takes a wife from among the women of this land, from Hittite women like these, my life will not be worth living"* (Genesis 27:46). Isaac agreed by telling Jacob not to marry a Hittite woman, but to go to *Paddan Aram, to the house of your mother's father* and *take a wife for yourself there* (Genesis 28:2).

Jacob *left* his home in *Beersheba and set out for Haran,* four hundred miles away (Genesis 28:10). Jacob had to have felt very isolated on this journey, for he had never been alone, not even in his mother's womb. When the sun began to set he reached a *certain place* (v. 11) and put a stone beneath his head to lie down to sleep.

He dreamed of *a stairway resting on the earth, with its top reaching to heaven, and the angels of God were ascending and descending on it* (v. 12). The Lord God was above the stairway and said to Jacob: *"I am the LORD, the God of your father Abraham and the God of Isaac. I will give you and your descendants the land on which you are lying"* (v. 13). God let Jacob know that He would give all this land to him and his descendants. Not only that but they would *spread out to the west and to the east, to the north and the south. "All peoples on earth will be blessed through you and your offspring"* (v. 14).

God then told Jacob that He was with him and would watch over him wherever he went, letting Jacob know that He would eventually bring him back home. Jacob's heart must have danced all over the place hearing these words and God's promise that He would not leave Him. Yes, indeed, God was in that place even though Jacob was not aware of it when he arrived there.

No matter what is happening in our lives, how threatening it is or horrendous it might be, rest assured God is forever with His children, never leaving them nor forsaking them. It is His promise to us.

When our God opens our eyes as He did Jacob's, we do will say, *"How awesome is this place! This is none other than the house of God; this is the gate of heaven* (Genesis 28:17).

MARCH 27

Keep your lives free
from the love of money
and be content with what you have,
because God has said,
"Never will I leave you;
never will I forsake you."
So we say with confidence,
"The Lord is my helper;
I will not be afraid.
What can mere mortals do to me?"
HEBREWS 13:5–6

L ife is filled with all kinds of twists and turns, often causing us to look elsewhere for relief rather than placing our trust in God, remembering what He had told us multiple times: *"Never will I leave you; never will I forsake you."* Instead, we seek relief from this temporal world in which we live, especially depending on things we can see and feeling safe because of it.

What enters our life, whether in the spring, summer, fall, or winter, or during the day or at night, is inconsequential. We can look at what seems to envelop us and shout with confidence, *"The Lord is my helper!"*

Even if surrounded by a battalion of enemies, we confidently proclaim, "I'm not afraid. God is with me!" And then turn heavenward, whispering to our Heavenly Father, "What can man do to me? I am a child of the King! Thank You, Jesus."

I lift up my eyes to the mountains—where does my help come from?
My help comes from the LORD, the Maker of heaven and earth.
PSALM 121:1–2

MARCH 28

Pray continually.
1 Thessalonians 5:17

After reading these two words from God, we sometimes ponder them and wonder how anyone can do anything continually—meaning constantly, all the time. Our Lord never instructs us to do anything without empowering us to do so.

It is only when we remain in our present moments in our Heavenly Father's presence that obeying any of His commands is possible through Jesus Christ, who always strengthens us to do what God is training us to do. As we walk His path of sanctification and forsake worrying about what our future might hold and quit traveling back into the past trying to repair it instead of focusing on our present moments with Him, we are able to fill our minds with His Presence in us.

Praying continually is a given. For when we see Him in all things, knowing we are strengthened by our Lord Jesus Christ and the Holy Spirit in us, with nothing impossible for God, we are enabled to pray continually. This brings us the peace that *transcends all understanding* (Philippians 4:7).

And God is faithful; he will not let you be tempted beyond what you can bear.
1 CORINTHIANS 10:13

MARCH 29

We live by faith,
not by sight.
2 Corinthians 5:7

All of us have petitioned our Heavenly Father for something or other. We wait and wait for God to respond, but as time moves on nothing seems to happen. We awaken each morning looking for what was requested, and finding it nowhere in sight some throw their heads into their hands and mumble and grumble, "I give up, Lord. I just give up."

God whispers into their ears and into ours as well, "Do you not remember, My child, I instructed you to *live by faith* and *not by sight?*"

"Yes, Lord."

His voice softly whispers into our minds, "My apostle Paul put to paper these very words I told him to write to the church in Corinth."

"But what does that have to do with me, Lord? I'm just tired of waiting for You to respond to what I've requested!"

"*Fix* your *eyes not on what is seen,* My child, *but on what is unseen*" (2 Corinthians 4:18).

"I don't understand, Lord."

"It means to have faith in Me—to trust Me, My child," He whispers. "In My time, not your, I make all things beautiful (Ecclesiastes 3:11)."

Shame floods our beings and soft tears stream down our cheeks as we tenderly mumble, "Yes, Father, I remember and I understand. Trust is number one, followed by hope, which is number two, and then grasping and holding tightly to Your hand while waiting for You to respond."

> Therefore we do not lose heart. Though outwardly we are wasting away,
> yet inwardly we are being renewed day by day. For our light and momentary troubles
> are achieving for us an eternal glory that far outweighs them all. . . .
> since what is seen is temporary, but what is unseen is eternal.
>
> 2 CORINTHIANS 4:16–18

MARCH 30

Let us then approach
God's throne of grace
with confidence,
so that we may receive mercy
and find grace to help us
in our time of need.

HEBREWS 4:16

From time to time worry and anxiety come calling at the doors of our hearts, seemingly determined to break into our minds, hoping to gain control of our thoughts. Far too often we let them succeed, allowing ourselves to become consumed with this or that or the other. Even when trying as hard as we can to dump the load of garbage they brought with them, we can't seem to figure out how to do it. We may even call a friend or anyone else we believe might be able to get our minds back on track.

It is then that we remember *we have a great high priest who has ascended into heaven, Jesus the Son of God,* who reaches down to us and reminds us we must let ourselves *hold firmly to the faith we profess* (Hebrews 4:14). God's Word *is alive and active. Sharper than any double-edged sword . . . it judges the thoughts and attitudes of the heart* (v. 12).

Hallelujah! *Nothing in all creation is hidden from God's sight. Everything is uncovered and laid bare before the eyes of him to whom we must give account* (v. 13).

For we do not have a high priest who is unable to empathize with our weaknesses,
but we have one who has been tempted in every way, just as we are—yet did not sin.
HEBREWS 4:15

MARCH 31

Show me the way I should go,
for to you I entrust my life.
PSALM 143:8

King David, the one God said was a man after His own heart, knew what it was like to be in the midst of hopelessness and depression. In Psalm 143, David pleaded with God, *"Hear my prayer, listen to my cry for mercy; in your faithfulness and righteousness come to my relief"* (v. 1). Apparently David had reached a fork in his road, not knowing in which direction to go.

He confessed to God that his *heart* was *dismayed* and his *spirit* was growing *faint* (v. 4). He felt crushed. While meditating on God, David brought to memory His *works* and what His *hands have done* (v. 5), even pleading with God to *let the morning bring me word of your unfailing love, for I have put my trust in you* (v. 8). David knew nothing else to do but seek God's help for what was troubling him. He pleaded, *"Rescue me from my enemies, LORD, for I hide myself in you"* (v. 9).

And then David requested something from God that God is teaching us through His words He put into David's heart: *Teach me to do your will, for you are my God; may your good Spirit lead me on level ground* (v. 10).

Answer me quickly, LORD; my spirit fails. Do not hide your face from me
or I will be like those who go down to the pit.
PSALM 143:7

APRIL

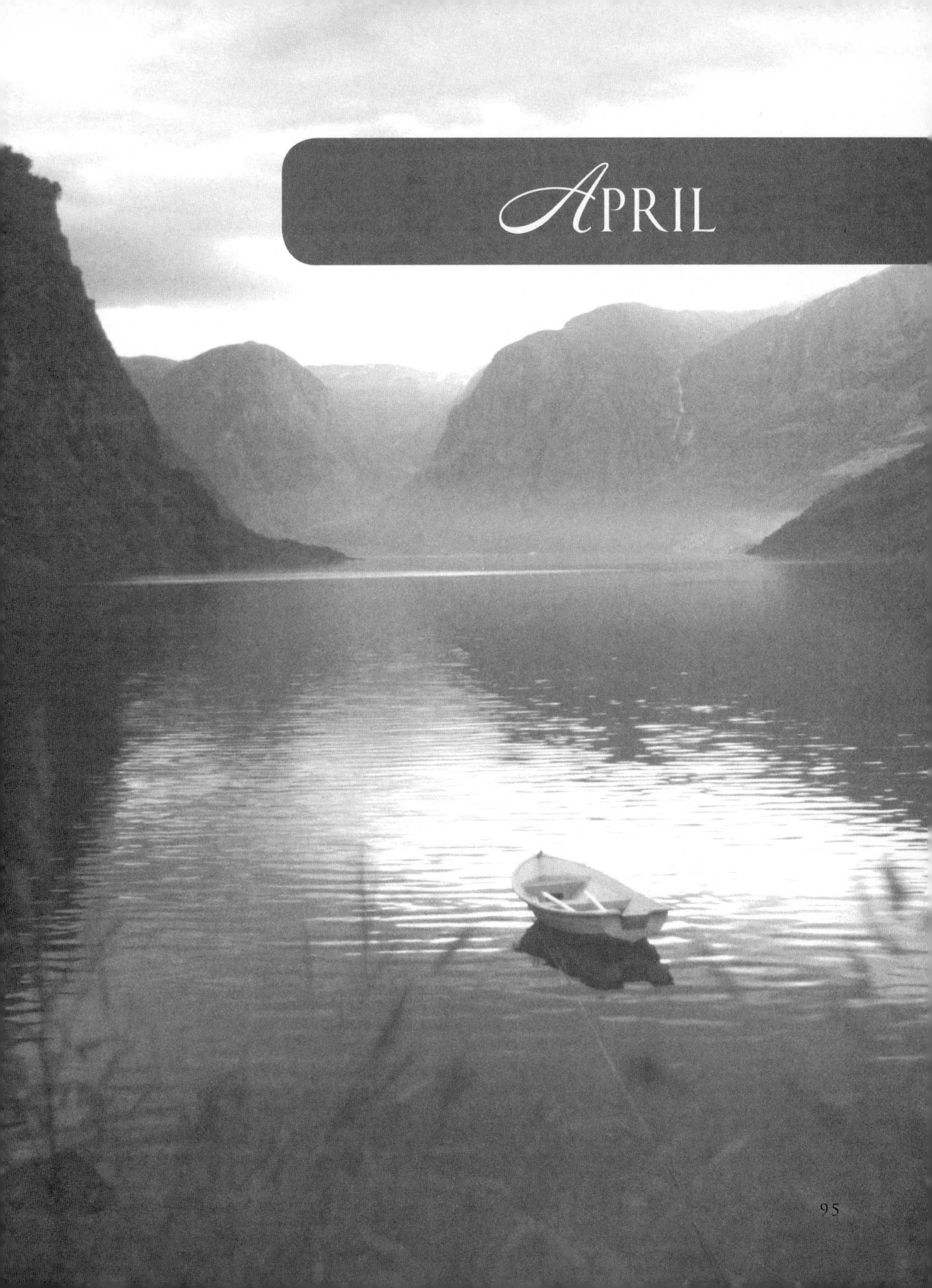

APRIL 1

Now the Lord is the Spirit,
and where the Spirit of the Lord is,
there is freedom.
2 CORINTHIANS 3:17

God the Father, God the Son, and God the Holy Spirit—the Trinity dwells in and around us. Through God's words written to the church at Corinth by His apostle Paul, God tells us that when we have been saved through the death, burial, and resurrection of Jesus Christ our Lord and Savior we receive a part of Him who now continually resides in us—God's Holy Spirit. It is His Spirit in us who leads, guides, and directs our paths.

God lets us know *there is freedom where the Spirit of the Lord is* present. This means God gives us a choice—we can either follow and obey His Spirit in us or not follow and obey. We can also quench His Spirit in us or grieve His Spirit in us or accept the Spirit's leading us.

What a precious treasure God has given us—the Holy Spirit continually in us, not just visiting us now and then like the Holy Spirit did in Old Testament times, but permanently residing in us, keeping us on track with our Heavenly Father's will for our lives.

Praise the LORD, Praise the LORD, my soul. I will praise the LORD all my life;
I will sing praise to my God as long as I live.
PSALM 146:1–2

APRIL 2

Sacrifice thank offerings to God,
fulfill your vows to the Most High,
and call on me in the day of trouble;
I will deliver you, and you will honor me.

PSALM 50:14–15

When our hearts reach up to our Lord God in thanksgiving for all He is and all He does, it pleases Him and bestows deep joy in our hearts as well—a joy that passes all our understanding. Not only are we instructed to *sacrifice thank offerings to God,* but we also are to *fulfill* our *vows to the Most High.* We all make promises to God, and when we do He expects us to honor them.

God also invites us to *call on* Him *in the day of trouble.* This is not a difficult invitation to accept, but as we do so we must trust Him to honor His word in His time, not in our time. We honor Him when we acknowledge that in His time He makes all things beautiful.

He has made everything beautiful in its time.
ECCLESIASTES 3:11

APRIL 3

I will lift up my eyes to the mountains—
where does my help come from?
My help comes from the LORD,
the Maker of heaven and earth.

PSALM 121:1–2

When trudging through a slimy mud pit, sinking ankle deep in oozing misery, it's extremely challenging to focus our eyes on the hills above; however, it is doable. All it takes is a fleeting glance Godward, with our wordless tongues and downcast eyes pleading, "Help!"

The Maker of heaven and earth immediately responds. He enfolds us in His heavenly arms, singing His sweet love song and assuring us He *will never leave* us *nor forsake* us (Deuteronomy 31:6).

It is then we know that in His time and in His way He will cause that which now engulfs us to bloom into something we never envisioned it could be, causing us to gasp at its breathtaking brilliance.

Wait for the LORD; be strong and take heart and wait for the LORD.
PSALM 27:14

APRIL 4

*Nevertheless, God was not
pleased with most of them;
their bodies were scattered
in the wilderness.*
1 CORINTHIANS 10:5

Who would have thought the descendants of our country's early immigrants would one day become the kind of people they now are—living far from our Lord God, not remaining the one nation under God the founders of our country set out for us to be. God tells us through His apostle Paul as he wrote to the church at Corinth that *God was not pleased with most of them.* Many of them were like the Israelites of bygone days: idolaters, immoral people, seeking their own way, straying from the Lord God's way.

Let us ask ourselves if God is pleased with the road many of us are on today. If we're honest with ourselves we know He is not.

**If my people, who are called by my name, will humble themselves
and pray and seek my face and turn from their wicked ways, then will I hear from heaven,
and I will forgive their sin and will heal their land.**
2 CHRONICLES 7:14

APRIL 5

And the Lord's servant
must not be quarrelsome
but must be kind to everyone.
2 TIMOTHY 2:24

We, who are God's children, are His servants. It is the desire of our hearts to willingly and completely obey Him. And as such, God has instructed us not to quarrel. Instead, we are to *be kind to everyone*—everyone. Regardless of what they've said or done to us? Absolutely! And not quarrel? Without question!

"But . . . but . . . ," we quibble, "it's impossible to be kind to everyone! How can I not quarrel with a quarreler or how can I be generous or compassionate with someone who has purposefully stepped on my toes, much less wronged my loved ones?"

Do we not know, do we not remember, what God so faithfully reminds us in His Word? We can do nothing in our own strength that our Heavenly Father calls us to do, but we can do everything *through Him* who gives us strength to do so (Philippians 4:13).

No temptation has overtaken you except what is common to mankind.
And God is faithful; he will not let you be tempted beyond what you can bear. But when you are tempted,
he will also provide a way out so that you can endure it.
1 CORINTHIANS 10:13

APRIL 6

But as for me,
I watch in hope for the LORD,
I wait for God my Savior;
my God will hear me.
MICAH 7:7

Sometimes we wait and wait and wait for God to respond to our pleas. When this happens, let us remember to trust Him to do what He tells us He will do—to grasp tightly to His gentle hand of hope as we're watching in faith for Him to respond to our requests. God always shows us what is good and lets us know what He requires of us.

Faith—Hope—Wait. This is what our Lord expects of us. Trust Him in any and all circumstances. Hope for that which we desire to arrive, and then wait for it to take place. Our Heavenly Father will never disappoint us.

He has shown you, O mortal, what is good. And what does the LORD require of you?
To act justly and to love mercy and to walk humbly with your God.
MICAH 6:8

APRIL 7

Peace I leave with you;
my peace I give you.
I do not give to you
as the world gives.
Do not let your hearts be troubled
and do not be afraid.
JOHN 14:27

Far too often, many of us search for peace in the wrong places, like shopping till we drop, stuffing our mouths with food, immersing ourselves in television, and so on. Unfortunately, some even turn to alcohol or drugs, elicit sexual acts, or a variety of wayward behaviors—things that can never bring God's peace.

How absurd for us to turn to worldly ways when our Heavenly Father very plainly tells us that He leaves His *peace* with us, meaning all we have to do is open our eyes to His precious gift already in our hands.

It is only when we acknowledge and accept His peace gift that we can refuse to let our hearts *be troubled and afraid.*

Because God has said, "Never will I leave you; never will I forsake you." So we say with confidence,
"The Lord is my helper; I will not be afraid. What can mere mortals do to me?"
HEBREWS 13:5–6

APRIL 8

This is how we know what love is:
Jesus Christ laid down his life for us.
And we ought to lay down our lives
for our brothers.
1 JOHN 3:16

Godly love is not a feeling or an emotion. It is Christ in us that enable us to love others the way God loves everyone: *For God so loved the world that he gave his one and only Son, that whoever believes in him shall not perish but have eternal life* (John 3:16). Our Heavenly Father plants His love in our hearts when we accept what Jesus accomplished on His cross for us—redeeming us to walk in newness of life.

We cannot love the way God wants us to love until we accept Jesus Christ as our Lord and Savior. Even with the love of God in our hearts, our Heavenly Father allows us to choose to use it His way or use it our way. The choice is ours, even if it means laying down our physical lives for our brothers and sisters in Christ.

Sometimes we might be called on to do so; nevertheless, all of us are called to die to ourselves in order for others to live in Christ. This means we must put ourselves at the bottom of our agenda, thinking more highly of others than of ourselves and willing to be put down if it means lifting another up. We all know that this is not an easy thing to do, but we also know that we can do all things through Christ who strengthens us (Philippians 4:13).

God is love. Whoever lives in love lives in God, and God in them.
1 JOHN 4:16

APRIL 9

You make your saving help my shield,
and your right hand sustains me.
PSALM 18:35

We become God's Christian soldiers when we accept Jesus Christ as our Lord and Savior. As we enter spiritual battles, our Commander equips us with His weapons of warfare. As we fight our skirmishes against His enemy, it is only when we use His Weapons that we are victorious. He is forever on our side.

This doesn't mean that from time to time we won't feel overcome with what stands in front of us, threating to do us in. Sometimes we might accidentally drop our shield of faith then scurry about trying to pick it up. This is when we hear our Commander's voice whisper into our ears, "Trust me, My child. Trust me," while pointing directly to His shield that He picks up and places back in our hands.

Never fear, warriors of God, His right hand forever and always sustains us, for we are His soldiers, marching as to war under the direction of our Commander-in-Chief.

Guide me in your truth and teach me, for you are my God my Savior,
and my hope is in you all day long.
PSALM 25:5

APRIL 10

With joy you will draw water
from the wells of salvation.
ISAIAH 12:3

During the times of deep desperation and despair, we don't understand or comprehend that a day is coming when the broken pieces of our hearts will mend, and as they do we discern something in ourselves never before recognized. As the agony of our hearts subsides and we *draw water from* His *wells*, God's *joy* fills our souls.

The joy of this water is vastly different from anything we've tasted before. We know that we could never have become what we now are becoming had our Heavenly Father not opened His door of affliction, traveling with us down its pathway. Long ago we were redeemed by the blood of His precious Lamb; now we are becoming more of what our Lord created us in Jesus Christ to be.

Those who sow with tears will reap with songs of joy.
Those who go out weeping, carrying seed to sow,
will return with songs of joy, carrying sheaves with them.
PSALM 126:5–6

APRIL 11

For with the measure you use,
it will be measured to you.
LUKE 6:38

We reap what we sow, more than we sow, and later than we sow. We have heard these words multiple times and experienced them as well. Yet the measuring cups we use are frequently small, with us somehow expecting more in return than we have given. If we want our garden to bloom with God's stunning flowers and vegetables and be saturated with joy, peace, love, kindness, gentleness, compassion, and understanding, then that is what we must sow—His bountiful variety of seeds He places in our hands, not the ones we choose. If we do so, our cups will overflow, pouring His blessings into our laps.

Give and it will be given to you. A good measure, pressed down,
shaken together and running over, will be poured into your lap.
LUKE 6:38

APRIL 12

Although the Lord gives you
the bread of adversity
and the water of affliction,
your teachers will be hidden no more;
with your own eyes you will see them.
ISAIAH 30:20

Most of us have an extremely difficult time understanding how our Lord God could possibly be responsible for *the bread of adversity and the water of affliction* that engulfs us. We have no choice but to eat and drink of it, producing such misery and agony that we almost choke just looking at it.

It takes time to digest it, but we cannot completely grasp the meaning of its presence in our lives until all but a few fragments are left. Then we understand that God either allowed or placed it in our lives for His reason—to grow us into what He created us in Christ to become.

Our confrontational bread and troubled waters are our Heavenly Father's sacred teachers, once hidden from our sight, but now seen and understood as His blessings, producing is us what we could never have become without them.

> **Whether you turn to the right or to the left, your ears will hear a voice behind you,**
> **saying, "This is the way; walk in it."**
> ISAIAH 30:21

APRIL 13

> *For in him you have been enriched in every way—*
> *with all kinds of speech and with all knowledge—*
> *God thus confirming our testimony*
> *about Christ among you.*
> 1 CORINTHIANS 1:5–6

Many of us don't recognize the importance of our Christian testimony to those whose paths we cross each and every day. Our words and behaviors are critical. Not even realizing it, we are constantly being observed by those around us. We don't have to become a Sunday School teacher or a missionary or in full-time Christian service to bring others to Christ or help others grow in Christ. All we need do is grab hold of God's Words and obey them.

Once we become a child of God, our Heavenly Father enriches us in every way, enabling us to grow in the knowledge of Him, thereby speaking and behaving in a way that brings honor to His name. When we speak mean, cruel, and destructive words; act disgracefully; and ignore God's gift of living for Him, we drive those away who are in deepest need of His grace and bring tears to the eyes of God's Holy Spirit in us.

> **May these words of my mouth and this meditation of my heart**
> **be pleasing in your sight, LORD, my Rock and my Redeemer.**
> PSALM 19:14

APRIL 14

Yet the Lord longs
to be gracious to you;
therefore he will rise up
to show you compassion.
For the Lord is a God of justice.
Blessed are all who wait for him!
ISAIAH 30:18

How many times has God whispered in our ears, "Wait, my child," and we ignored His words, much preferring to go our own way instead of waiting for Him? At some time or other we all are guilty of this. Our Heavenly Father wants each of His children to know that He absolutely *longs* not only *to be gracious* to us, but compassionate as well. Perhaps we don't grasp His words because we allow ourselves to judge quickly and often harshly, forgetting that our *Lord is a God of justice.*

No matter how long we have to wait or what it is we're waiting for, our Heavenly Father will *be gracious and compassionate* to us, permeating our hearts with His love and *justice* that is beyond understanding.

Wait for the LORD; be strong and take heart and wait for the LORD.
PSALM 27:14

APRIL 15

I say to myself,
"The LORD is my portion;
therefore I will wait for him."
LAMENTATIONS 3:24

Sometimes we feel cheated. We convince ourselves that what is due us is withheld, which fills us with resentment and bitterness. We've all walked this road at one time or another. Perhaps it might be difficult for us to turn away from these emotions, but it is not impossible to do so. It is more than doable by saying aloud to ourselves, "God *is my portion. I will wait for Him* to work this out. In His time, He will make this beautiful. I trust Him to make it right."

Our Lord God *will never leave* us *nor forsake* us (Deuteronomy 31:6). It is our impatience inside us that runs from His Presence, seeking our own way in our own time.

So I say to you: Ask and it will be given to you; seek and you will find;
knock and the door will be opened to you. For everyone who asks receives; the one who seeks finds;
and to the one who knocks, the door will be opened.
LUKE 11:9–10

APRIL 16

I led them with
cords of human kindness,
with ties of love.
To them I was like one who lifts
a little child to the cheek,
and I bent down to feed them.

HOSEA 11:4

God tells us that the more He *called* His children Israel to follow Him, the more they strayed from Him. They turned to the gods of *the Baals*, burning incense to these idols. Yet God went on to inform them that it was He *who taught Ephraim to walk, taking them by the arms* and healing them, but they didn't heed his call to follow Him (Hosea 11:2–3). Our Heavenly Father desires we know what He did for those whom He loved then, just as He wants us to know what He is doing for His people today.

As He placed His *cords of human kindness with ties of love* on Ephraim (v. 4), enabling them to walk with Him, He does likewise for us. In His kindness and love, He redeems us through Christ and declares us His children. As God lifted the yoke of heaviness from Israel's necks during that time, He does the same today when He tells us, *"Take my yoke upon you and learn from me, for I am gentle and humble in heart, and you will find rest for your souls. For my yoke is easy and my burden is light"* (Matthew 11:29–30). In Ephraim's day God bent down to feed Israel (v. 4). He also feeds us today with His Holy Words from His Holy Book—something they didn't fully have at that time, but something we have in completeness yet, unfortunately, too often ignore.

I will sing to the Lord all my life; I will sing praise to my God as long as I live.
May my meditation be pleasing to him, as I rejoice in the Lord.
PSALM 104:33–34

APRIL 17

This is the confidence we have
in approaching God:
that if we ask anything
according to his will,
he hears us.

1 JOHN 5:14

When we approach God in prayer and petition Him for our heart's desire, *He* always *hears us* when *we ask according to His will*, not our will for ourselves. Many times, however, what we request of Him is not His will for us. His plans are not our plans; neither is His ways our ways (Isaiah 55:8). When what we ask doesn't happen, we might think God hasn't heard us. Nothing could be further from the truth. It takes time, and sometimes a lot of it, for us to realize we've asked amiss, not considering if our request is God's will for our lives.

As Jesus agonized in the Garden of Gethsemane, He prayed, *"Abba, Father, everything is possible for you. Take this cup from me. Yet not what I will, but what you will"* (Mark 14:36). Yes, Lord, not my will but Your will.

APRIL 18

Everything is possible
for one who believes.
MARK 9:23

How many times have we been overwhelmed with a problem, discussed it with any-one available, and found no solution whatsoever? This is what a man did who had a mute son possessed by an evil spirit. At times the boy would have seizures, fall to the ground, foam at the mouth, and become rigid. Then, apparently seeing some of Jesus' disciples in a large crowd, the man approached them with the hope they would be able to help his son.

When Jesus came down from the mountain with His disciples Peter, James, and John, they saw the other disciples surrounded by the crowd and the teachers of the law arguing with them

(Mark 9:14). Seeing Jesus approach, the other disciples ran to greet Him. Jesus asked them a question, *"What are you arguing with them about?"* (v. 16).

The man stepped forth and told Jesus what was wrong with the boy and that His disciples couldn't heal him. After asking the father to bring the boy to Him, the lad fell to the ground in a seizure. When asked how long the boy had been this way, the dad replied, *"From childhood. It often has thrown my boy into fire or water to kill him"* (v. 21).

The man then asked Jesus a request we often ask: *"But if you can do anything, take pity on us and help us"* (v. 22).

Let us ask ourselves a question: Do we not do the same thing? Do we not go to our Heavenly Father and request His help after we've become exhausted and the help we've sought cannot help at all?

"'If you can?'" said Jesus. "Everything is possible for one who believes" (v. 23).

Our Heavenly Father asks us the same question. We, like the father in this story have also approached His throne as a last resort, rather than immediately exclaiming, "Help me, Lord! Help me!"

After healing the boy, Jesus went indoors, where his disciples asked him in private, "Why couldn't we drive it out?" (v. 28).

Jesus told them, *"This kind can come out only by prayer"* (v. 29).

> Ask and it will be given to you; seek and you will find;
> knock and the door will be opened to you. For everyone who asks receives; the one who seeks finds;
> and to the one who knocks, the door will be opened.
> MATTHEW 7:7–8

APRIL 19

I sought the LORD,
and he answered me;
he delivered me
from all my fears.
PSALM 34:4

As a small child, I once asked my mother why there were stars in the night sky and who put them there. Either becoming weary of my frequent questions or not knowing what to say, my mother responded, "Don't think about such things. It'll drive you crazy." My little mind figured out that if my mother didn't answer my questions then no one else would either.

Years later when I came to know Jesus as my Lord and Savior, I gained a glorious Heavenly Father who not only answers all my questions but who gave me a Book that explained much of what my tiny mind wanted to know as I was growing up. I not only learned it was not crazy-making to seek answers to anything but also discovered that my Father would comfort me whenever I became frightened and wanted responses to questions no one could or would answer.

You will seek me and find me when you seek me with all your heart.
JEREMIAH 29:13

APRIL 20

But as for me,
I watch in hope for the LORD,
I wait for God my Savior;
my God will hear me.
MICAH 7:7

Hope is having confidence, anticipating that what we seek will occur. When something we've hoped for and waited and waited for God to send our way doesn't appear, others might tell us to let it go, forget it, and move on; but we believe we know better. This is when we tell ourselves, "I watch and I wait because God my Savior hears me," which He does.

But in the interval we might wonder why our Heavenly Father doesn't respond to us if He has heard our cry. As we wait, however, we learn a tremendous lesson—if that for which we petition God doesn't arrive then it is not God's will for us to have. It can then no longer remain the desire of our heart. As time moves on, we began to comprehend that if God had given us the thing we asked it would have been disastrous for us. This is when we tell ourselves, "*I watch in hope for the Lord; I wait for God my Savior* for my God hears me, and He knows what is best for me. Thank You, Lord, in Jesus' name."

Trust in the LORD with all your heart and lean not to your own understanding;
in all your ways submit to him, and he will make your paths straight.
PROVERBS 3:5–6

APRIL 21

You will keep in perfect peace
those whose minds are steadfast,
because they trust in you.
ISAIAH 26:3

Why is it vital that we keep our minds in a *steadfast* mode? Are we really capable of doing this? We know that we can do all things through the strength of Christ in us (Philippians 4:13); however, we can do nothing without trusting Him to do what He says He will do. God's perfect peace is a byproduct of our trusting Him in everything and in all things.

It is imperative that we keep our trust-broom handy so that we can quickly sweep away the clutter that the evil one scatters into our thoughts. Sometimes, no matter how hard we work on keeping the floor of our mind cleared, it overflows with the junk that the evil one tosses our way. God's solution to this problem is simply to petition His help: "Help me, Lord! Help me!"

His perfect peace fills our heart and soul as we come to Him in our time of need. His peace that passes all understanding permeates every fiber of our being and enables our thoughts to rest at the foot of His throne, heads bowed, thanking Him and singing praises to His name.

Trust in him at all times, you people; pour out your hearts to him, for God is our refuge.
PSALM 62:8

APRIL 22

My son, do not despise the LORD's discipline
and do not resent his rebuke,
because the LORD disciplines those he loves,
as a father the son he delights in.
PROVERBS 3:11–12

When we punish our children, seldom do they look our way with a smile on their faces. Usually a gloomy frown swallows them whole, with them gulping down their dismay at being reprimanded. Their thoughts are also easy to read: *I hate you! You're mean!*

Of course, it's hurtful for us to sense these emotions in our children, but it is because we love them and want them to become all they can be that we correct them. We know that no one wants to be around a spoiled brat.

The same is true for God's children. Unfortunately, there are lots of little "holy terrors" who would never become what God created them in Christ to become if He did not discipline them, getting them back on His track. Our Heavenly Father tells His children the same thing we want our children to know: "Do not resent what I have allowed or sent into your life. It is meant for your good. It is because I love you that I bring you back to me whenever you stray. In time, you will pick up the *beauty* I have laid at your feet in exchange for your *ashes*."

To bestow on them a crown of beauty instead of ashes, oil of joy instead of mourning,
and a garment of praise instead of a spirit of despair. They will be called oaks of righteousness,
a planting of the LORD for the display of his splendor.
ISAIAH 61:3

APRIL 23

He will wipe away every tear from their eyes.
There will be no more death
or mourning or crying or pain,
for the old order of things has passed away.
REVELATION 21:4

The day is coming when there will be no more pain or crying. There will be no more death, therefore no more mourning. Our Heavenly Father will wipe away all tears. Our glorious New World will be saturated with His presence and His forever peace.

In the meantime, in the midst of pain, crying, deaths, mourning, and a fallen and forsaken world, we can gaze into His majestic face, saturated in His holy love for us, and raise our hands in praise and thankfulness to Him for His gift of salvation through the shed blood of His Son, Jesus Christ. As God's children we are blessed indeed. Our Holy Shepherd directs every step we take, with our having no need to be anxious or upset or worried about anything. He leads us in *the paths of righteousness for His name's sake*, anoints our heads with His oil, and makes our cups overflow (Psalm 23:3, 5 NKJV).

Surely your goodness and love will follow me all the days of my life,
and I will dwell in the house of the LORD forever.
PSALM 23:6

APRIL 24

And do not grumble,
as some of them did.
1 CORINTHIANS 10:10

Far too often, we are grumblers and complainers. No one can ever raise his or her hand, proclaiming innocence of moaning and groaning, for none of us are without guilt. When we catch ourselves engaged in such activity, the wise thing to do is fall to our knees and seek God's forgiveness for our lack of trust. Nothing ever enters our lives that He has not directly sent or allowed.

No matter how distressing circumstances are, it is far better to look at them as a gift from God—one that enables us to grow more into what He created us in Christ to become. It takes diligence and time to keep our mouths and minds on God's track, not allowing ourselves to become agitated and upset. But through the strength of Christ it is doable.

> **May these words of my mouth and this meditation of my heart be pleasing in your sight,**
> **Lord, my Rock and my Redeemer.**
>
> **PSALM 19:14**

APRIL 25

Let the beloved of the Lord
rest secure in him,
for he shields him all day long,
and the one the Lord loves
rests between his shoulders.

DEUTERONOMY 33:12

When we notice a dad running about carrying his child on his shoulders, it delights our hearts. It's hard to tell who's enjoying the experience more—the father or the child. Both laugh wildly, enjoying their trek together. There's no doubt about their love for each other as the child rests safely in his father's care.

God's children experience the same with Him. We feel secure with our Heavenly Father and trust Him to put us on His shoulders, give us rest, and shield us. We laugh with Him and we also cry with Him. Our journey together is breathtaking. It comforts us to know He is always with us and will never leave us, no matter what. It relieves us to know that, unlike our earthly father, our Heavenly Father never has to rest or put us down. Our ride with Him is a forever ride.

It also thrills our hearts to know that at the same time our Heavenly Father carries us on His eternal shoulders all of our brothers and sisters are there along with us too.

> **Sing to the Lord, all the earth; proclaim his salvation day after day.**
>
> **1 CHRONICLES 16:23**

APRIL 26

The integrity of the upright guides them,
but the unfaithful are destroyed by their duplicity.
PROVERBS 11:3

Our Heavenly Father grants us the freedom to choose His way or our way. We can be truthful and honest living the way the Lord wants us to live, or we can be dishonest, deceitful, and disloyal. It's far better to be known as a man or a woman of integrity than one dedicated to lies, schemes, and deception.

Let us all remember He is our Potter and we are His clay. *Does the clay say to the potter, "What are you making?"* As our Lord God is molding us and shaping us into the image of His Son, let us agree with Him and go His way in His work, for we never want to ask ourselves, *"Does your work say, 'The potter has no hands'?"* (Isaiah 45:9).

This is what the LORD says—the Holy One of Israel, and its Maker: Concerning things to come, do you question me about my children, or give me orders about the work of my hands?
ISAIAH 45:11

APRIL 27

Truly my soul finds rest in God;
my salvation comes from him.
Truly he is my rock and my salvation;
he is my fortress,
I will never be shaken.
PSALM 62:1–2

Too many of us flitter here, there, and yonder, yawning and scratching our heads and wondering how we are going to be able to complete all the tasks that lie at our feet. It is only as we awaken each morning saying, *"This is the day the LORD has made. We will rejoice and be glad in it"* (Psalm 118:24 NKJV), and mean it, that His peace infiltrates us and reigns in our hearts.

If God alone is our Hope and the Rock beneath our feet, is it not insanity for us to step into a slimy mud hole instead of resting in His fortress that surrounds us and assures us we will not be shaken?

Our Heavenly Father has given us His key that always opens His door—Jesus Christ! Grip it tightly. Never let it go.

And that rock was Christ.
1 CORINTHIANS 10:4

APRIL 28

Jesus stopped and called them.
"What do you want me to do for you?" he asked.
MATTHEW 20:32

After leaving Jericho with His disciples, a large crowd followed Jesus. Sitting on the side of the road were two blind beggars. When they heard that Jesus was approaching they yelled, *"Lord, Son of David, have mercy on us!"* (Matthew 20:29). When the crowd told the men to hush and be quiet, the beggars shouted even louder, *"Lord, Son of David, have mercy on us!"* (v. 30–31).

Jesus stopped and called out to the men, *"What do you want me to do for you?"* (v. 32).

Do we not know, do we not understand that—whatever we face, whatever overwhelms us, whatever we need or think we need—all we have to do is the same thing these two blind beggars did even as they were reprimanded for doing it? They simply said, *"Lord, we want our sight"* (v. 33).

In His compassion, Jesus touched their eyes, and they immediately regained sight. But their story didn't end there, for afterwards they followed Jesus (v. 34).

Ask and it will be given to you; seek and you will find;
knock and the door will be opened to you. For everyone who asks receives; the one who seeks finds;
and to the one who knocks, the door will be opened.
LUKE 11:9–10

APRIL 29

He gives strength to the weary
and increases the power of the weak.
Isaiah 40:29

All of us experience feelings of weariness and weakness. We have times when we want to quit, shouting, "I give up, Lord. I just give up. I'm sick of it."

What does our Heavenly Father do as He listens to us? Rather than directly responding to us, He quickly picks us up in His Heavenly arms and asks us two questions that He answers himself: *"Do you not know? Have you not heard?"* There is no time for us to respond because He quickly adds, *"The Lord is the everlasting God, the Creator of the ends of the earth. He will not grow tired or weary, and his understanding no one can fathom"* (Isaiah 40:28).

No matter what is going on in our lives, it is our Heavenly Father who strengthens us, decreasing our weakness. Regardless of our age, whether we're young or old or in between, God assures us that it is He who keeps us from stumbling and growing weary. But He requires something of us. That something is called hope. God lets us know that it is our hope, our faith, our trust in Him that renews our strength.

They will soar on wings like eagles; they will run and not grow weary, they will walk and not be faint (Isaiah 40:31). Hallelujah! Thank You, Lord!

APRIL 30

Let them give thanks to the LORD
for his unfailing love
and his wonderful deeds for mankind.
Let them sacrifice thank offerings
and tell of his works with songs of joy.
PSALM 107:21–22

When life is moving along smoothly, thankfulness for His wonderful deeds fills our hearts and souls with joy. However, we don't easily proclaim our thankfulness when life seems to be nothing but a miserable train wreck. God always knows what is happening in us or to us, for He witnesses our aching hearts and suffering souls before we ever approach Him with our dilemmas.

This is the time when it is imperative for us to offer our Heavenly Father a sacrifice of thanksgiving and praise, singing His songs of joy and allowing others to see that with God nothing is impossible (Mark 10:27)—even the ability to sing and praise Him during a time of deep sorrow and pain.

Come, let us sing for joy to the LORD; let us shout aloud to the Rock of our salvation.
Let us come before him with thanksgiving and extol him with music and song.
PSALM 95:1–2

May

MAY 1

Commit your way to the LORD;
trust in him and he will do this:
He will make your righteous reward
shine like the dawn,
your vindication like the noonday sun.

PSALM 37:5

T he way in which we walk with the Lord is comparable to binding ourselves with strong and unbreakable cords to Him and to His Ways. As we trust Him with everything in our lives, He promises us that He will make our uprightness and honesty shine like the dawn, bringing delight to others and to ourselves as well. Not only this, but even before noonday our acts and words will fill us with the integrity that radiates from us through His work in us, spreading His joy to all whom we encounter.

Let us *commit* our *way to the Lord.*

Take delight in the LORD and he will give you the desires of your heart.
PSALM 37:4

MAY 2

The bolts of your gates will be iron and bronze,
and your strength will equal your days.

DEUTERONOMY 33:25

S inking these Words of God into our minds, how could we not realize that what Moses proclaimed about Asher is also true for all of God's children? No matter our age or predicaments, let us claim this promise: *Your strength will equal your days.* It may not feel as if our physical bodies are like bolts of *iron and bronze* or that our *strength* has not diminished with aging, but God has been, now is, and always will be our *shield and helper* as well as our *glorious sword* (v. 29).

So do not fear; for I am with you; do not be dismayed, for I am your God.
I will strengthen you and help you; I will uphold you with my righteous right hand.

ISAIAH 41:10

MAY 3

Not that we are competent in ourselves
to claim anything for ourselves,
but our competence comes from God.

2 CORINTHIANS 3:5

From time to time, all of us have been assigned a task we know we are incapable of accomplishing, much less completing. Perhaps we weren't given a choice of whether to agree to it or not; nevertheless it's ours. Unwilling to dive in and attempt to put together the pieces of this complicated puzzle, we moan and groan, hoping beyond hope that somehow we can undo what we've been called to do.

It is only when we comprehend the words of the apostle Paul to the church at Corinth that we are able to relax and breathe more freely, knowing that where we cannot God always can and does. His hand is forever reaching down to us. Let up reach up and grasp it as our Heavenly Father enfolds us in His loving arms and whispers His words of encouragement into our ears.

I can do all this through him who gives me strength.
PHILIPPIANS 4:13

MAY 4

Therefore we do not lose heart.
Though outwardly we are wasting away,
yet inwardly we are being renewed day by day.
2 CORINTHIANS 4:16

Regardless of what is happening in our lives, whether a terminal illness, or the death of a loved one, or bankruptcy, or the loss of a job, or the consequences of an earthquake or a flood or a fierce tornado, let us take heart. God not only is with us, He is in us as well. Even though our bodies are *wasting away*—attempting to sweep away all our hope—or our homes are waterlogged or torn to shreds by high winds, or we're tossed on the streets seeking shelter and food, let us grasp His hope in us. God is continually with us, renewing us *day by day*. Even if isolated, surrounded by nothing but broken pieces of lumber and wood scattered beneath our feet, we are never alone. God is with us.

Trust in the Lord with all your heart and lean not on your own understanding;
in all your ways submit to him, and he will make your paths straight.
PROVERBS 3:5–6

MAY 5

If you remain in me
and my words remain in you,
ask whatever you wish,
and it will be done for you.
JOHN 15:7

We cannot remain in God if we've never given our hearts to Him, and there is no way His words can remain in us if we never read or study them. This is why it is so critical for us to recognize and confess to our Heavenly Father the sins we commit against Him, knowing He forgives us when we ask.

It's also critical for us to study the Bible, letting His words sink deeply into our souls and keeping them close to our hearts, saturating us with His love and mercy. If we do not, we will never know how to correctly petition Him for that which He so eagerly provides. When we stay close and connected to Him, marinating His words in our hearts with His love for us, whatever we wish or ask of Him will be granted.

But some might think, *Not so. God hasn't always given me everything for which I've asked.*

Of course not! Will a parent give a diabetic child a candy bar simply because the child begs and whines for it? Our Heavenly Parent only grants His children that which is good and healthy for them, not something they cannot handle or that will harm them. The more His words remain is us and our hearts remain with Him, the more skilled we become in knowing for what to ask, trusting Him to give us what is best for us.

Have you ever opened a gift you so desperately wanted and discovered that it was not the thing for which you hoped but something far more wonderful than anything you could have ever imagined?

Be still and know that I am God.

PSALM 46:10

MAY 6

Though he brings grief,
he will show compassion,
so great is his unfailing love.

LAMENTATIONS 3:32

As we grow in Christ, becoming more of what God created us in Him to become, the more our pathways seem cluttered with troubles and sorrows. However, our paths are also saturated with deep hope and peace, soaked in His unfailing love.

If God asked us if we wanted to experience these particular pathways, our response more than likely would be negative, for who wants to shed tears and experience such trials tagging their heels?

Only when we've completed a particular learning highway on which God has put us can we discern what we are becoming. We realize that we could never be who we are growing into being had His unfailing love and compassion during our travels with Him not filled us with His peace, love, and hope.

Though the Lᴏʀᴅ's mercies we are not consumed, Because His compassions fail not.
They are new every morning; Great is Your faithfulness.
LAMENTATIONS 3:22–23 ɴᴋᴊᴠ

MAY 7

Not only so, but we also rejoice in our sufferings,
because we know that suffering produces perseverance;
perseverance, character; and character, hope.
Rᴏᴍᴀɴs 5:3–4

Not many of us raise our arms into the air and dance joyfully when we experience deep anguish, pain, and grief. Yet the apostle Paul tells us there is a reason for us to rejoice in everything—regardless of what is going on in us and around us. The reason for rejoicing in suffering is the outcome of our miseries: *perseverance* that produces a transformed *character* in us, and renewed *character* that blossoms into a more confident *hope*—a kind never before experienced.

If we're attentive to God's work in us—knowing He never sends or permits anything in our lives that does not help transform us into what He created us in Christ to become—let us welcome adversities with open arms, dancing joyfully in our minds, knowing we are becoming more in Christ than we ever imagined we could be.

This new true grit in us attracts those around us and enables us to take them by their hands and encourage them along the same paths we've trod. With our renewed faith, our inner beings become more confident that, with the strength of Christ in us, we can do all the things our Heavenly Father calls us to do.

Therefore we do not lose heart. Though outwardly we are wasting away,
yet inwardly we are being renewed day by day. For our light and momentary troubles are achieving
for us an eternal glory that far outweighs them all. So we fix our eyes not on what is seen,
but on what is unseen, since what is seen is temporary, but what is unseen is eternal
2 CORINTHIANS 4:16–18

MAY 8

And hope does not put us to shame,
because God's love has poured out
into our hearts
through the Holy Spirit,
who has been given to us.
ROMANS 5:5

Too often we compare God's love with human love. There is no comparison. God's love is closely tied to faith—trust, confidence in His Word—knowing in our heart of hearts that our Heavenly Father loves us, no matter what. Yes, we sin *and fall short of the glory of God* (Romans 6:23), but as *we confess* our wrongdoings to our Heavenly Father, He forgives us (1 John 1:9). In fact, our confessed sins are removed *as far as the east is from the west* (Psalm 103:12). Unfortunately, we often hold on to them even when His Word tells us that He remembers them no more.

The Lord has gloriously poured out His love into our hearts when we become His children. The gift of His Holy Spirit in us continually guarantees His love for us. It is we, not our Heavenly Parent, who shrink away from His ever-loving arms, somehow convincing ourselves we are unworthy of such a magnificent gift—God's love in us.

And so we know and rely on the love God has for us. God is love.
Whoever lives in love lives in God, and God in them.
1 JOHN 4:16

MAY 9

But we have this treasure in jars of clay
to show that this all-surpassing power
is from God and not from us.
2 CORINTHIANS 4:7

The weeping prophet, Jeremiah, tells us in the eighteenth chapter of his book that the Lord instructed him to *go to the potter's house* and listen to the words God would speak to him there. Of course, when Jeremiah got there he saw the potter at work at his wheel, making a vessel out of clay. The vessel the potter was making became flawed, so the potter remade the lump of clay again into the vessel he designed for it to become. (Jeremiah 18:1–4).

God then asked Jeremiah a question: *"Can I not do with you, Israel, as this potter does?"* The Lord went on to say, *"Like clay in the hand of the potter, so are you in my hand"* (v. 6). As children of God, we are in His hands on His Potter's wheel. He is fashioning us into the image of His Son, Jesus Christ. When we sin, our clay image becomes stained, but our Potter does not throw us away. He just keeps working on what He is fashioning us to become.

We can even become damaged when horrendous events enter our lives, prompting us to ask our Heavenly Father why He allowed such sufferings to come our way. Only as His hands keep molding us and shaping us do we eventually grasp that our anguish and pain came from His working out the flaws in our jars of clay, which was necessary for us to grow more into what our Potter wants us to come to become in Christ.

The Potter doesn't complete His work in us until we arrive at heaven's gate and fix our eyes on our Heavenly Potter. It is then we see what a magnificent vessel we have become! Praise God from whom all blessings flow.

And we all, who with unveiled faces contemplate the Lord's glory,
are being transformed into his image with every-increasing glory,
which comes from the Lord, who is the Spirit.
2 CORINTHIANS 3:18

MAY 10

Be joyful in hope,
patient in affliction,
faithful in prayer.
ROMANS 12:12

Our hope is not always decked out in joyful clothing. Sometimes what we feel is nothing less than fear and terror. We say things like, "I hope that tornado doesn't come my way," or "I hope I don't fail this test," or "I hope I don't lose my job." But regardless if a tornado is heading our way, or a test is too difficult for us to pass, or we might be fired, our Lord tells us to be joyful in hope. We know He is not only in us but also with us and *will never leave* us *nor forsake* us (Deuteronomy 31:6), regardless of what might or might not come about.

It isn't always easy to be patient when our lives are not going smoothly, much less when difficulties arise, but we can do all things through Christ. If we remain faithful in communicating with our Heavenly Parent every nanosecond of time, His joy infiltrates us and His peace permeates us.

This doesn't mean we are on our knees in constant prayer. It simply means we are living in God's presence in our present moments, seeking His guidance in everything we say or do. His Holy Spirit in us enables us to be joyful in hope, patient in afflictions, and faithful in prayer.

You will go out in joy and be led forth in peace; the mountains and hills
will burst into song before you, and all the tress of the field will clap their hands.
ISAIAH 55:12

MAY 11

For it is God
who works in you
to will and to act
in order to fulfill
his good purpose.
PHILIPPIANS 2:13

Sometimes we are like rebellious children who absolutely refuse to do what they have been asked or told to do. As children of God, however, even in our defiance we are never alone in the decisions we make like a disobedient child is. God's Holy Spirit in us constantly directs our paths. When God places His words in our minds, His Holy Spirit in us walks along beside us and enables us to be obedient to our Heavenly Father. It is when we refuse to listen and obey that we quench and grieve God's Spirit by rejecting His guidance.

Do we not grasp, do we not appreciate that God has a plan for us—and that plan is to grow us into what He created us in Christ to become? It is only when we stay in His Word, obeying it, clutching His outstretched hand, and remaining in His presence in our present moments that we realize what God's ultimate plan is for us and all of our brothers and sisters in Christ.

I keep my eyes always on the Lord. With him at my right hand, I will not be shaken.
You have made known to me the path of life; you will fill me with joy in your presence,
with eternal pleasures at your right hand.
PSALM 16:8, 11

MAY 12

There is no fear in love.
But perfect love drives out fear,
because fear has to do with punishment.
The one who fears
is not made perfect in love.
1 JOHN 4:18

John, the apostle and beloved disciple of Jesus, tells us, *"God is love"* (1 John 4:16). God's love is perfect—flawless, without blemish. We can rely on the love God has for us; we are able to love because God first loved us (v. 19). Children who are deeply loved and cherished by their parents learn to love in return. They do not fear punishment. Of course, they don't want it and certainly don't look forward to it, but they don't fear it because deep within they know whatever their parents say or do to them or for them is because their parents love them. Unfortunately, not all children experience this kind of parental love, with many being mistreated. Perhaps this is why some of God's children have a difficult time comprehending and relating to His love for them.

However, no matter what kind of childhood we have experienced, we can rely on God's love. We have nothing to fear because His love is perfect. His *love drives out fear.* In God's love we have confidence that, no matter what comes, He is forever at our side, leading, guiding, and directing us in His love for us, every nanosecond of time.

This is how God showed his love among us: He sent his one and only Son
into the world that we might live through him. This is love: not that we loved God, but that he loved us
and sent his Son as an atoning sacrifice for our sins.
1 JOHN 4:9–10

MAY 13

For the revelation awaits
an appointed time;
it speaks of the end
and will not prove false.
Though it linger, wait for it;
it will certainly come
and will not delay.
HABAKKUK 2:3

All of us ask our Heavenly Father questions. We also appeal to Him for the desires of our hearts. God has answers to everything we ask and He fulfills that for which we plea. However, everything is accomplished in God's time, not ours. God knows what we think, what we need, and what we want, but He also knows what is necessary for us to know, what is essential for us to have, and the perfect time for Him to respond.

Unfortunately, we shove aside His Words telling us there is a time for everything and a season for every activity under heaven, and He makes everything beautiful in its time (Ecclesiastes 3:1, 11). We are an impatient lot. In our way of thinking, it seems our Lord must respond immediately to give us that for which we plead.

In the meantime, let us wait for the Lord, knowing however long it takes God will respond. When He does, we will fall to our knees with thanksgiving and praise to Him in our hearts for all the amazing things He does for us.

I will stand at my watch and station myself on the ramparts;
I will look to see what he will say to me, and what answer I am to give to this complaint.
HABAKKUK 2:1

MAY 14

Therefore the LORD will wait,
that He may be gracious to you;
And therefore He will be exalted,
that He may have mercy on you.
For the LORD is a God of justice;
Blessed are all those who wait for Him.
ISAIAH 30:18 NKJV

When God does not immediately respond to our petition, it is for a reason. We often need time to understand whether what we seek is His will for us—whether it's good for us to have. In His graciousness He allows us time to grasp why He delayed His response or refused our request. Hopefully, as time goes on, we gain wisdom and understand His responses to us. *The holy God will be proved holy by his righteous acts* (Isaiah 5:16).

Whether we *turn to the right or to the left,* our *ears will hear a voice behind* us *saying, "This is the way; walk in it"* (Isaiah 30:21). Our Lord God is a God of righteousness. *In repentance and rest is* our *salvation, in quietness and trust is* our *strength* (Isaiah 30:15). Blessed are all who wait on Him.

Although the Lord gives you the bread of adversity and the water of affliction,
your teachers will be hidden no more; with your own eyes you will see them.
ISAIAH 30:20

MAY 15

He will be the sure foundation
for your times,
a rich store of salvation
and wisdom and knowledge;
the fear of the LORD
is the key to this treasure.
ISAIAH 33:6

Regardless of God's timeframe for our lives, our Lord God has given us the keys to His Kingdom—His treasures while walking with Him through this life. He is our *sure foundation*. He is *a rich store of salvation and wisdom and knowledge*. Our time of receiving His keys does not begin the moment we are born; it occurs when we are reborn in Christ. As we begin our pilgrimage with Him, He bestows on us a magnificent store of His salvation, giving us the wisdom and knowledge we need to follow Him in the way we should go.

The key to this treasure in Him is faith and trust in our Almighty God, the One who enables us to walk the paths of righteousness in peace, the One who fills our hearts with His eternal love. For *we have this treasure in jars of clay to show that this all-surpassing power is from God and not from us* (2 Corinthians 4:7).

Therefore we do not lose heart. Though outwardly we are wasting away,
yet inwardly we are being renewed day by day. For our light and momentary troubles are achieving
for us an eternal glory that far outweighs them all. So we fix our eyes not on what is seen, but on what is
unseen, since what is seen is temporary, but what is unseen is eternal.

2 CORINTHIANS 4:16–18

MAY 16

Devote yourselves to prayer,
being watchful and thankful.
COLOSSIANS 4:2

God tells us through His apostle Paul to *devote* ourselves *to prayer*. We are to give our-selves over to prayer, to dedicate ourselves to prayer. How do we accomplish this? Our Heavenly Father never gives us a command that He does not enable us to do, because He tells us we *can do all things through Christ who strengthens* us (Philippians 4:13 NKJV).

Because of the verbal prayers we hear from others or even our own, sometimes we fall into the trap of believing we need to be in a specific place, at a certain time, under particular circum-stances, speaking elegantly and spiritually for God to take note of what we say.

Nothing could be further from the truth. Our Lord God not only listens to what we ver-balize, but to what we think as well. Even while driving down the street, we're communicating with God as we voice or think our thankfulness for His beauty in nature, or ask Him to assist a wayward driver, or seek His help to reach a destination, or pray we don't run out of gas before spying a gas station, or a multitude of things.

Devoting ourselves to prayer means we are aware of His presence in us in whatever we're doing. This is how God enables us to take note of our surroundings and become watchful and thankful for everything our Heavenly Father does for us.

And pray in the Spirit on all occasions with all kinds of prayers and requests.
EPHESIANS 6:18

Pray continually.
1 THESSALONIANS 5:17

MAY 17

Though the mountains be shaken
and the hills be removed,
yet my unfailing love for you
will not be shaken
nor my covenant of peace be removed,
says the LORD,
who has compassion on you.
ISAIAH 54:10

Regardless of the tragedies that descend on us, or the things we view and hear on newscasts that fill our hearts with despair, or predictions of disasters, we have no need to fear. Our Lord God is forever with us. His love is unfailing; it will never be shaken. Our Heavenly Father has compassion for us—He cares what happens to us. As children of God, we are forever under His covenant of peace.

So let us raise our hands to Him in thanksgiving for all He has done for us, is doing for us, and will continue to do for us until He returns again or we meet Him in heaven.

Because your love is better than life, my lips will glorify you.
I will praise you as long as I live, and in your name I will life up my hands.
PSALM 63:3–4

MAY 18

Every good and perfect gift is from above,
coming down from the Father of the heavenly lights,
who does not change like shifting shadows.
JAMES 1:17

We all receive gifts—some wanted and some not. As God's ways are not our ways and His thoughts not our thoughts (Isaiah 55:8), so too are His gifts. No other gift can rival God's gift of eternal life to us through the shed blood of His Son, Jesus Christ.

The gifts He showers on His children are *good and perfect*, descending from our *Father of heavenly lights* to strengthen us and grow us into that which He created us in Christ to become.

Others may come and go in our lives—sometimes as a friend and sometimes as an enemy, but our Heavenly Parent *is the same yesterday, today, and forever* (Hebrews 13:8). He never changes *like shifting shadows*. The gift of His presence in us, His words to us, and His unfailing love forever surpasses all other gifts we have been given.

He chose to give us birth through the word of truth,
that we might be a kind of firstfruits of all he created."
JAMES 1:18

MAY 19

Why do you look
at the speck of sawdust
in your brother's eye
and pay no attention
to the plank in your own eye?
LUKE 6:41

This is a question Jesus asked His disciples and one He also asks each of us. None of us can shake our heads from side to side believing we're not guilty. None of us are innocent, for all of us have spied specks of sawdust in our brother's or sister's eye while paying no attention to the planks in our own. We don't like to admit it, but from time to time we're hypocrites, opening our mouths before thinking, and pointing out others faults—things of which we are just as guilty.

Let us all hesitate before saying a word, look heavenward and inward, and wait for our Heavenly Father to put His thoughts into our minds and His words into our mouths before we speak. Jesus tells us that *no good tree bears bad fruit, nor does a bad tree bear good fruit* (Luke 6:43). We are all recognized by our own fruit.

A good man brings good things out of the good stored up in his heart. . . .
For the mouth speaks what the heart is full of.
LUKE 6:45

MAY 20

We do not know what to do,
but our eyes are on you.
2 CHRONICLES 20:12

There are times when we don't know what to do. We feel frightened, stranded, and abandoned. We often think words similar to those of King Jehoshaphat of Judah: *We have no power to face this vast army that is attacking us* (2 Chronicles 20:12). Too often we feel helpless, not knowing in which direction to go or what to say or what to do. As far as we're concerned, we're up the creek without a paddle.

Never! Not so! Our Heavenly Father is forever with us and always on our side. He promised: *"Never will I leave you; never will I forsake you"* (Hebrews 13:5). King David, the man after God's own heart, said, *"Therefore let all the faithful pray to you while you may be found"* (Psalm 32:6).

Our Lord God is our *hiding place*; He *will protect us from trouble and surround us with songs of deliverance* (Psalm 32:7). To top it off, God *will instruct us and teach us in the way* we *should go* and *counsel us and watch over us* (v. 8).

As God instructed us through David, so let's do it: *"Do not be like the horse or the mule, which have no understanding"* (v. 9). *"Do not be afraid or discouraged . . . For the battle is not yours, but God's"* (2 Chronicles 20:15).

Give thanks to the LORD, for his love endures forever.
2 CHRONICLES 20:21

MAY 21

Now faith is confidence
in what we hope for
and assurance about
what we do not see.

HEBREWS 11:1

When conversing with our Heavenly Father through prayer, we often petition Him for something we long for with all of our hearts, souls, and beings. We so desperately want to see what we requested come to pass. As we wait, however, and wait and wait some more, our hope begins to dwindle. Sometimes we surrender to the thought that perhaps God doesn't want us to have that for which we asked, and maybe we become upset with Him, tossing aside our faith and giving up on God responding to us.

Possibly what we need to do in these kinds of circumstances is to remember what faith is. Faith is trust. When we trust, really trust, we never give up on what we've been promised or told. We're positive beyond any kind of doubt that we won't be let down. Unfortunately, we live in a broken world, and all of us have been betrayed by someone's damaged words. Fortunately, our Heavenly Father is not someone—He is the Great I AM! He is totally, completely trustworthy.

We can be sure, knowing beyond a shadow of doubt, that He has heard our request and in His time will respond to our petition. In the meantime, we look Godward, knowing He loves us and being certain of what we do not see.

Trust in the LORD with all your heart and lean not on your own understanding;
in all your ways submit to him, and he will make your paths straight.

PROVERBS 3:5–6

MAY 22

Trust in him at all times, you people;
pour out your hearts to him,
for God is our refuge.
PSALM 62:8

We can go to God anytime, under any and all circumstances, and pour our hearts out to Him. He hears every word we speak and even reads our thoughts before we verbalize them. Our Lord God is trustworthy. We find shelter in His presence in our present moments while resting at His feet.

No matter the troubles that infiltrate our hearts and minds, God stands between us and whatever threatens to overwhelm us. God only requires that we trust Him all the time—always, which means exactly what it says, always.

He has made everything beautiful in its time.
Also He has put eternity in their hearts, except that no one can find out
the work that God does from beginning to end.
ECCLESIASTES 3:11 NKJV

MAY 23

If I rise on the wings of the dawn,
if I settle on the far side of the sea,
even there your hand will guide me,
your right hand will hold me fast.
PSALM 139:9–10

Let us pray as did King David, *"You have searched me, LORD, and you know me. You know when I sit and when I rise; you perceive my thoughts from afar. You discern my going out and my lying down; you are familiar with all my ways"* (Psalm 139:1–3).

No one can hide from God; however, many of us try to do so. Perhaps we are not happy about what He calls us to do or where He tells us to go or what He asks us to say, such as instructing us to forgive—something repugnant to so many of us.

"No way," we mumble as we crawl into the closet of our minds, hiding from Him and somehow believing He can't find us.

Our Heavenly Father always knows where each of His children is and what is in their hearts and on their minds. No matter where we flee, He is with us and in us. We fool no one but ourselves. We can never escape His presence or His Spirit who indwells us. In fact, who in his or her right mind would even consider such a thing?

From time to time, we all do. So, let us grasp the hands of our brothers and sisters in Christ and stand united together, assuring each other that no matter our circumstances His *hand will guide* us and His *right hand will hold* us *fast*.

Search me, God, and know my heart; test me and know my anxious thoughts.
See if there is any offensive way in me, and lead me in the way everlasting.
PSALM 139:23–24

MAY 24

You, LORD, are my lamp;
the LORD turns my darkness into light.
With your help I can advance against a troop;
with my God I can scale a wall.
2 SAMUEL 22:29–30

From time to time, worries by the dozens land on our doorsteps and threaten to blow us up if we don't tread lightly. Darkness completely consumes us and we believe we're done for. Even the flicker of a tiny candle clutched in our hands produces no comfort whatsoever, for we can see nothing but gloom and doom and believe no one can or will relate to what is happening in our lives.

We forget what God did for King David when his enemies and the hand of Saul threatened to do him in. David said: *"The LORD is my rock, my fortress and my deliverer; my God is my rock, in whom I take refuge, my shield and the horn of my salvation. He is my stronghold, my refuge . . . and my savior . . . I called to the LORD, who is worthy of praise, and have been saved from my enemies"* (2 Samuel 22:2–4).

These are the kind of words that illuminate our darkness and turn it into God's light. It is then, as it was with David, that we know He reaches down from on high and takes hold of us. He draws us out of deep waters . . . and rescues us from our powerful enemy, from the foes who were too strong for us. God always bring us into His spacious place, rescuing us because he delights in us (2 Samuel 22:20).

The LORD lives! Praise be to my Rock! Exalted be my God, the Rock, my Savior!
2 SAMUEL 22:47

MAY 25

See, I have refined you,
though not as silver:
I have tested you
in the furnace of affliction.
ISAIAH 48:10

When the going gets rough, far too many of us want to quit. We want absolutely nothing to do with the path on which we find ourselves. Try as we might, we cannot grasp why our Heavenly Father has allowed this incident, or that disease, or a multitude of infirmities or griefs to enter our lives. Not only do we fall into the depths of despair, but, baffled and angry, we plead: "O, Lord God why, why have you allowed this to happen to me?"

Jeremiah of the Old Testament was ordered by God to abandon whatever he was doing and go immediately to the potter's house, for God had words to say to him there. Jeremiah watched as the potter's wheel spun around and around. *But the pot he was shaping from the clay was marred in his hands; so the potter formed it into another pot, shaping it as seemed best to him* (Jeremiah 18:1–4). The potter could have tossed the lump of clay away and begun anew on a fresh lump, but he chose not to do so. The decision to start over rested solely with the potter.

God asks us the same question He asked the house of Israel, *"Can I not do with you, Israel, as this potter does?. . . Like clay in the hand of the potter, so are you in my hand"* (Jeremiah 18:5–6).

We are God's lump of clay on His Potter's wheel. Our sins and the harsh circumstances that God allows in our lives mar our lump of clay. But our Potter does not toss us away, for He is molding and making us into the image of His Son, Jesus Christ. Our pods of clay must go through fire to beautify us as He completes us. We enter heaven's gate fashioned as He intended us to become when He placed us on His wheel.

As He refines and tests us in His furnace of afflictions, fear not, for He is with us and will never leave us and will dry every tear that falls on our cheeks.

> Even to your old age and gray hairs I am he, I am he who will sustain you.
> I have made you and I will carry you; I will sustain you and I will rescue you.
>
> ISAIAH 46:4

MAY 26

> *I will sacrifice a thank offering to you*
> *and call on the name of the LORD.*
> PSALM 116:17

At times life can be unbearable. We feel as if God has somehow abandoned us, leaving us in a gully of despair. We know, however, that God never puts more on us than we can bear. At such times, nothing brings such joy to His ears than for us to sacrifice a thank offering to Him and call on His name.

As we do, we discover joy saturating our souls even though the valley is still there, but we are not walking in it alone because we know He is with us and forever will be. Our jubilation bursts forth, for our Lord God is pleased with our sacrifice of thanksgiving.

> Through Jesus, therefore, let us continually offer to God a sacrifice of praise—
> the fruit of lips that openly profess his name.
>
> HEBREWS 13:15

MAY 27

*And Elisha prayed, "Open his eyes, L*ORD*, so he may see."*
*Then the L*ORD *opened the servant's eyes,*
and he looked and saw the hills full of horses
and chariots of fire all around Elisha.

2 KINGS 6:17

After conferring with his officers when Aram was at war with Israel, the king of Aram said, *"I will set up my camp in such and such a place"* (2 Kings 6:8). God revealed to the prophet Elisha the king's words soon after he spoke them. Elisha then warned the king of Israel to be careful not to go to a particular place because the Arameans would be there. Time and again Elisha warned Israel's king so that he was on his guard in such places (v. 9–10).

The king of Aram became angry because he thought one of his officers was betraying him to the Israelites. His officers told their king they weren't guilty but that the informer was the prophet Elisha, who told the king of Israel exactly what he said even while in his bedroom. The king then ordered the officers to find Elisha so he could capture him (v. 11–13).

When the king discovered Elisha was in Dothan, he sent horses and chariots and a strong force, who surrounded the city during the night. The next morning when Elisha's servant got up and spied the horses and chariots, it petrified the servant. He asked Elisha what they were now going to do (14–15).

Elisha's response then was the same one God always speaks to us in alarming times: *"Don't be afraid. . . . Those who are with us are more than those who are with them."* Elisha's servant was dumfounded. Elisha prayed, *"Open his eyes, L*ORD*, so he may see."* When God opened the servant's eyes, *he looked and saw the hills full of horses and chariots of fire all around Elisha* (v. 16–17).

Elisha prayed to the Lord again, asking Him to strike the soldiers with blindness. He then told the blind soldiers they were in the wrong place and to follow him to the right one. He led them to Samaria. Once there, Elisha asked the Lord to open their eyes so that they could see they were in Samaria (v. 18–20).

When the King of Israel saw the men, he asked Elisha, *"Shall I kill them, my father? Shall I kill them?"* (v. 21).

Elisha responded negatively, asking the king if he would kill men he had captured with his own sword. He instructed the king to give them food and water so that they could eat and drink before going back to their master. After the soldiers of Aram returned to their land, the bands of soldiers from Aram stopped raiding Israel's territory (v. 22–23).

In this story God is teaching us to lean on Him, to trust Him in any and all things, for when our surroundings are full of His horses and chariots of fire nothing can harm us without obtaining His permission to do so.

> I will lift up my eyes to the hills—From whence comes my help?
> My help comes from the LORD, who made heaven and earth.
> PSALM 121:1–2 NKJV

MAY 28

When he had gone indoors,
the blind men came to him,
and he asked them,
"Do you believe
that I am able to do this?"
MATTHEW 9:28

As Jesus was leaving one place heading for another, *two blind men followed Him call-ing out, "Have mercy on us, Son of David!"* (Matthew 9:27). Jesus did not respond. He entered a house and the men followed Him. This is when Jesus asked them a question, one He frequently asks us: *"Do you believe I am able to do this?"*

Jesus knew the men were blind, but how did He know this? They never said they were blind. They just asked for Him to have mercy on them—compassion, pity, benevolence. Our circum-stances are not as essential to our Lord as is our trust in Him to do that which we seek. Regard-less of what is happening to us, in us, or around us, all that is needed is for us to respond as did the blind men to Jesus' question about whether we believe. "Yes, Lord," they replied" (v. 28).

> Then he touched their eyes and said, "According to your faith let it be done to you."
> MATTHEW 9:29

MAY 29

Are not two sparrows
sold for a penny?
Yet not one of them
will fall to the ground
outside your Father's care.
MATTHEW 10:29

A sparrow is a rather small songbird, so insignificant that in Jesus' day when two of them were sold they cost the buyer only a penny. Jesus used this example to encourage His disciples and those who follow Him. He urges us not to fear—to be anxious for nothing. The very hairs of our heads are numbered (Matthew 10:30). Not even one tiny sparrow will fall to the ground apart from God's will.

Then why do so many of us walk around with a cloud of dread hovering over our heads? Why do we tremble as we head into the unknown? We are never alone on any path on which our Lord and Savior places us. Absolutely nothing in our lives occurs without God knowing it and approving it.

His ultimate plan is to grow us into the image of Jesus Christ, His Son. We are children of the King. As such, we are to listen to His voice, because *there is nothing concealed that will not be disclosed, or hidden that will not be made known* (v. 26).

As His children, let us step up to God's plate with eagerness and enthusiasm, even if the demonic enemy's ball is heading our way, threatening to do us in. *Not one* sparrow falls to the ground apart from the will of God. *All things are possible with God* (Mark 10:27).

So don't be afraid; you are worth more than many sparrows.
MATTHEW 10:31

MAY 30

Trust in him at all times, you people;
pour out your hearts to him,
for God is our refuge.
PSALM 62:8

It seems we've no sooner come through one bumpy situation than another confronts us. We moan and groan, complaining up one side and down another. We are sick and tired of everything. Others may encourage us to look on the bright side and leave what was behind and move forward, and they're exactly right. *There is . . . a season for every activity under the heavens,* which includes *a time to be silent and a time to speak* (Ecclesiastes 3:1, 7).

However, as we speak, God tells us to pour out our hearts to Him because we can trust Him. He is our refuge. God knows our thoughts—every one of them. Far better to seek His presence, opening up our hearts to Him and verbalizing exactly what we feel, than to keep our misery bottled up. He never tells us to hush. However, *there is a season for every activity under heaven*. Thankfully, our Heavenly Father knows when our season is complete, for He is the One who quietly instructs us to be quiet and to move on.

He has healed our wounds and placed us on a new path—one filled with His presence in our present moments.

He has made everything beautiful in its time.
ECCLESIASTES 3:11

MAY 31

My grace is sufficient for you,
for my power is made perfect in weakness.
2 CORINTHIANS 12:9

The apostle Paul had some sort of *thorn in his flesh* (2 Corinthians 12:7). We're not told what it was, but apparently it was chronic and from time to time kept him from God's work. However, Paul viewed it as keeping him focused and on track, enabling him to do what God had called him to do.

Whatever our Lord has asked of us, it seems that we, too, can discover a thorn in our flesh. Perhaps it's anxiety, not believing we're up to what God enables us to do, or feeling we're not educated enough to do it, or thinking we're not even good enough to do it. God's grace is always sufficient, and His *power is made perfect in* our *weakness.* God's unmerited favor rests on us. What others might say about us or how they judge us is inconsequential. *If God is for us, who can be against us?* (Romans 8:31).

Those to whom Paul ministered found no fault with him or his ministry. Only those who opposed him and what he proclaimed from God were his critics. The same is also true for us.

Therefore I will boast all the more gladly about my weaknesses,
so that Christ's power may rest on me. That is why, for Christ's sake, I delight in weaknesses,
in insults, in hardships, in persecutions, in difficulties. For when I am weak, then I am strong.
2 CORINTHIANS 12:9–10

JUNE

JUNE 1

Let perseverance finish its work
so that you may be mature and complete,
not lacking anything.
JAMES 1:4

No matter what arises in our walk with the Lord, we must persevere—hang on with all our might, determined to keep on keeping on through whatever God either sends or allows in our lives. God's *thoughts are not* our *thoughts, neither are* His *ways* our *ways.* He has a mission for each and every one of us, and that is to bring us into the image of His Son, Jesus Christ. To accomplish His work in us, we must be persistent and unwavering in our walk with Him, regardless of what occurs along the way.

God never puts more on us than we can bear. He wants us to mature in His plan for us and not lack anything. In order to mature, we will experience trials and tribulations. When we reach the end of a difficult path, we realize we're more than we ever thought we could become had we never developed His gift of perseverance in us.

"For my thoughts are not your thoughts, neither are your ways my ways," declares the LORD.
ISAIAH 55:8

JUNE 2

Yet I am always with you;
you hold me by my right hand.
PSALM 73:23

Remember when you were a little child and your mother held your hand? When you entered adolescence you no longer wanted her to do this. Rather, you preferred exploring the world around you, surrounded by your friends. When adulthood arrived, you no longer lived with your parents or siblings. You were on your own.

No matter what comes or goes in our lives, whether desolations or joys, our Heavenly Father is with us every step of the way. God never leaves us nor forsakes us (Deuteronomy 31:6). We may not be aware of it, but He is always holding our hand.

Just as it delights us to envision the times while growing up when our parents were always there for us, it brings even greater joy, peace, and comfort to feel the softness of His hand embracing our own, assured He is with us. No matter where we are on our earthly pilgrimage, God will always be there too—something no earthly being could ever accomplish.

But thanks be to God! He gives us the victory through our Lord Jesus Christ.
1 CORINTHIANS 15:57

JUNE 3

He has caused his wonders to be remembered;
the LORD is gracious and compassionate.
PSALM 111:4

The writer of Psalm 111 wrote: *Great are the works of the LORD; they are pondered by all who delight in them* (v. 2). No one who has entered His presence and reached for His outstretched hand can ever forget even God's tiniest miracle, which penetrated their hearts and souls as if searing them. It's unforgettable. It's exquisite, like holding a pot of gold that glimmers in the sunlight. It's remarkable beyond description.

Our Lord God is gracious and compassionate. He never leaves us or forsakes us (Deuteronomy 31:6). If there's any leaving or forsaking, it is we who do it, not our Holy Savior.

Great is your faithfulness.
LAMENTATIONS 3:23

JUNE 4

You are the salt of the earth . . .
You are the light of the world.
MATTHEW 5:13–14

After explaining His Beatitudes to the crowds to whom He spoke His Sermon on the Mount, Jesus admonished them to be *the salt of the earth* and *the light of the world.* Salt is to bring out the flavor of food. *If the salt loses its saltiness, how can it be made salty again?* (Matthew 5:13). Just as salt is meant to liven up food, we are to do the same for those we encounter as well as for ourselves. If we do not stay in communication with our Heavenly Father, listening to His words and obeying His Spirit, our salt will lose its flavor and we are *no longer good for anything, except to be thrown out and trampled underfoot* (v. 13).

Likewise, we cannot hide God's light in us. Unlike an earthly light bulb that has only a specific lifespan, God's light in us never runs out. It is we who hide it when we stray from Him and go our own way, preferring rather to place our light beneath a bowl instead of letting it shine from His glorious lampstand. God wants everyone to see His light in us. We are to let our lights *shine before others, that they may see* our *good deeds and glorify* our *Father in heaven* (v. 16).

We will serve the LORD our God and obey him.
JOSHUA 24:24

JUNE 5

For with you is the fountain of life;
in your light we see light.
PSALM 36:9

Total darkness, not even being able to see our hands in front of our faces, is alarming—so much so that we struggle to grab hold of anything that will keep us balanced. It is the same with thirst, especially when there is no water in sight and we crave nothing but to quench our thirst. At such times of need, all we have to do is look Godward, knowing that

Jesus Christ is our fountain of life, who pours out His lifesaving water on our heads and lights the path beneath our feet.

With God nothing is impossible. He assures us that we *can do all things through* the strength of *Christ* in us (Philippians 4:13 NKJV). Regardless of what we encounter on His precious road of salvation, we are never alone. He is our fountain of life and in Him we have light.

How priceless is your unfailing love, O God!
People take refuge in the shadow of your wings.
PSALM 36:7

JUNE 6

*In your unfailing love
you will lead the people
you have redeemed.
In your strength
you will guide them
to your holy dwelling.*
EXODUS 15:13

When we take Jesus Christ as our Lord and Savior, our Heavenly Father adopts us into His royal family. We are redeemed by the shed blood of Jesus, thereby becoming saturated in God's unfailing love. God cancels out all our sins. He remembers them no longer. Unfortunately, we hang on to many of them, not forgiving ourselves and doubtful God could ever love someone who has done what we have done.

Our Heavenly Father never makes a promise that He does not keep. We might fail others and ourselves, but God never fails us! As His children we are on His redemptive road headed for His holy dwelling, where we will see Him face-to-face in heaven.

In the strength of Christ in us, we can do all things. Let us not hold on to anything our Heavenly Father has forgiven. If we refuse to let go then we have committed another sin, one of not believing His love is unfailing, for He has redeemed us through the shed blood of His Son.

If we confess our sins, he is faithful and just and will forgive us our sins
and purify us from all unrighteousness.
1 JOHN 1:9

JUNE 7

For through the Spirit
we eagerly await by faith
the righteousness
for which we hope.
GALATIANS 5:5

Many people believe that if they are good enough God will be pleased with them and take them to heaven when they die. They trust in what they can do to please God rather than trusting what God can and does do in them. It is the Holy Spirit He places in us at the time of our redemption who enables us to grow into what God created us to be—righteous through the shed blood of Jesus Christ, growing us moment by moment in our walk with Him, and shaping us into the image of His Son.

It is our faith—our trust in our Heavenly Father—that grows our hope of becoming who He created us to be. All we have to do is listen to Him, obey Him, and walk with Him along the paths he places beneath our feet.

For God so loved the world that he gave his one and only Son,
that whoever believes in him shall not perish but have eternal life.
JOHN 3:16

JUNE 8

I have been crucified with Christ
and I no longer live,
but Christ lives in me.
The life I live in the body,
I live by faith in the Son of God,
who loved me
and gave himself for me.
GALATIANS 2:20

Getting off track is not a difficult thing to do. The apostle Peter did so when he decided not to continue to eat with Christian Gentiles. Some Jewish believers had come into Peter's life and rebuked him for eating gentile food. Peter's decision to refrain from such behavior implied he was violating the gospel by eating it and that Christ alone was not enough for salvation, but the Jewish law also had to be followed (Galatians 2:11–13). From time to time we do likewise because we want to fit in with everyone else.

When the apostle Paul publically confronted Peter regarding this, Paul said, *"You are a Jew, yet you live like a Gentile and not like a Jew. How is it, then, that you force Gentiles to follow Jewish customs?"* (v. 14). Peter awakened to his sin of hypocrisy, and he repented. Paul did well to reprimand Peter, and Peter did well to heed his rebuke.

Let us do likewise and listen to our Christian brothers and sisters, who love us enough to take us by the hand and lead us back to God's path. We must pay strict attention to God's way and not attempt to please others by walking away from it.

I live by faith in the Son of God, who loved me and gave himself for me.
GALATIANS 2:20

JUNE 9

Speaking to one another with
psalms, hymns, and songs from the Spirit.
Sing and make music in your heart to the Lord,
always giving thanks to God the Father for everything,
in the name of our Lord Jesus Christ.
EPHESIANS 5: 19–20

We are to *be careful how* we *live—not* being *unwise but wise, making the most of every opportunity* (Ephesians 5:15–16). God instructs us not to be foolish but to listen to Him so that we can understand what His will is. What we say, what we do, and how we respond to the adversities of life reverberate not only to us but to those around us as well.

We are to encourage one another with God's words, *make music* in our hearts *to the Lord,* and *always* give *thanks* to Him *for everything, in the name of Jesus Christ* (Ephesians 5:19–20). Yes, we will experience trials and tribulations on our walk with our Heavenly Father, and we will feel as if we don't have the energy or the desire to continue walking His path, much less singing and thanking Him in our struggles.

God knows we will get to the other side of what He has either sent or allowed into our lives, regardless of how long it takes to get through it. When we reach the point of understanding God was equipping us to help those who are now going through their own trials, our hearts once again overflow with His *psalms, hymns*, and spiritual *songs*. As others gather around listening to us praise Him for walking with us through the dark valley, they too will come out on the other side of their sorrow more of what God created them in Christ to become.

We are to continue *speaking to one another with psalms, hymns, and songs from the Spirit*; making music as we give *thanks to God the Father for everything* He sends our way.

Come, let us sing for joy to the LORD; let us shout aloud to the Rock of our salvation.
Let us come before him with thanksgiving and extol him with music and song.
PSALM 95:1–2

JUNE 10

The LORD has done great things for us,
and we are filled with joy.
PSALM 126:3

Sometimes we feel so low we have to stretch our necks to see upward. But when we do, it is well worth the effort. Seeing God's face looking down on us while also clutching our hand encourages our minds to be filled with the great things He has done for us. As our Shepherd He has met all our needs, led us beside still waters, and made us *lie down in green pastures*. We can't even begin to count the times He refreshed our souls and *guided us along the right paths* (Psalm 23:1–3).

When He walked us *through the darkest valley*, we weren't afraid because He was with us, comforting us. And the times He prepared *a table* surrounded by our enemies and anointed our heads with His oil of joy and peace, our cups absolutely overflowed because we know His *goodness and love will follow* us *all* our *days* (Psalm 23:4–6).

His promise that we would *dwell in* His *house forever* washes away feelings of lowliness because our Shepherd will never abandon us. He is forever at our side.

How great are your works, LORD, how profound your thoughts!
PSALM 92:5

JUNE 11

*Call to me
and I will answer you
and tell you great
and unsearchable things
you do not know.*
JEREMIAH 33:3

We live in a busy world. We seek answers to our questions, but far too often no one seems to want to take time to raise our spirits, much less lift us up. Our Heavenly Father is forever waiting for our call. All we have to is ring Him up, for we never get a busy signal. It matters not what we want to ask Him or discuss with Him. He is faithfully there for us, regardless of the time of day or night, and we can remain on the line with Him as long as we like because time with Him is not only unlimited but free as well.

Why is it then that far too many of us neglect dialing His number, for it is so simple to remember? It's called falling to our knees, crying out, "Help me, Jesus." He always promptly responds.

How abundant are the good things that you have stored up for those who fear you,
that you bestow in the sight of all, on those who take refuge in you.
PSALM 31:19

JUNE 12

But you are a chosen people,
a royal priesthood,
a holy nation,
God's special possession,
that you may declare the praises
of him who called you
out of darkness
into his wonderful light.

1 PETER 2:9

As children and teenagers, many of us were passed by as others were selected to play on an athletic team or chosen to perform in a drama production or other activities that required an elimination process. We felt left out, alienated from the goings on around us.

But when God selected us to be on His team, it was a different matter altogether. We were no longer overlooked. We became His *chosen people.* Everyone receives an invitation to come and join His team. No one is ever eliminated. We have been *called out* of the *darkness* that once engulfed us to walk with Him in His magnificent *light.*

We belong to God. We are His *royal priesthood.* All that is required of us is to sing His praises to those around us, telling them of His unfailing love and His desire for them to accept His invitation to join us on His team.

Come, let us sing for joy to the Lord; let us shout aloud to the Rock of our salvation.
Let us come before him with thanksgiving and extol him with music and song.

PSALM 95:1–2

JUNE 13

I will never leave you
nor forsake you.
JOSHUA 1:5

After Moses died, his successor, Joshua, was given the job of leading over two hundred million people of God into the Promised Land and conquering those who inhabited it. Quite a challenge! Probably none of us will ever face one like it, but all of us will encounter our own trials, fears, and troubles during our lifetimes. It's a given.

God said to Joshua: *"As I was with Moses, so I will be with you"* (Joshua 1:5). Our Heavenly Father says the same thing to His children today. Regardless of what comes into our lives, He is continually with us. He *will never leave* us *nor forsake* us. Yes, others will leave us, for we are never guaranteed of remaining with our loved ones. They die, or they can walk away from us, leaving us with feelings of abandonment—but our Lord God *never* leaves us nor forsakes us. He is with us every step on our earthly travels, with His Holy Spirit in us guiding us and leading us to His final destination for us—heaven.

Be strong and courageous. Do not be afraid; do not be discouraged,
for the LORD your God will be with you wherever you go.
JOSHUA 1:9

JUNE 14

You may ask me
for anything in my name,
and I will do it.

JOHN 14:14

Did God say we can *ask* Him *for anything in* His *name and* He *will do it*? Yes, but as we do so, we must take note of the three words wrapped around His promise of asking for anything. They are "*in My name.*" In other words, what we ask of Him must be His will for our lives.

The only way we are guaranteed of knowing His will for us and being in His will is to stay in close contact with Him. This means reading from His Word and talking with Him daily. It also means listening to His Holy Spirit as He directs our paths, putting us on the right track, letting us know in which direction to go and what to say or not say and what to do or not do.

No one has to tell us when we grieve His Spirit or quench Him. We know when we're off track, but far too often we refuse to acknowledge it, much preferring to go our way instead of going His way.

Nothing is more comforting to our spirits than trusting God and obeying Him because, as we do, we are in His will and as such we can *ask* Him *for anything* since we know His will for us.

You make known to me the path of life; you will fill me with joy in your presence,
with eternal pleasures at your right hand.

PSALM 16:11

JUNE 15

The LORD makes firm the steps
of the one who delights in him;
though he may stumble,
he will not fall,
for the LORD upholds him
with his hand.
PSALM 37:23–24

P arents rejoice to see their children make wise choices throughout their lifetimes. By laying a solid foundation for children on which to build their futures, parents long for their children to pay close attention to what they select as they build their lives on the foundation that has been laid for them.

It is the same with our Heavenly Father. When we take Jesus Christ as our Lord and Savior, God lays a solid foundation on which we are to build the kind of life He desires for us to live. Nothing delights Him more than when we follow through, building on His groundwork that which pleases Him. God makes our steps firm, knowing we will stumble along His way—often taking a nosedive. If we do, God does for us something our parents cannot do—upholds us with His hand. Our time with our parents is limited. Our time with Heavenly Father is limitless.

Our Heavenly Parent always gives us a choice about what to build on His foundation. We can do it His way or we can do it our way. Nothing is lovelier than His way.

Commit your way to the LORD; trust in him and he will do this:
He will make your righteous reward shine like the dawn, your vindication like the noonday sun.
PSALM 37:5–6

JUNE 16

But you are to hold fast
to the LORD your God,
as you have until now.
JOSHUA 23:8

Joshua was 110 when he died and was buried in the Promised Land. God had given him an enormous task to accomplish during his lifetime, and he not only did it, but he did it well. God had instructed Joshua to *be strong and very courageous* (Joshua 1:7). As Joshua prepared himself for his home going, he summoned all of Israel—the elders, leaders, judges, and officials—and commanded them to *be very strong; be careful to obey all that is written in the Book of the Law of Moses, without turning aside to the right or to the left* (Joshua 23:6).

Our Lord God gives each and every one of us a task to accomplish during our lifetimes. It may not be as enormous as was Joshua's, but it is as important as his was, and we must take it as seriously as did Joshua. Remember, we *can do all things through Christ who strengthens* us (Philippians 4:13 NKJV). God has implanted His Holy Spirit in us to complete that which He began is us—to grow us into the image of His Son, Jesus Christ.

We will experience many trials and tribulations along our paths with Him, but God is forever with us, enabling us to keep going no matter what comes our way. When the time comes for Him to call us home, we can say to those we leave behind the same words God spoke to Joshua and the words Joshua repeated to His people: *Be very strong; be careful to obey all that is written in the Book of the Law of Moses, without turning aside to the right or to the left.*

Rejoice in the LORD always. I will say it again: Rejoice!
PHILIPPIANS 4:4

JUNE 17

Therefore, since we are surrounded
by such a great cloud of witnesses,
let us throw off everything that hinders
and the sin that so easily entangles.
And let us run with perseverance
the race marked out for us.
HEBREWS 12:1

Let us imagine ourselves being surrounded by the *great cloud of witnesses* to whom the writer of the Book of Hebrews is referring—people like Noah, Abraham, Sarah, Isaac, Jacob, Joseph, Moses, David, and many others well-known for their faith in spite of their trials and tribulations. Now let us add the countless people throughout all generations who have endured the race God placed before them.

As we look into their eyes and hearts, we can comprehend more completely we are not the only ones who have walked the challenging paths our Heavenly Father has marked out for us. As we do, *let us throw off everything that hinders* us from what He has called us to do, especially *the sin that so easily entangles* us—the one well-known by the evil one, who delights in tossing it our way, hoping we will give in to it.

We are to *run with perseverance*, determined in our heart of hearts to continue on no matter what. And as we do so, let us repeat over and over to ourselves: *"I can do all this through him who gives me strength"* (Philippians 4:13).

As we pray for His help and thank Him for everything that comes our way, our anxiousness will be replaced by *the peace of God, which transcends all understanding* and will *guard* our *hearts and minds in Christ Jesus* (Philippians 4:6–7).

Fixing our eyes on Jesus, the pioneer and perfecter of faith. For the joy set before him he endured the cross, scorning its shame, and sat down at the right hand of the throne of God.
HEBREWS 12:2

JUNE 18

I have loved you
with an everlasting love;
I have drawn you
with unfailing kindness.
JEREMIAH 31:3

Have you ever noticed how conditional human love is? Think about it. Yes, we do have those in our lives we love unconditionally, don't we? But do we really? Do we not take love back or refuse to express it when the one loved does not meet our expectations, even our demands? Yes, we can and do love with an enduring love—but it has its drawbacks. It's conditional, depending on circumstances in our lives.

Praise God, His love is never restrictive! No matter how unloving we are or what sins we commit or words we say, God's love is everlasting—no shortcomings whatsoever. His love is so breathtaking that it is impossible for us to grasp. It is beyond our intellectual capacity. God pours it out on us by His bucketsful. He draws us to Him with His lovingkindness, forever expressing His love in ways far beyond our comprehension.

It is through faith in Him that we receive His perfect and everlasting love. He remains with us through thick and thin. Let us raise our hands in praise to Him for his everlasting, unending, and eternal love!

Let us come before him with thanksgiving and extol him with music and song.
PSALM 95:2

JUNE 19

I will turn all my mountains into roads,
and my highways will be raised up.
ISAIAH 49:11

America's Great Smoky Mountains are astounding. Mountain peak after mountain peak looms upward, causing many of us to want to climb all of them, but we cannot. Yet all of us have climbed our own mountains of despair, hopelessness, and gloom, to name only a few. It was an arduous task, one that almost drained us dry.

As we look back on our challenging climbs, we are astounded—speechless. The road God put beneath our feet, as we pressed upward and onward, enabled us to grow more into what He created us in Christ to become. We were never alone. His highway raised us up so we could become more than we ever dreamed we could be as we desperately desire to follow Him wherever He leads. God always creates roads that intersect His highways on all His mountains of growth for us.

My sheep listen to my voice; I know them, and they follow me.
JOHN 10:27

JUNE 20

They will still bear fruit in old age,
they will stay fresh and green,
proclaiming, "The LORD is upright;
he is my Rock,
and there is no wickedness in him."
PSALM 92:14–15

The writer of Psalm 92 tells us: *The righteous will flourish like a palm tree, they will grow like a cedar of Lebanon; planted in the house of the LORD, they will flourish in the courts of our God* (v. 12–13). As children of God, we have been made righteous through the shed blood of Jesus Christ, God's son. We become like the cedar trees of Lebanon—rock-solid, resilient, and secure—even when tossed about through the fierce and devastating winds of life's circumstances. And like palm trees, as we age we endure, standing tall regardless of what comes our way or what people might say.

No matter how old we get or what discouraging events flock toward us, we will remain fresh and green, joyfully proclaiming: *"The Lord is upright; he is my Rock."*

We have this hope as an anchor for the soul, firm and secure.
HEBREWS 6:19

JUNE 21

Why, my soul, are you downcast?
Why so disturbed within me?
Put your hope in God,
for I will yet praise him,
my Savior and my God.
PSALM 43:5

During problematic times let us ask ourselves the same questions as did the sons of Korah, who were appointed by King David to serve as choir leaders and temple musicians: *"Why are you downcast,* feeling so disheartened? What causes you to be so anxious and worried?" More than likely we won't be able to come up with a definite response to these questions because our minds are in an uproar, confusing us.

Regardless of what brings about blue thoughts and feelings of discouragement, let us take note: There is only one response to these questions. It is what the choir leaders directed their temple members to sing: *"Put your hope in God."* Praise Him for anything and everything, for nothing brings up a downcast spirit as does praising God for His blessings.

Be strong and take and take heart, all you who hope in the Lord.
PSALM 31:24

JUNE 22

I keep my eyes always on the Lord.
With him at my right hand,
I will not be shaken.
PSALM 16:8

As King David declared that God was his *portion* and his *cup*, making him secure, so let us raise our hands in praise to the Lord, saying the same. Our Lord God set *boundary lines in pleasant places* for King David, and David proclaimed he had a *delightful inheritance* (Psalm 16:5–6). So it is with every child of the King.

God counsels us continually, instructing us how to live the life He has given us through His Son, Jesus Christ. How can we, as God's children, not rejoice? How can we not rest secure, knowing He will never forsake us? Our Lord God will never leave us. Thank You, Lord. Amen.

You make known to me the path of life; you will fill me with joy in your presence,
with eternal pleasures at your right hand.
PSALM 16:11

JUNE 23

I will be fully satisfied
as with the richest of foods;
with singing lips
my mouth will praise you.
PSALM 63:5

No matter what circumstances come into our lives, we can say along with King David that regardless of what our Heavenly Father either allows to come or directly sends our way, we are *satisfied as with the richest of foods* and sing praises to Him even in the depths of despair, for our Father is forever with us and will never leave us.

Even when walking through the valley of the shadow of death, He holds us securely in His everlasting arms, singing His love song to us and mending our broken hearts. We know that we know that we know the gruesome path beneath our feet will not last forever, for in His time God makes all things beautiful (Ecclesiastes 3:11).

You, God, you are my God, earnestly I seek you;
I thirst for you, my whole being longs for you,
in a dry and parched land where there is no water.
PSALM 63:1

JUNE 24

Since no man knows the future,
who can tell someone else what is to come?
ECCLESIASTES 8:7

Our futures are in God's hands. Mulling over what is to come is a waste of precious time—moments we could spend in God's presence, conversing with Him about His will for our lives and thanking and praising Him for who He is and what He does. The only One who can reveal our future to us is the One who is presently with us, guiding and directing the paths we are currently on with Him at our sides.

Let us take the hand He extends to us and walk with Him along our roads together, for in Him we trust whatever our futures might hold.

He has made everything beautiful in its time.
He has also set eternity in the human heart; yet no one can fathom
what God has done from beginning to end.
ECCLESIASTES 3:11

JUNE 25

For our light and momentary troubles
are achieving for us an eternal glory
that far outweighs them all.
2 CORINTHIANS 4:17

When we are traveling down the roads of the shadows of death, we sink to rock bottom, feeling as if we're being swallowed by the mud-covered waters of wretchedness. No matter what another says to encourage us, there is no way we believe the circumstances we experience are *light and momentary troubles*. Our hearts are crushed, filled with grief.

It is not until we reach the other side of our sufferings that God's light shining in us awakens us, enabling us to raise our hands in praise to Him because we now know He has achieved for us *an eternal glory that far outweighs* everything He has allowed to cross our paths.

We are now more of what He created us in Christ to become. *Surely goodness and mercy will follow* us *all the days of* our lives (Psalm 23:6 NKJV), with our Heavenly Father and King of kings walking with us every step of the way. Hallelujah!

For with God nothing will be impossible.
LUKE 1:37 NKJV

JUNE 26

For God, who said,
"Let light shine out of darkness,"
made his light shine in our hearts
to give us the light
of the knowledge
of God's glory
displayed in
the face of Christ.
2 CORINTHIANS 4:6

*I*n the beginning God created the heavens and the earth *and darkness was over the surface of the deep,"* and *God said, "Let there be light"* (Genesis 1:1–3). He has also commanded *His light* to *shine in our hearts to give us light* as well. Our *light* is *the knowledge of God's glory* glowing *in the face of* our Lord and Savior, Jesus *Christ.*

Let us never believe we are alone because He is always in us, with us, and for us. His light forever and ever shines in and through us, letting us know that we can do everything through Christ who gives us the strength to do so. Everything! So, let us never allow ourselves to grow weary of any assignment He gives us, any place He puts us, or any words He commands us to speak.

Never will I leave you; never will I forsake you.
HEBREWS 13:5

JUNE 27

But God demonstrates
his own love for us in this:
While we were still sinners,
Christ died for us.
ROMANS 5:8

How could we ever become oblivious to God's love for us? His love completely surrounds us. it envelopes us in the brilliance of the Holy Spirit that our Heavenly Father places in us when we accept His gift of eternal life through the sacrificial blood of Jesus Christ. God's love remains with us forever, regardless of the sins we commit.

Perhaps it is difficult for many of us to absorb the complexities of such love because our love is far too conditional. We often require perfection from those who seek our love, sometimes willing to dish it out and sometimes furiously clamping it off. Never so with our Heavenly Father—His love is eternally in us and with us. His well never runs dry.

And so we know and rely on the love God has for us. God is love.
Whoever lives in love lives in God, and God in them.
1 JOHN 4:16

For God so loved the world that he gave his one and only Son,
that whoever believes in him shall not perish but have eternal life.
JOHN 3:16

JUNE 28

Whoever believes in me,
as the Scripture has said,
rivers of living water
will flow from within them.
JOHN 7:38

On the last and greatest day of the Feast of Tabernacles, *Jesus stood* up to the crowd *and said in a loud voice, "Let anyone who is thirsty come to me and drink"* (John 7:37). Some of the listeners declared Jesus was a prophet, while others said, *"He is the Messiah."* Still others declared He couldn't be *the Messiah* because He was *from Galilee,* not *Bethlehem, the town where David* once *lived* (v. 40–42).

The chief priests and the Pharisees had sent temple guards to arrest Jesus, but they didn't do so, even though some in the crowd wanted Him seized. When the temple guards went back to the priests and Pharisees empty-handed, the leaders wanted to know why the guards hadn't brought Jesus with them (v. 44–45).

The temple guards stated, *"No one ever spoke the way this man does"* (v. 46).

No one can quench our thirst the way Jesus can. And no one can fill our hearts *with rivers of living water* flowing *from within* us as does God's Holy Spirit, who indwells us once we accept Jesus Christ as our Lord and Savior.

Without God's *rivers of living water* flowing *from within* us we cannot accomplish what our Heavenly Father desires we do after becoming children of the King.

Love the Lord your God with all your heart and with all your soul and
with all your mind and with all your strength.
MARK 12:30

JUNE 29

She said to herself,
"If I only touch his cloak,
I will be healed."
MATTHEW 9:21

A woman who had been bleeding for twelve years came up behind Jesus as He busied himself with those who sought His healing. She said nothing. All she did was touch the edge of His cloak, believing that was all she needed to do to become well. When Jesus turned and saw her, He said, *"Take heart, daughter, your faith has healed you"* (Matthew 9:20–22).

How many times have we, like this woman, believed our Lord and Savior Jesus Christ knows what we seek before asking, and then received it without speaking a word?

As the woman was healed from that moment on, so shall we if we take hope in the Lord, trusting in His love for us to do that which will make us whole again. This doesn't mean trust necessarily brings physical healing the way we expect it. It simply means that trust brings spiritual healing and growth in us, making it possible for us to wait on the Lord, knowing in His time He makes all things beautiful—whatever those things might be.

Whether we are physically or emotionally healed when seeking God's help, He says to us the same as He did to this woman: *"Take heart; your faith has healed you."* All we need to do to become well is in faith touch the edge of His cloak.

If you have faith as small as a mustard seed, you can say to this mountain,
"Move from here to there," and it will move. Nothing will be impossible for you.

MATTHEW 17:20

We live by faith, not by sight.
2 CORINTHIANS 5:7

JUNE 30

As for God, his way is perfect;
The LORD's word is flawless.
He shields all
who take refuge in him.
2 SAMUEL 22:31

Our Lord God declared that King David was a man after His own heart—and he was. Yes, David sinned deeply by committing adultery and fathering a child with Bathsheba, who was married to Uriah. Yes, he also had Uriah killed after bringing him home from the battlefield so that he would sleep with his wife, whom Uriah refused to see in honor of his comrades left on the battlefield. *But the thing David had done displeased the LORD* (2 Samuel 11:27).

However, our Lord God's way is perfect and His words are flawless. God is a shield to *all who take refuge in Him* (2 Samuel 22:31). When God's prophet Nathan rebuked David for his sins of adultery and murder and told David what he had done in secret God would reveal openly, bringing calamity on his household, David responded, confessing, *"I have sinned against the LORD"* (2 Samuel 12:13).

Our Heavenly Father knows everything about us—everything! We can always take refuge in Him for He is our shield. He *will never leave* us *nor forsake* us (Deuteronomy 31:6). But we will reap what we sow, as did King David.

He reached down from on high and took hold of me; he drew me out of deep waters.
He brought me out into a spacious place; he rescued me because he delighted in me.
2 SAMUEL 22:17, 20

July

JULY 1

Therefore, holy brothers and sisters,
who share in the heavenly calling,
fix your thoughts on Jesus,
whom we acknowledge
as our apostle and high priest.
HEBREWS 3:1

In the times in which we live, it is not always a simple matter to control our thinking. Our minds are bombarded by what we read in the daily news; hear on TV newscasts; and witness while working, eating in restaurants, or even strolling up and down the street. Our minds seem to flit here, there, and yonder.

Our Heavenly Father never instructs us to do anything that He does not equip us to accomplish. We *can do all things through Christ who* gives us the strength (Philippians 4:13 NKJV). Yet far too many of us submit to worldly, mind-boggling thoughts—ones joyfully implanted by the evil one, who knows how vulnerable we are to his sly and wicked ways.

It is more than possible to *fix* our *thoughts on Jesus.* All that is needed is to pay strict attention when our minds begin wandering and to grasp the hand that is always outstretched, waiting for us to reach up and take hold of it.

LORD **Almighty, blessed is the one who trusts in you.**
PSALM 84:12

JULY 2

*I will extol the L*ORD
at all times;
his praise will always
be on my lips.
PSALM 34:1

I t is only as we live in God's presence in our present moments that we can worship Him in a way that pleases Him. Our past and our future can be booby traps for us if we linger in either place longer than necessary. Many of us much prefer living in the past or dwelling in the future more than applauding our Heavenly Father for what He is presently accomplishing in us, for us, and through us.

God was in our past when the past was present and God will be in our future when it becomes the present. Presently He is with us as we clutch His hand in our present moments with Him.

Yes, we may *exalt His name* for the wonders of the past or the hopes for the future, but more importantly, we worship Him most completely in our present moments, with Him leading, guiding, and directing our lives.

Glorify the LORD **with me; let us exalt his name together.**
PSALM 34:3

JULY 3

Why, my soul, are you downcast?
Why so disturbed within me?
PSALM 42:5

A ll of us have asked ourselves these two questions, wondering why we are so sad and troubled and what it is that distresses us. At such moments we spend far too much time searching for answers rather than seeking God's help. His Holy Spirit abides in us and is available all the time. It takes only a split second to reach out to Him. We can trust Him because He knows exactly what to say to us and do for us.

Just say, "Help me, Jesus"—three words, four syllables. So simple, and yet we make it so complicated. And in the process, don't forget to praise Him and thank Him for all He has done, is doing, and will continue to do in us and for us.

While in the shower this morning I fell and landed on my back. Terrified, I thought I might have broken a bone in my back or my hip. As hard as I tried, it seemed I could not get up. In desperation, I cried out, "Help me, Jesus!" Immediately He came to my aid and enabled me to get back on my feet. The remarkable thing about it is: I was in perfect condition, with no pain and no bruises whatsoever.

God is so good! Praise His Holy name!

> Put your hope in God, for I will yet praise him, my savior and my God.
> PSALM 42:5

JULY 4

I instruct you in the way of wisdom
and lead you along straight paths.
PROVERBS 4:11

Many of our paths have been more than challenging; they have been wearisome, to say the least. It seems we no sooner leave a mud-soaked, rock-cutting trail that our wounded and blood-saturated feet are planted on, when yet another walkway fills us with sorrow and pain. Tossing our hands skyward, we shout, "Enough is enough already."

It takes time for us to grasp that these roadways weren't crooked at all, but straight as an arrow and sharp as any two-edged sword. They result in great wisdom, for we learn that God is growing us into what He created us in Christ to become. His straight and narrow pathways open our minds to understand that His highways are never twisted at all.

During those thought-provoking times our hearts fill with praise and thanksgiving to our Heavenly Father for who He is and what He is accomplishing in our lives. In His great love for us, God allows us to walk through His shadows of death, fearing no evil for He is with us every step of the way.

> When you walk, your steps will not be hampered; when you run, you will not stumble.
> PROVERBS 4:12

JULY 5

Above all else,
guard your heart,
for everything you do
flows from it.
PROVERBS 4:23

Not only does God instruct us to *pay attention* to everything He tells us, listening very closely to His words and not letting them out of our sight but keeping them within our hearts, but He also lets us know they are *health* to our bodies. We are not to *turn to the right or the left*, but keep our *eyes straight ahead*, fixing our gaze directly on Him. It is then and only then that we can cast *perversity* from our mouths and *keep corrupt talk far from* our *lips* (Proverbs 4:20–27).

When we do this our Lord guards our hearts, allowing them to be the fountainhead of His love flowing from within us into the lives of those around us.

Such confidence we have through Christ before God.
2 CORINTHIANS 3:4

JULY 6

"Though the mountains be shaken
and the hills be removed,
yet my unfailing love for you
will not be shaken
nor my covenant of peace be removed,"
says the LORD, who has compassion on you.
ISAIAH 54:10

God's *peace* continually surrounds us, saturating our hearts with His *unfailing love.* Even though the economy may fail, or jobs grow scarce, or the stock market continue to plummet, or even the sale of houses spiral further downward, God's peace in us and His love for us remain with us forever—meaning, no matter what, God is with us, in us, and for us. *The Sovereign LORD is my strength, he makes my feet like the feet of a deer, he enables me to tread on the heights* (Habakkuk 3:19).

Let us shout these words of God: *Though the fig tree does not bud and there are no grapes on the vines, though the olive crop fails and the fields produce no food, though there are no sheep in the pen and no cattle in the stalls, yet I will rejoice in the LORD, I will be joyful in God my Savior* (Habakkuk 3:17–18).

Holy, holy, holy is the LORD Almighty; the whole earth is full of his glory.
ISAIAH 6:3

JULY 7

So keep up your courage, men,
for I have faith in God
that it will happen
just as he told me.
ACTS 27:25

These words of the apostle Paul are just as important for us today as they were for the centurion aboard the ship who was in charge of bringing Paul as a prisoner to Rome. The sea storms had violently raged, and Paul had warned the centurion what would happen if they continued on. Instead of listening to Paul, the man followed the advice of the pilot and the owner of the ship, which was to continue onward, hoping to reach Phoenix and stay there for the winter. *Before very long a wind of hurricane force, called the Northeaster, swept down from the island,* and *the ship could not head into the wind.* So the sailors *gave way to it and were driven along.* Having taken *a violent battering from the storm, they began to throw their cargo overboard,* and then continued on in the raging storm many days, finally giving up *all hope of being saved* (Acts 27:9–20).

Everyone aboard the ship had gone without food for a long time when *Paul stood up before them and said, "Men, you should have taken my advice not to sail from Crete; then you would have spared yourselves this damage and loss."* He told them to be courageous *"because not one of you will be lost; only the ship will be destroyed."* He then let them know that he had encountered *"an angel of the God to whom I belong and whom I serve,"* who told him, *"Do not be afraid, Paul. You must stand trial before Caesar; and God has graciously given you the lives of all who sail with you"* (v. 21–24).

Then Paul said, *"So keep up your courage, men, for I have faith in God that it will happen just as he told me"* (v. 25). He let them know they would *run aground on some island* (v. 26), which they eventually did. This is when *the soldiers planned to kill the prisoners to prevent them from swimming away and escaping. But the centurion wanted to spare Paul's life and kept them from carrying out their plan* to kill the prisoners (v. 42–43).

Three months later these men and Paul traveled to Rome, where Paul was allowed to live by himself and able to preach, while a soldier guarded him (Acts 28).

Regardless of whatever comes into our lives, our Lord God assures us that, irrespective of what happens to us, we are to be courageous and keep the faith—for He is with us, in us, and for us.

For two whole years Paul stayed there in his own rented house
and welcomed all who came to see him. He proclaimed the kingdom of God
and taught about the Lord Jesus Christ—
with all boldness and without hindrance!

ACTS 28:30–31

JULY 8

Give thanks in all circumstances,
for this is God's will for you
in Christ Jesus.

1Thessalonians 5:18

Thanking our Lord God for everything is not always easy, but, rest assured, it is doable. We can do *all things through Christ who* gives us the strength to do it (Philippians 4:13 NKJV). Our Almighty God never puts more on us than we can handle. Thanking Him in any and all circumstances is more than we can imagine as we walk with Him, holding His outstretched hand while on the pathways He puts beneath our feet as He leads us every step of His way. But He will help us do this.

As we know, the roads beneath our feet are not always pleasant. But, as we also know, whatever is there is there for a purpose—to grow us into what God created us in Christ to become. Far better to raise our hands in thanksgiving to Him, rather than grumbling and complaining and keeping our minds on ourselves instead of on God's will for our lives.

How could we not be continually thankful that God is making us whole? Let us thank our Heavenly Father in all circumstances.

Always giving thanks to God the Father for everything, in the name of our Lord Jesus Christ.
EPHESIANS 5:20

JULY 9

The LORD Almighty is with us.
PSALM 46:7

O ur Lord God is always in us, with us, and for us. Let us never let go of holding His right hand of righteousness as He walks beside us. Let us revel in His Spirit's guidance and the gift of eternal life bestowed on us through the death and resurrection of His Son, Jesus Christ.

We never have anything to fear, for He *is our refuge and strength, an ever-present help in trouble* (Psalm 46:1). God *will never leave* us *nor forsake* us (Deuteronomy 31:6). Let us raise our hands in praise to our Heavenly Father for who He is and what He does for us.

> **"Be still, and know that I am God I will be exalted among the nations,**
> **I will be exalted in the earth."**
> **PSALM 46:10**

JULY 10

"Be joyful in hope,
patient in affliction,
faithful in prayer.
ROMANS 12:12

E ven if our feet fall from beneath us and we have to look up just to see the bottom of the pit in which we find ourselves, let us joyfully grab hold of *hope*—for hope is always in us, as is God's joyfulness. They might not ring loudly, making a racket, but they are forever in us. God's Holy Spirit who dwells in us is joyfully hopeful, constantly singing God's sweet songs to us. If we listen closely, we can jubilantly hear His voice of encouragement through our deepest afflictions.

Our prayer may simply be three words: "Help me, Jesus," but nevertheless this cry is most effective. We are encouraged to be faithful as we trust in His guidance, for He has never failed us and He never will fail us.

I will sing to the LORD all my life; I will sing praise to my God as long as I live.
Praise the LORD, O my soul. Praise the LORD.

PSALM 104:33, 35

JULY 11

"Like clay in the hand of the potter, so are you in my hand."
JEREMIAH 18:6

Whatever a potter desires to create, he does so by selecting a lump of clay and placing it on his potter's wheel. Once we become children of God, our heavenly Potter does the same with us. We are His lump of clay, swirling around on His wheel. His hands are continually on us, molding us and shaping us into what He created us in Christ to become.

Our clay, however, is unlike all the other lumps that our Potter selects to create His magnificent work. No two lumps of His clay are the same. He knows exactly what it takes to mold each one and fashion it into what the misshapen piece of clay could never envision becoming were it not in the hands of this particular Potter, for He is well known for His passionate love, faithfulness, gentleness, and kindness.

Yet He withholds nothing to shape the clay's forthcoming beauty, even if it means placing great pressure to the point of smashing it down so that He can rebuild it again, creating a thing of beauty.

Not until the piece of clay on the Potter's wheel is complete does it know that its Maker is well pleased with its beauty, as He places it in one of His rooms in His great house. The piece of clay rejoices, knowing the Potter is delighted at what His bumpy-lumpy clay has become.

Yet you, LORD, are our Father. We are the clay,
you are the potter; we are all the work of your hand.

ISAIAH 64:8

JULY 12

Humble yourselves
before the Lord,
and he will lift you up.
JAMES 4:10

It doesn't take much effort to allow ourselves to become pigheaded, thinking we know exactly what to do or say under any and all circumstances. Nothing could be further from the truth. In and of ourselves we can do nothing, but through Christ's strength we can do anything.

It matters not the situations in which we find ourselves. Regardless of how complicated, embarrassing, complex, or problematic they are, God always has the answer for everything. It is only when we patiently turn to God, waiting for His Words and guidance and submitting to His Spirit in us, that we let go of our prideful brashness and joyfully take the hand of Jesus, knowing as we do so He is directing our paths. It is God who lifts us up, not we ourselves.

Come near to God and he will come near to you.
JAMES 4:8

JULY 13

Sorrowful, yet always rejoicing.
2 CORINTHIANS 6:10

Regardless of our *troubles, hardships, and distresses,* or our *hard work, sleepless nights, and hunger,* or the threat of death (2 Corinthians 6:4–5), let us say with the apostle Paul that though we have *nothing,* through Christ in us we possess *everything* (v. 10). Even as we walk through the valley of the shadow of death, we are admonished to rejoice in our sorrow.

We never know how encouraging we are to those around us when we allow nothing to stand in the way of demonstrating *Christ in* us—*the hope of glory* (Colossians 1:27). They may be poor in spirit but they become rich in Christ as we exhibit Christ regardless of the broken pieces of our hearts.

This doesn't mean we will not grieve. It simply means as we walk through the valley of the shadow of death we hold tightly to our Heavenly Father's hand, trusting Him not only to lead, guide, and direct our paths, but to sustain us along the way.

> Now the one who has fashioned us for this very purpose is God,
> who has given us the Spirit as a deposit, guaranteeing what is to come.
> For we live by faith, not my sight.
> 2 CORINTHIANS 5:5, 7

JULY 14

> *For my yoke is easy*
> *and my burden is light.*
> MATTHEW 11:30

Only the master or owner of an ox places his yoke on his ox's shoulders. There is no way an ox can do this for itself. I imagine if it could, it would select a very soft and comfortable piece of wood that was not heavy and burdensome to wear—but something it might even be pleased to carry on its shoulders. Just like an ox, we cannot select our own yoke either. However, unlike an ox, we often insist on doing so, even though our Master and Lord does not approve of the yoke we have chosen for ourselves instead of allowing Him to harness us.

It is the Lord who gives us rest—not we ourselves. We cannot learn from ourselves what we need to know as we walk with our Master. He is *gentle and humble in heart*. We *find rest for* our *souls* only through Him (v. 29). So let us wait for God to place His yoke on us rather than selecting our own before going to work for Him.

> We wait in hope for the LORD; he is our help and our shield.
> PSALM 33:20

JULY 15

You came near when I called you,
and you said, "Do not fear."
LAMENTATIONS 3:57

Regardless of what comes our way, no matter how overwhelming or terrifying it appears, we can forsake the horrendous terror that suddenly grasps us by the throat. Our Lord God, who is always with us and will never leave us, faithfully comes to our rescue. All we have to do is call out to Him, silently or aloud: "Help me, Jesus."

He softly whispers into our hearts, "Take My hand, child. Do not be afraid."

It is then we know that irrespective of what comes into our lives, we have nothing to fear, regardless of how devastating it is. God in us is with us every step of the way.

So do not fear, for I am with you; do not be dismayed, for I am your God.
I will strengthen you and help you;
I will uphold you with my righteous right hand.
ISAIAH 41:10

JULY 16

By faith Abraham,
when God tested him,
offered Isaac as a sacrifice.
HEBREWS 11:17

Why did God test Abraham? And why does our Lord God, who knows us through and through, test us? Doesn't He already know everything about us—what we think, what we say, and what we do? He tests us so that we can know ourselves, opening our hearts and eyes to who we really are and to whom we belong. God instructs us to put *no other gods before* Him (Exodus 20:3). This is His first and greatest commandment; but from time to time all of us break it, perhaps not even realizing we do. An idol can be a person or a place or a thing or an event—anything that consumes us, with us believing we cannot survive without it, thereby putting it first and foremost in our lives.

Abraham waited countless years to have a child by his wife, Sarah, who was barren. I can only imagine how precious that boy was to him when Sarah gave birth to Isaac. His long-awaited son had finally arrived. Abraham's child could not become an idol to him so, to alert Abraham, God intervened.

For Abraham to grasp who came first in his life, God had to open his eyes to the necessity of obeying Him, regardless of what He asked of him. God told Abraham to take his *only son, whom you love—Isaac—and go to the region of Moriah,* where Abraham was to *sacrifice* Isaac *as a burnt offering* on one of the mountains there (Genesis 22:2).

Abraham did as God instructed. He took Isaac, along with two of his servants, and a loaded donkey, along with some cut wood for the burnt offering to the place God directed him. When Abraham saw the place in the distance, he told his servants to stay behind with the donkey while he and Isaac went onward. He told the servants that after he and his son worshiped there they would come back to them (v. 3–5).

Arriving at the place, *Abraham built an altar there and arranged the wood on it. He bound his son Isaac and laid him on the altar, on top of the wood. He reached out his hand and took the knife to slay his son. But the angel of the Lord called out to him from heaven, "Abraham! Abraham! Do not lay a hand on the boy. Do not do anything to him. Now I know that you fear God, because you have not withheld from me your son, your only son"* (Genesis 23:9–12).

The Lord God wanted Abraham to grasp—to completely comprehend—what could become more to him than God was to him. Our Lord God does the same for us today. Our idols can be our spouses, our children, our families, our careers, or anything that we place number one in our lives. If or when we do so, it becomes an idol.

Do you remember that Abraham told the servants he and Isaac would meet them back at the place he had left them? Abraham put his faith in God. He trusted God, knowing somehow that even when he sacrificed his son, God would intervene and keep Isaac safe, even if it meant bringing him back to life again. Let us do likewise—sacrifice to God anything that we might put before our Heavenly Father.

I am the Lord your God, who brought you out of Egypt, out of the land of slavery.
You shall have no other gods before me. You shall not make for yourself an image in the form of anything in heaven above or on the earth beneath or in the waters below. You shall not bow down to them or worship them; for I, the Lord your God, am a jealous God, punishing the children for the sin of the parents to the third and fourth generation of those who hate me, but showing love to a thousand generations of those who love me and keep my commandments

EXODUS 20:2–6

JULY 17

*I have received full payment
and have more than enough.*
PHILIPPIANS 4:18

If Paul—who underwent beatings, imprisonments, and harsh words from the religious leaders of his day, even living in the darkness and loneliness of prison cells—could say he had gotten full payment for His mission from God then we, who may have never experienced Paul's kind of anguish, must say likewise.

We have been chosen to reach out to the world, extending God's invitation to others to become our brothers and sisters in Christ. More than likely we will never experience the kind of life the apostle Paul lived. Nevertheless, we have been chosen to be God's children, and as we travel down God's highways we know in the depths of our beings that we are receiving God's full payment and even more because of what we have allowed God to do in us and through us.

To our God and Father be glory for ever and ever. Amen.
PHILIPPIANS 4:20

JULY 18

*My grace is sufficient for you,
for my power
is made perfect in weakness.*
2 CORINTHIANS 12:9

All of us have an area that seems like quicksand and know if we approach it we're done for because we don't have the ability to walk through it without sinking. It scares the daylights out of us even thinking about it. None of us wants to go there.

But, like the apostle Paul, our Lord God places His *thorn in* our *flesh* (2 Corinthians 12:8), and no matter how many times we ask Him to remove it He will not. He has put it there to keep us on track so we won't think too highly of ourselves while we strut around with a sinful grin of pride on our faces.

Whatever our weaknesses are, like Paul let us exclaim, *"I will boast all the more gladly about my weaknesses, so that Christ's power may rest on me"* (v. 9). This is why Paul knew he could *delight in* his *weaknesses, insults, hardships, persecutions, and difficulties* (v. 10).

For when I am weak, then I am strong.
2 CORINTHIANS 12:10

JULY 19

Love the LORD your God
with all your heart
and with all your soul
and with all your strength.
DEUTERONOMY 6:5

Perhaps if we ask ourselves—before we say a word or do anything that comes our way—what our words and actions are demonstrating to others, we might become more mindful of what the Lord asks us to do: *Love* Him *with all of our heart and soul and strength.*

Children of God are always on display—always. It doesn't matter where we are or what we're saying or doing, everyone around us is taking it in and analyzing it to see if it fits our testimony.

We love our spouses, children, and families with everything in us. We would even give our lives for them. We never want to do anything that would discredit our love for them, and yet far too often we live carelessly with the Love of our life—our Lord and Savior, Jesus Christ. If we love Him with all of our heart, soul, and strength then we would also give up our life for Him by living every moment for Him.

Jesus said, "Father, forgive them, for they do not know what they are doing."
LUKE 23:34

JULY 20

Whoever believes in me,
as Scripture has said,
rivers of living water
will flow from within them.
JOHN 7:38

Whenever we take God's outstretched hand and follow Him wherever He leads, we discover His *beauty for ashes* (Isaiah 61:3 NKJV), whether they are our own or those belonging to someone else. Everyone needs God's *living water* flowing in them. We thirst for it as if our lives depend on it, and they do.

It is only when we process the sad and difficult times we have endured with our Lord and Savior and receive His *rivers of living water* flowing through us that His living water then seeps from within us into other people's lives.

The LORD has done great things for us, and we are filled with joy.
PSALM 126:3

JULY 21

And without faith
it is impossible to please God,
because anyone who comes to him
must believe that he exists
and that he rewards those
who earnestly seek him.
HEBREWS 11:6

When we slip into a mode of not trusting our Lord God, it is impossible for us to please Him. Our Heavenly Father rewards us when we cling to our trust in Him for everything that enters our lives, regardless of what it is. Having faith in

God—trusting Him—is essential for our well-being. It enables us to keep on keeping on, no matter what.

When God tells us to wait on Him while in a dilemma or to respond to our urgent requests, then that's exactly what we need to do because in His time He will make everything beautiful (Ecclesiastes 3:11). God is always with us, in us, and for us and *will never leave* us *nor forsake* us (Deuteronomy 31:6). This is what faith is all about—trusting Him as He wills and works in us for His *good pleasure* (Ephesians 1:5).

But as for me, I trust in you.
PSALM 55:23

JULY 22

*Let the peace of Christ
rule in your hearts,
since as members of one body
you were called to peace.
And be thankful.*
COLOSSIANS 3:15

Our Heavenly Father's words are explicit—very clear. He admonishes us to let His peace rule in our hearts, and He gives us a reason for doing so. As His children we are all members of one body, sometimes alone and sometimes grouped together in various places—like at home, in churches, schools, or work environments, etc. Regardless of where we are and in what situations surround us, we have been called to peace. As we let His peace rule in our hearts, we will not be so quick to allow others to ruffle our feathers or drag us into heated debates when a huge disagreement raises its ugly head and demands we fight it out to the bitter end.

God's solution for this is very simple: a thankful heart. We cannot focus on God's bountiful blessings with twisted minds, for that is what they become when we argue and fight.

Let us be thankful, praising our Heavenly Father for who He is and what He has done for us, is doing for us, and will do in our lives in the future when we *let* His *peace rule in* our *hearts.*

**And the peace of God, which transcends all understanding,
will guard your hearts and your minds in Christ Jesus.**
PHILIPPIANS 4:7

JULY 23

Don't you know
that you yourselves
are God's temple
and that God's Spirit
dwells in your midst?
1 CORINTHIANS 3:16

If we grasped that our bodies *are God's temple* in which His Spirit lives, then perhaps we would be more respectful and cautious with what we do with them and how we take care of them. People don't walk into a church sanctuary irreverently, turning a blind eye to the purpose of it—a meeting place for worshipers of the Trinity: God the Father, God the Son, and God the Holy Spirit. It is also where God's work is carried out—meeting needs, reaching out, and helping others as well as encouraging ourselves.

When we envision ourselves as *God's temple*, with His Holy Spirit in us guiding and leading us every nanosecond of time, we will grow into what our Heavenly Father created us in Christ to become.

We, ourselves, are God's holy temple. Hallelujah!

I will extol the LORD at all times; his praise will always be on my lips.
PSALM 34:1

JULY 24

Set a guard over my mouth, LORD;
keep watch over the door of my lips.
PSALM 141:3

From time to time we are all careless with our tongues. We speak before thinking, and, when we do, troubles by the dozens come calling. This is why it is so imperative to ask for God's help in keeping a *watch over the door of* our *lips*. We can never undo the damage of our thoughtless and insensitive words. Regardless of how many times we apologize, or if we ask for forgiveness at all, our careless words are glued to where they landed, deep in another's heart.

Yes, Lord, *guard* our mouths and *keep watch over the door of our lips.*

Like apples of gold in settings of silver is a ruling rightly given.
PROVERBS 25:11

JULY 25

Be joyful in hope,
patient in affliction,
faithful in prayer.
ROMANS 12:12

God tells us that *hope deferred makes the heart sick, but a longing fulfilled is a tree of life* (Proverbs 13:12). He also says: *Anyone who is among the living has hope—even a live dog is better off than a dead lion!* (Ecclesiastes 9:4). Not only are we saved by hope, *but hope that is seen is no hope at all* (Romans 8:24).

When we hope for what we don't already have, *we wait for it patiently* (Romans 8:25). How could we not be joyful when we know what God's hope is—delightful—and, as Paul says, well worth waiting for. But hope must be faithfully pursued in prayer.

Our Lord God never tires of hearing us converse with Him. It delights His heart, especially when we thank Him for even the dark times in our lives. So no matter what our life circumstances are, let us raise our hands to our Lord in thanksgiving, for, even if we feel like a trampled dog, we're much better off than being a lifeless lion.

And we know that in all things God works for the good of those who love him,
who have been called according to his purpose.
ROMANS 8:28

JULY 26

Peace I leave with you;
my peace I give to you.
I do not give it to you as the world gives.
Do not let your hearts be troubled
and do not be afraid.
JOHN 14:27

The Holy Spirit is our Counselor. Wow! Think about it—He is our Therapist! He teaches us all things and constantly reminds us of everything God has told us in His Holy Word (John 14:26). All we have to do is have faith in Him—trust Him for any and all things He either sends or allows into our lives. It is only when we obey Him that we are able to heed His reminder to keep on keeping on, directing us in the ways He wants us to go.

The world can never give us what God gives us—His wonderful and powerful peace that is beyond understanding. If and when we grasp this, then we know that we know that we know that our hearts will not be troubled and we will not be afraid.

If you love me, keep my commands.
JOHN 14:15

JULY 27

*Every good and perfect gift
is from above,
coming down from
the Father of the heavenly lights,
who does not change
like shifting shadows.*

JAMES 1:17

We know that life continually changes. As King Solomon wrote: *There is a time for everything, and a season for every activity under the heavens* (Ecclesiastes 3:1). We are not the same person we were twenty or thirty years ago, much less last year. Activities and events come and go in our lives, and as they do we adjust to them or change with them. Change is a given. Because we have changed, perhaps this is why when someone gifts us with something we adored in our past we are not too pleased or grateful for it today.

However, no matter how much we've changed or grown, any gift God lays at our feet is perfect and timely, regardless of when it arrives. He is the only One who knows us perfectly, even more fully than we know ourselves.

We change throughout our lifetimes, but God never changes. He is the same yesterday, today, and tomorrow (Hebrews 13:8). He is the great I AM.

Let us come before him with thanksgiving and extol him with music and song.

PSALM 95:2

JULY 28

But where can wisdom be found?
Where does understanding dwell?
JOB 28:12

How do we gain wisdom and an ability to better understand the circumstances of our lives and those around us? Job pondered this question. He asked it while at the bottom of a spiritual pit, one allowed by God Almighty after Satan had approached God while *roaming throughout the earth, going back and forth in it* (Job 1:7).

God asked Satan if he had considered His servant Job because *there is no one on earth like him; he is blameless and upright, a man who fears God and shuns evil* (Job 1:8). Of course, God knew what Satan was up to—discrediting Job. Satan accused God of putting a hedge around Job and his household and everything else. In other words, "Why wouldn't he trust You? You've given him everything" (v. 10).

Our Lord God allowed Job to lose it all—his children, his servants, his herdsmen, and his home, and, to top it off, his health. His wife even told him to *curse God and die*, probably something she felt like doing (Job 2:9).

Hearing of Job's circumstances, three of his friends approached him to comfort him. Comfort they did not. They brought accusations that his sins had brought him to where he now was.

While talking with his friends Job asked them where wisdom could be found and where understanding dwelt (Job 28:12). Then he made a profound statement: *"No mortal comprehends its worth; it cannot be found in the land of the living"* (v. 13). Apparently Job had searched for wisdom and understanding everywhere because he concluded, *"The deep says, 'It is not in me'; the sea says, 'It is not with me'"* (v. 14).

While going through the trials and tribulations God allows in our lives, we also search for that which Job did: to understand, being able to grasp why God has sent such misery our way. We want no part of it. Sometimes, unlike Job, we even accuse God of being unfair.

It is not until we, like Job, get to the end of our wretched roads that we grasp God's explanation to our asked questions. He tells us He is willing and working in us *according to His purpose* to bring us *into the image of His Son*, Jesus Christ (Romans 8:28–29)—words we never could have understood unless He allowed us to travel His roads of anguish and sorrow, the places that opened our eyes to what wisdom is and where understanding dwells.

The Lord answered Job's questions and says to all His children, *"The fear of the Lord—that is wisdom, and to shun evil is understanding"* (Job 28:28).

The LORD blessed the latter part of Job's life more than the former part.
He had fourteen thousand sheep, six thousand camels, a thousand yoke of oxen
and a thousand donkeys. And he also had seven sons and three daughters.
After this, Job lived a hundred and forty years;
he saw his children and their children to the fourth generation.
JOB 42:12–13, 16

JULY 29

Like one who takes away a garment on a cold day,
or like vinegar poured on a wound,
is one who sings songs to a heavy heart.
PROVERBS 25:20

Far too many of us sing songs like "Don't Worry, Be Happy" to those who are burdened and heavyhearted, immersed in the blackest of black in the deepest part of their souls. It's far better to take our hands and place them gently over our closed mouths, and open up our empathic ears to quietly listen to those who are down and out.

One of the greatest gifts we can give others is to sit quietly in their presence while they pour out their hearts to us and we absorb every word they speak. If necessary to keep from blurting our harmful words, we should stick duct tape over our mouths—much better to say nothing at all than to *take away a garment on a cold day.*

There is a time for everything.
ECCLESIASTES 3:1

My command is this: Love each other as I have loved you.
JOHN 15:12

JULY 30

Now there is in store for me
the crown of righteousness,
which the LORD, the righteous Judge,
will award to me on that day—
and not only to me,
but also to all who
have longed for his appearing.
2 TIMOTHY 4:8

No matter what kind of awards or ribbons or crowns we trained to achieve and strived to win during our lifetimes, we take none of them with us when we leave the world—for we brought nothing with us when we came and we can take nothing with us when we leave. However, as children of God, we receive His *crown of righteousness* when we arrive at our final destination—heaven!

This is the crown we so longed to see placed on our heads when we meet our Savior face-to-face. Nothing will please us more than to realize all we worked for, all we made every effort to accomplish for Jesus' sake on our earthly travels, we now see—His *crown of righteousness* resting on our head.

It is the most exquisite item imaginable. We join all of our brothers and sisters in Christ in His heavenly realm praising Him for His sacrifice that qualifies us to walk into eternity with Him with such magnificence surrounding us—His righteousness in us and with us.

For Christ also suffered once for sins, the righteous for the unrighteous, to bring you to God.
1 PETER 3:18

JULY 31

Put on the full armor of God,
so that you can take your stand
against the devil's schemes.
EPHESIANS 6:11

Our struggles are *not against flesh and blood* (Ephesians 6:12). They are against satanic demons, who fiercely pursue us in our race for the Lord. These demons are powerful and determined to outmaneuver the work of Christ in us. The more dedicated we are to our calling, the more ferocious they are in attempting to take us down. Nothing pleases them more than watching us crawl into a shell, terrified of their satanic schemes.

We are soldiers for Christ; therefore God has admonished us to put on His whole *armor* so that we can *stand* our ground and, no matter how fiercely pursued, keep standing. The Holy Spirit in us enables us to buckle His *belt of truth* around us and assures us *His breastplate of righteousness* is in place. He checks our feet, inspecting them to make sure they are ready to run with *the gospel of peace* (v. 14–15).

Most of the time, He has to shove His *shield of faith* in front of our faces, making sure that we hold it correctly so we can *extinguish all the flaming arrows of the evil one* (v. 16). And to top it off, He adjusts our *helmet of salvation* and makes sure the Word of God we have studied permeates every fiber of our being.

Last of all, He admonishes us to *pray in the Sprit on all occasions with all kinds of prayers and requests . . .* and *be alert and always keep on praying for all the Lord's people* (v. 18).

Onward, Christian soldiers! March as to war, for God *will never leave* us *nor forsake* us (Deuteronomy 31:6).

Grace to all who love our Lord Jesus Christ with an undying love.
EPHESIANS 6:24

AUGUST

AUGUST 1

Commit to the Lord whatever you do,
and he will establish your plans.
PROVERBS 16:3

King Solomon's words, written through the direction of our Lord God, are not only essential but absolutely meaningful and helpful. Whatever we do or are involved with will succeed when we *commit* ourselves and our plans to God. God's ways are not our ways, nor are His plans our plans (Isaiah 55:8), but when we bind His Word in our hearts and commit ourselves to keep His Word hidden in our hearts, whatever we do will be successful.

Those who trust in the Lord are like Mount Zion, which cannot be shaken but endures forever.
PSALM 125:1

AUGUST 2

My son, do not despise the Lord's discipline
and do not resent his rebuke,
because the Lord disciplines those he loves,
as a father the son he delights in.
PROVERBS 3:11–12

Many of us fear discipline because while we were growing up those who corrected us may have done it in unhealthy ways. Perhaps those who reprimanded us only copied what they learned as they were growing up and did not seek a better way. Regardless of how we're disciplined, few of us appreciate correction, much less look forward to it.

When we understand that our Holy Father loves us more deeply than any love known to mankind, it blows our minds, for we frequently ask ourselves how God could possibly love us after what we did or said or thought.

God *will never leave* us *nor forsake* us (Deuteronomy 31:6). His love is forever in us and with us. When we allow His love-thoughts into the deepest part of our souls, then and then only do we comprehend that He *delights* in us and, because He does, He keeps us on track with Him through His loving discipline.

God is love. This is how God showed his love among us:
He sent his one and only Son into the world that we might live through him. This is love: not that
we loved God, but that he loved us and sent his Son as an atoning sacrifice for our sins.
1 JOHN 4:8–10

AUGUST 3

The LORD your God is with you,
the Mighty Warrior who saves.
He will take great delight in you,
in his love he will no longer rebuke you,
but will rejoice over you with singing.
ZEPHANIAH 3:17

Absolutely nothing is more calming and soothing than to hear the words, *God is with you.* Not only is God with us, but He is mighty to save. No matter what happens or what circumstances come our way, He is with us and in us, leading and guiding us every step of the way regardless of how gruesome or ghastly or horrific our situation might be.

The Holy One takes *great delight* in His children and, irrespective of what happens, He soothes us with His presence and whispers His love songs in our ears. Even if we know a horrifying ending awaits us, He enfolds us in His loving arms and rejoices over us. The Lord our God is forever with us. Praise the Lord!

Let everything that has breath praise the LORD. Praise the LORD.
PSALM 150:6

AUGUST 4

Now get up
and stand on your feet.
ACTS 26:16

These are Christ's words to the apostle Paul and for us today. The Lord appeared to Paul to appoint him as a servant and as a witness of what he had seen of Jesus and what Jesus was going to show him. It was Paul's mission *to open* everyone's *eyes* and persuade them to *turn from* their *darkness to* His *light*, away from Satan to God, so they could be forgiven and become *sanctified by* their *faith* in Jesus (Acts 26:18).

God has called each and every one of us to do likewise.

"Who me?" we question.

Yes, you and me also.

"But . . . but . . . I don't have the ability to do this," we whisper. "That is not my calling. That's not my spiritual gift."

Regardless of the spiritual gift or gifts God has vested in every one of His children, the end result of that gift is to demonstrate through our service to Him that God is love and He gave His only begotten Son so that we may live in Christ.

It's a simple task. Live for Christ so that others will see Christ in us.

Now, let's rise and stand for Jesus' sake today.

Love the LORD your God with all your heart and with all your soul and with all your mind.
This is the first and greatest commandment.
MATTHEW 22:37–38

AUGUST 5

Therefore we do not lose heart.
2 CORINTHIANS 4:16

No one has ever had a time in their lives that they haven't felt like giving up. We've all been tired and discouraged and sick of putting one foot in front of the other. We just want to slink away from the circumstances that have drained us. It feels useless to keep on keeping on. Everyone knows these feelings.

Let us recall Paul's words regarding losing heart. God is renewing us day by day. We may not feel it, but He is. He tells us *our light and momentary troubles are achieving for us an eternal glory that far outweighs them all* (2 Corinthians 4:17). Even though we know God continually renews us, assuring us that what we are experiencing are only *momentary troubles* and that our future hope far outweighs them all, we somehow remain down and out—feeling drained.

It isn't until God reminds us to *fix our eyes not on what is seen, but on what is unseen* (v. 18) that we wake up, suddenly grasping that what we now see is only temporary and will not last forever.

But what is unseen is eternal.
2 CORINTHIANS 4:18

AUGUST 6

But you are a chosen people,
a royal priesthood,
a holy nation,
God's special possession,
that you may declare
the praises of him
who called you
out of darkness
into his wonderful light.

1 PETER 2:9

So many do not fully grasp what our Heavenly Father means when He tells us we *are a chosen people*—especially declaring we are *a royal priesthood* and *a holy nation*. But we are. Once we accept God's Son, Jesus Christ, and what He accomplished for us on His cross, we belong to the family of God. Our Father has a mission for each and every one of His children—to proclaim His praises for rescuing us from our darkness and to draw others to Him.

The way in which we carry out this mission is quite simple: Open our eyes to what God has done for us and live our lives in such a way that His light in us shines through us, calling others to follow Him.

But whoever lives by the truth comes into the light,
so that it may be seen plainly that what they have done has been done in the sight of God.

JOHN 3:21

AUGUST 7

But few things are needed—
or indeed only one.
LUKE 10:42

F ar too many of us flit here, there, and yonder fretting over what is on today's docket, wondering how we will get everything done. We grumble and become more than irritated when the day ends without our having completed that which we set out to do. However, when we begin our day seeking a quiet place to sit at Jesus' feet, meditating on His Words and listening intently to what the Holy Spirit directs us to do, our day ends quite differently.

Our energy is not exhausted. In fact, we are strengthened, totally satisfied that we accomplished more than we ever imagined we could. We even had quiet intervals, stunned that we were able to engage in those things that bring such joy to our hearts.

Only one thing is needed each and every day of our lives: *Seek the LORD while He may be found; . . . for* His *thoughts are not* our *thoughts,* and His ways are higher than our ways (Isaiah 55:6, 8).

Mary has chosen what is better, and it will not be taken away from her.
LUKE 10:42

AUGUST 8

*If you pay attention to
the commands of the LORD your God
that I give you this day
and carefully follow them,
you will always be at the top,
never at the bottom.*
DEUTERONOMY 28:13

What a magnificent promise God made to His people whom Moses was leading to His Promised Land. That assurance is also for us today. When we do not pay attention to what God tells us each and every nanosecond of our time, there is no way we can ever be at the top of what God wants for us. As we *trust* our *Lord* God *and do* what He tells us to do, it pleases Him so much that He gives us *the desires of* our *heart* (Psalm 37:3–4). Do we not remember that our Lord God *delights* in the way we go, making our feet *firm* beneath us, even keeping us from falling if we *stumble* (v. 23–24)?

However, God also asks us to *be still before* Him as we *wait patiently for Him* in our moment-to-moment walk with Him and *not fret when people succeed in their wicked schemes* (v. 7). Remember, the Lord tells us *the salvation of the righteous comes from the LORD; he is their stronghold in time of trouble* (v. 39). When we *take refuge* in God, He always *helps* us and *delivers* us (v. 40).

Do not turn aside from any of the commands I give you today,
to the right or to the left, following other gods and serving them.
DEUTERONOMY 28:14

AUGUST 9

If anyone, then, knows
the good they ought to do
and doesn't do it,
it is sin for them.
JAMES 4:17

Everyone has committed sins of omission—knowing the good we ought to do but not doing it. These kinds of sins eventually sting us to the very core of our beings. We knew ahead of time what we should have done, but we somehow convinced ourselves it wasn't important we do it. So now we've committed yet another sin—lying to ourselves.

We also persuade ourselves that it's such a minor thing not to volunteer to do the thing that comes our way or even say a word of encouragement to someone in need. After all, we assure ourselves, are not our schedules already filled to the brim with undertakings God had called on us to do?

Come on, brothers and sisters in Christ, let's quit fooling ourselves. When we know *the good* we *ought to do*, then skip all the rest and just do it!

Submit yourselves, then, to God. . . .
Come near to God, and He will come near to you.
JAMES 4:7–8

AUGUST 10

But if from there you seek
the Lord your God,
you will find him
if you seek him
with all your heart
and with all your soul.
Deuteronomy 4:29

From time to time we allow ourselves to wander away from our Lord God, seeking comfort in people, places, or things, even though we know in the depths of our beings it's useless to do so—for without God we can do nothing. No matter how far away we stray, peace and comfort cannot be found. We become like the Israelites of God's Promised Land and walk away from God—the One who never walks away from us.

When this happens, our Heavenly Father tells us as He did His people, "Know this, my child. If you look for Me *with all your heart and soul, you will find* Me. No matter how long or how far away you have wandered, I can be found. Do you not know that my Spirit who dwells in you will show you the way?"

But seek first his kingdom and his righteousness,
and all these things will be given to you as well.
MATTHEW 6:33

AUGUST 11

Those who look to him
are radiant.
PSALM 34:5

People who are radiant surround us. They may have been hit over the head with a sledge-hammer, so to speak; nevertheless, their eyes glow with joy and peace that surpass all understanding. We want what springs from within them, but we don't desire to walk the roads they travelled to get it—ones of deep loss, or perhaps humiliation, or even degradation or embarrassment and shame, not to mention the valleys of the shadows of death.

As they hold their heads high, looking heavenward, we begin to grasp that their glow is a result of their walk with God, who was with them every step of the way. Had they not gripped His outstretched Hand, trusting and believing Him, they would never be what our Heavenly Father created them in Christ to become. They learned something we have yet to learn: Our Lord God *will never leave* us *nor forsake* us (Deuteronomy 31:6). We are never alone.

Even though I walk through the darkest valley, I will fear no evil,
for you are with me; your rod and your staff, they comfort me.
PSALM 23:4

AUGUST 12

Let us hold unswervingly
to the hope we profess,
for he who promised
is faithful.
HEBREWS 10:23

Have we ever noticed how many times God admonishes us through His Word to *let* ourselves do this, that, or the other? And He cautions us to be steadfast as we do so. Our Heavenly Father always gives us a choice—we can do things His way, or we can do them our way. And have you noticed how perfect and simple His way is? All we have to do is allow God to will and work in us according to His good pleasure to be what He created us in Jesus Christ to become.

In Hebrews 10:23 God tells us to engage ourselves completely in our battle for His hope in us, validating it to others by the way we live. Sounds simple, doesn't it? Yet far too many of us don't hang in there. We don't let ourselves *hold unswervingly to the hope we profess,* thereby turning away from God's promises. God is forever faithful. He never reneges on anything He promises us.

Therefore, let us hold fast to His Word.

> May the God of hope fill you with all joy and peace as you trust in him,
> so that you may overflow with hope by the power of the Holy Spirit.
> ROMANS 15:13

AUGUST 13

For it has been granted to you
on behalf of Christ
not only to believe on him,
but also to suffer for him.
PHILIPPIANS 1:29

The moment we accept Jesus Christ as our Lord and Savior is not the moment we understand that we will suffer for Him. This knowledge comes later, and it happens in God's time and in His way. Sometimes it arrives swiftly and sometimes it delays before becoming evident. Nevertheless, it will land at our feet, and when it does, hopefully our eyes open widely to what suffering for Him means. Its purpose is grow us into what God created us in Christ to become, which gradually happens over time but is not completed until we see Him in heaven or raise our hands in praise to Jesus at His second coming.

Our Lord God allows many trials and tribulations to enter our lives in our walk with Him. No matter how agonizing, heartbreaking, or excruciatingly painful they are, let us remember the reason they are there—to grow us into what He recreated us in Christ to become.

> In you, LORD my God, I put my trust. I trust in you.
> PSALM 25:1–2

AUGUST 14

For in him we live and move
and have our being. . . .
We are his offspring.
ACTS 17:28

As children of God *we live and move in Him*, yet we are our individual selves. God made the heavens and the earth, *and He is not served by human hands.* He doesn't need anything from us. It is God who *gives everyone life and breath.* God determines our lifespans and exactly where we are to live on earth. Our Lord God wants us to *seek Him* and live for Him, for *he is not far from any one of us* (Acts 18:24–27).

Knowing we *live and move and have our being* through Him is such an awesome blessing that it is sometimes hard to comprehend. But, as Paul stated in many of his biblical writings, we who have accepted Jesus Christ as our Lord and Savior are God's children.

No one fools with a mother bear's cubs, and no one fools with a child of God. No one and no circumstance can harm us unless our Father has given His permission. Just ask Job of Old Testament times. Satan had to go before our Holy God to ask His permission to bring agony, trials, and tribulations into Job's life. At that time Satan accused God of putting a hedge around Job, his family, and his possessions, saying to God, *"But now stretch out your hand and strike everything he has, and he will surely curse you to your face"* (Job 1:11).

After Job had suffered, the Lord God *blessed the latter part of Job's life more than the former part* (Job 42:12).

After this, Job lived a hundred and forty years; he saw his children and their children
to the fourth generation. And so Job died, an old man and full of years.
JOB 42:16–17

AUGUST 15

Be strong and take heart,
all you who hope in the LORD.
PSALM 31:24

When traveling down the roads of heartbreak, disasters, sorrows, and despair, it isn't easy for us to be strong, much less uplift our hearts. But as we wait on our Lord, who is with us every nanosecond of the way, it is possible. It just takes time—a lot of it. As He grasps our hands and leads the way to the other side of our distressing roadway, we discover a hidden treasure awaiting us there—God's mirror.

When we pick it up and look at our reflection in it, we are stunned—speechless.

"Oh, yes, it is," God whispers into our ears. "It is you."

"But . . . but . . . Lord, it can't be. There's something . . . I don't know what . . . that is vastly different . . . more peaceful . . . more confident . . . stronger," we respond.

"Yes, My child," He continues. "You are growing in the image of My Son, and as we continue to travel these kinds of roads together the more I am growing you to look like Him."

"Thank You, Lord. Thank You!"

"*Be strong and take heart,*" He encourages. "Just remember, *I am always with you*—always!"

Since you are my rock and my fortress, for the sake of your name lead and guide me.
PSALM 31:3

AUGUST 16

He saw the disciples straining at the oars,
because the wind was against them.
MARK 6:48

After feeding five thousand people with only five loaves of bread and two fish and then dismissing the crowd, Jesus instructed His disciples to get into a boat and go ahead of Him to Bethsaida. Meanwhile He went up on a mountainside to pray (Mark 6:45–46). The disciples did as they were told, never expecting to meet such a strong wind that caused them to gasp at the difficulty of their mission. *The wind was against them.*

We all have times when we are in "God's boat," straining at our oars because the wind is against us. We mimic Jesus' disciples' frightful feelings of being so alone—and do not even recognize the Lord Jesus is close by. He walked on the lake toward them to rescue them (v. 48). He does the same for us today. When this happens, like His disciples, we too will be completely amazed.

May we all do as His disciples did—call out to Him, "Help me, Jesus." He will climb into our boat with us just as He did for His disciples.

Immediately he spoke to them and said, "Take courage! It is I. Don't be afraid."
MARK 6:50

AUGUST 17

See, I am doing a new thing!
Now it springs up;
do you not perceive it?
I am making a way in the wilderness
and streams in the wasteland.
Isaiah 43:19

Before our Lord tells us to look and see what *new thing* He is bringing our way, He instructs us to *forget* about *the past* and not to dwell on it (Isaiah 43:18). Even having experienced God making a way for us during extremely bewildering times, we often remain resistant to any new challenge He allows to enter our lives.

It's like God is telling us, "It's here. Don't you see it? This is the way I want you to go."

"Oh, no!" we exclaim. "I don't want and I don't need a new desert to walk through or another journey in inhospitable floods. Been there, done that too many times already, Lord!"

Silence. God does not respond.

Ashamed, we mumble, "Forgive me, Lord. You told me *not* to *dwell on the past*, and that's exactly what I'm doing, isn't it?"

"Yes, My child. Now take up your cross and follow Me," He responds softly and sweetly as He reaches out to take our trembling hands in His.

"Not my will, but Yours, Lord," we say. "Wherever You lead me I will follow."

My Father, if it is possible, may this cup be taken from me.
Yet not as I will, but as you will.
MATTHEW 26:39

AUGUST 18

What no eye has seen,
What no ear has heard,
and what no human mind has conceived—
the things God has prepared
for those who love him.
1 CORINTHIANS 2:9

It seems far too many of us dwell on the dark times of our lives, trying to drag our feet out of life's slimy pits. And it seems far too many of us allow ourselves to focus on the difficulties that might infiltrate our lives tomorrow. Far too many of us spend too many moments of time dwelling on what was and no longer is, not allowing ourselves to joyfully gallop as fast as we can into what our Lord now places beneath our feet.

Do we not know, do we not comprehend the acts of love, kindness, mercy, and peace our Heavenly Father faithfully sends our way? He *will never leave* us *nor forsake* us (Deuteronomy 31:6). It is we who abandon His presence, turning away from His face, desperately seeking security and comfort elsewhere.

Our Lord God who created us in His own image knows we don't need to know what is on our upcoming days or ruminate on what was in our past. All that is essential is for us to trust our Lord God with all our heart, will, and emotion, paying strict attention to the admonitions of His Holy Spirit in us, while taking hold of His outstretched hand and joyfully following Him wherever He leads us.

I will lead the blind by ways they have not known, along unfamiliar paths I will guide them;
I will turn the darkness into light before them and make the rough places smooth.
These are the things I will do; I will not forsake them.
ISAIAH 42:16

AUGUST 19

You did not choose me,
but I chose you
and appointed you
so that you might go
and bear fruit—
fruit that will last.
JOHN 15:16

God chose you and God chose me to come to Him. Everyone on the face of the earth receives His gracious and loving invitation to follow Him. He promises to give us His peace—a peace that passes all understanding. What man, woman, or child could refuse such a breathtaking and fantastic invitation? Unfortunately, many do.

Perhaps if we followed through with what He appointed us to do when we accepted Him as our Lord and Savior, those who refused His offer would reconsider and accept it and join us in bearing much fruit for Him—*fruit that will last.*

For God so loved the world that he gave his one and only Son,
that whoever believes in him shall not perish but have eternal life.
JOHN 3:16

AUGUST 20

As servants of God
we commend ourselves in every way:
in great endurance;
in troubles, hardships and distresses;
in beatings, imprisonments and riots;
in hard work, sleepless nights and hunger;
in purity, understanding, patience and kindness;
in the Holy Spirit and in sincere love;
in truthful speech and in the power of God;
with weapons of righteousness in the right hand and in the left;
through glory and dishonor, bad report and good report;
genuine, yet regarded as impostors;
known, yet regarded as unknown;
dying and yet we live on;
beaten and yet not killed;
sorrowful, yet always rejoicing;
poor, yet making many rich;
having nothing, and yet possessing everything.
2 CORINTHIANS 6:4–10

Wow! The apostle Paul experienced everything he described in these verses, which he wrote as directed by the Spirit of God. He encouraged the Corinthians and every one of us today with these words. Read through all thirty-four examples of what Paul took part in and what he endured. We have experienced a small number of them. Perhaps others not only have knowledge of all of them but have walked through the valley of shadow of death with most of them.

So what is our Heavenly Father teaching us through these words? He is willing and working in us through what He either sends or allows into our lives to grow into the image of His Son, Jesus Christ. Yes, we will suffer many trials, but we learn after walking through them that our nights turn to day. His majestic glory infiltrates every particle of our beings, causing us to know beyond a shadow of doubt we never could become what we are becoming in Christ without what we suffered and endured for His sake.

This is how we learn to be pure, understanding, patient, kind, sincere in love, and truthful in speech through the power of God in us. We raise our hands in thanksgiving to Him that we are learning to rejoice at all times and trust Him in all things, for in Him we possess everything even if our hands seem empty.

I can do all this through him who gives me strength.
PHILIPPIANS 4:13

AUGUST 21

And if I go and prepare a place for you,
I will come back and take you to be with me
that you also may be where I am.
You know the way to the place where I am going.
JOHN 14:3–4

Before His crucifixion, death, burial, and resurrection, Jesus assured His disciples He would have a place prepared for them when He called them home to be with Him in heaven. He tells us the same thing. When we know and understand and accept His plan for getting us where He wants us to be, He commissions us to follow in His footsteps and lead others to Him the way He instructs us to do.

Then he said to them all: "Whoever wants to be my disciple must deny themselves
and take up their cross daily and follow me."
LUKE 9:23

AUGUST 22

I will refresh the weary
and satisfy the faint.
JEREMIAH 31:25

Vacuuming floors fatigues many because of the constant pushing and pulling it requires. There is a relatively new invention in our marketplaces that can do this task for us. It's called an iRobot or Roomba. Just push the "clean" button on its top and it automatically sets about doing its job.

When its energy is drained, sometimes it stops working before it can find its way back to its home base to be recharged. When this happens, its owner must rescue it because it has no life left in it to do so for itself.

This is what our Heavenly Father does for each and every one of His tired, exhausted, and fatigued children—He picks us up in His loving arms and places us where we can rest while He recharges us. God promises He will refresh our weary souls and satisfy our faint hearts. Our Lord God *will never leave* us *nor forsake* us (Deuteronomy 31:6).

Thanks be to God for His indescribable gift!
2 CORINTHIANS 9:15

AUGUST 23

So we say with confidence,
"The Lord is my helper;
I will not be afraid.
What can mere mortals do to me?"
HEBREWS 13:6

While growing up it was comforting to know that no matter what came our way, our earthly parents would back us up. As time moved onward, however, we discovered the day would come for us to build our own lives apart from our parents. It became our job to supply our food and shelter and put clothing on our backs.

Even though countless things, people, and events frequently frightened us as we were growing up, we believed our mothers and fathers could always protect us. As we continued on, however, it became apparent they couldn't. Sometimes our anxieties would intensify to the point of our being scared to death, knowing we'd have to rescue ourselves.

Thankfully, we were introduced to our Heavenly Father and accepted His invitation to join His family. We know He is forever there to help us and rescue us! He is always with us and will never leave us, so there is never a reason for us to be afraid.

Jesus Christ is the same yesterday and today and forever.
HEBREWS 13:8

AUGUST 24

And I will ask the Father,
and he will give you another advocate
to help you and be with you forever—
the Spirit of truth.
JOHN 14:16–17

We are never alone. We are never without God's counsel and help. Jesus asked the Father to give us another Counselor after He completed His mission of redeeming us by dying for our sins. The Holy Spirit, God's *Spirit of truth*, lives in us and is always available to us.

The absolutely fantastic thing about our Counselor is that He already knows what we need even before we ask. If we would only grasp the awesomeness of His being with us forever—leading, guiding, and directing our paths and teaching us the way we should go—our walk with our Lord would be more fruitful.

Let us raise our hands in thanksgiving to Jesus for sacrificing Himself so that God's light shines in us and through us to those who cross our paths.

When Jesus spoke again to the people, he said, "I am the light of the world.
Whoever follows me will never walk in darkness, but will have the light of life."
JOHN 8:12

AUGUST 25

That is why I am suffering as I am.
Yet this is no cause for shame,
because I know whom I have believed,
and am convinced that
he is able to guard
what I have entrusted to him
until that day.
2 TIMOTHY 1:12

We reach a time on our earthly travels with our Heavenly Father when we encounter such fierce storms and opposition that we don't know where to turn or what to do. We are exhausted, depleted of every ounce of energy within us. If this is where you are now, sit down with the apostle Paul and read his second letter to Timothy, whom he called his *dear son* (2 Timothy 1:2.) As Paul recalled Timothy's tears and longing to see him to bring him joy, he wrote that he was reminded of Timothy's *sincere faith* and of his grandmother, Lois, and his mother, Eunice, knowing that such faith now lived in Timothy (v. 4–5).

Paul may have known this letter might be his last one to write because he told Timothy to *fan into flame the gift of God, which is in you through the laying on of my hands* (v. 6). Paul didn't want Timothy to be timid so he reminded him instead to have a spirit of *power, love, and self-discipline* (v. 7). He urged Timothy not to be *ashamed* to testify about Jesus or be mortified because he, Paul, was being held captive in prison (v. 8). Instead, Paul invited Timothy to join him *in suffering for the gospel* because God not only *saved* him but He *called* him and all His children to live *a holy life* (v. 9). He lets us, as well as Timothy, know that every child of God has a mission, through the strength of Christ in them, to persevere through God's grace—His unmerited favor.

Just as Paul was *appointed a herald and an apostle and a teacher* (v. 11), Timothy as well as we were appointed by God to use the spiritual gifts He implanted in us at the time of our redemption. Yes, often we will suffer as we use these gifts, perhaps not as violently as did the apostle Paul, but we will encounter distress. And we persevere because we *know whom* we *have believed and* we are *convinced that He is able to guard what* we *have entrusted to Him until that day* (v.12).

Do not be afraid; do not be discouraged.
DEUTERONOMY 1:21

AUGUST 26

And we know that in all things
God works for the good
of those who love him,
who have been called
according to his purpose.
ROMANS 8:28

There is no such thing as a coincidence in the life of a Christian. Nothing enters our lives happenstance, even though it may appear it does. Our Heavenly Father is continually at work in us, shaping us into what He created us in Christ to become. The roads He places us on to reach His destination for us are quite dissimilar. Our Lord God knows us through and through. No two of us are alike, and what works for one doesn't necessarily work for another.

However, whatever He selects to send our way is the exact thing we need to experience in order to grow in Christ, even though it can be quite painful and we want nothing to do with it, pleading with God to take it away or to make it vanish.

It is not until we get to the other side of what has brought such despair into our hearts that we begin to comprehend we could never be the person we are becoming in Christ had our Heavenly Father not allowed us to experience such devastation. Our pains and sufferings always work for our good. We praise Him for making us more than we could ever become without His hand on our lives.

For the Mighty One has done great things for me—holy is his name.
LUKE 1:49

AUGUST 27

A cheerful heart
is good medicine,
but a crushed spirit
dries up the bones.
PROVERBS 17:22

Medications don't all taste alike. Some pills and liquids are easy to swallow, while others make us gag and want to spit them out. King Solomon tells us *a crushed spirit dries up the bones,* and he is absolutely right. A crushed spirit will dry us up inside, and when this happens we need medication for it. We are spiritually sick. But if we refuse to take God's good medicine for our ailment, we will never reach His healing that's needed for us to experience His cheerful heart in us.

For it is God who works in you to will and to act in order to fulfill his good purpose.
PHILIPPIANS 2:13

AUGUST 28

For with God nothing will be impossible.
LUKE 1:37 NKJV

Absolutely *nothing* is *impossible with God*, who is in us, for us, and with us. If we truly took God's words to heart, we would know beyond any shadow of doubt that every word He speaks is completely true. Why is it that we so frequently doubt Him? Why do we wallow in the horrible mud of distrust? Our Holy Father has given every one of His children His weapons of warfare. All we have to do is pick them up and use them.

When demonic forces shoot their wicked arrows our way, let us immediately give a ride to His shield of faith—pick it up with His other weapons and use them. That's what they are there for. It doesn't matter how many times we put them into action, they never fail because they are created to last forever. All that is required is for us to trust Him and obey Him. So, let's pick up and use all of His weapons of warfare, joyfully praising our Father for them!

Such confidence we have through Christ before God.
2 CORINTHIANS 3:4

AUGUST 29

*And whoever does not
carry their cross and follow me
cannot be my disciple.*
LUKE 14:27

As Christians we are God's students, sitting in His classroom and listening as He instructs us in what we need to know to graduate from His school of discipleship. Our textbook is His cross, which we must carry with us everywhere we go. Even though it is burdensome at times, still we must clutch it, never letting it out of our hands. The harder we cling to it, the stronger we grow.

Even though we often protest and complain while sitting among other students doing likewise, we must continue onward. Somewhere in our Teacher's learning process we will absorb that our cross is not heavy to bear at all; rather it is quite a joy and a blessing to carry.

We must never ever hesitate to carry the cross He places in our hands when we enter His classroom. If we do, we will miss out on what He has put us in His classroom to learn.

I can do all this through him who gives me strength.
PHILIPPIANS 4:13

AUGUST 30

For a long time I have kept silent,
I have been quiet and held myself back.
ISAIAH 42:14

It takes quite some time for many of us who are sitting in God's classroom and soaking in His words, contemplating each and every one of them, to open ourselves up and intently listen to His Holy Spirit reveal the way we need to go. We remain silent, not participating in what is happening in class, perhaps instead holding ourselves back for fear of criticism or disapproval.

However, hopefully we will reach the time when we listen intently to the Holy Spirit in us, obeying Him and refusing to quench and grieve Him. When this time arrives, and it will if we wait patiently for it, then we completely open ourselves up and joyfully participate in every aspect of learning that our Heavenly Father sends our way.

There is a time for everything, and a season for every activity under the heavens.
ECCLESIASTES 3:1

AUGUST 31

For with much wisdom
comes much sorrow;
the more knowledge,
the more grief.
ECCLESIASTES 1:18

Human knowledge is not enough to get us through our lifetimes. No one is astute enough in and of themselves to figure out what to do in all of life's situations. It is our human mind and understanding that all too frequently brings sorrow and regret our way. The information, facts, or data we acquire is never enough to keep us on God's track.

Insight comes only from heeding the leading of the Holy Spirit. It's far better to have Him in us leading and directing our way than to have human wisdom without God's leadership. `It is God's wisdom in us that is needed, not our own intelligence and insight that so frequently leads us astray.

You will keep in perfect peace those whose minds are steadfast,
because they trust in you.
ISAIAH 26:3

September

SEPTEMBER 1

LORD, I know
that people's lives
are not their own;
it is not for them
to direct their steps.
JEREMIAH 10:23

When we can say with Jeremiah that a man's life is not his own, then we can embrace God's Holy Spirit in us and allow God Almighty to direct our steps. Such a picture-perfect life—and yet far too many refuse it, preferring their own way instead. Has not our Heavenly Father told us that His thoughts are not our thoughts and His ways are not our ways (Isaiah 55:9)? Why then, do we insist on doing what we want to do when we want to do it? Why do we invite the outside world into our innermost life, somehow believing it will fill us with joy and peace and comfort?

God's Word will not return to Him empty. He will achieve His purposes for our lives (v. 11), and as He does so we *will go out in joy and be led forth in peace; the mountains and hills will burst into song.* How wonderful to hear His *mountains and hills* singing their songs and *all the trees of the field* clapping *their hands* (v. 12). It's far better to rest beneath our Heavenly Father's awesome trees than to sink under our own thorns and briers (v. 13).

Come to me, all you who are weary and burdened, and I will give you rest.
Take my yoke upon you and learn from me, for I am gentle and humble in heart,
and you will find rest for your souls. For my yoke is easy and my burden is light.
MATTHEW 11:28–30

SEPTEMBER 2

Surely you have granted him
unending blessings
and made him glad
with the joy of your presence.
PSALM 21:6

Let us shout with David as he did when God delivered him from his enemies and he raised his hands in thanksgiving to God Almighty for saving him in battle. Our Heavenly Father does the same for us today. He watches over us and takes care of us, for we are His sheep. He is our Holy Shepherd. We shall never be in want. Our God absolutely provides everything we need. He even walks with us *through the darkest valley*, and He anoints our heads with oil as He refreshes our souls when we slip and fall (Psalm 23:1–5).

How could we not rejoice, knowing His *goodness* and His *love follow* us *all the days* of our lives? And, to top it off, we will live *in the house of the Lord forever* (v. 6).

Some trust in chariots and some in horses, but we trust in the name of the LORD our God.
PSALM 20:7

SEPTEMBER 3

Many are the plans
in a person's heart,
but it is the LORD's purpose
that prevails.
PROVERBS 19:21

Many of us go to bed each night with tomorrow's plans spinning around in our minds, embedding anxiety in our hearts. We ruminate over and over again, wondering if we will be able to fit our plans into tomorrow's schedule.

However, if we begin our day focusing on God's plans for us, meeting with Him, talking with Him, and petitioning His help throughout the moments of our day, it relieves us of anxiety, frustration, and burdensome feelings. Our Heavenly Father's plan is for us to stay in touch with Him, lean on Him, learn from Him—not lean on ourselves. He and we together make our days satisfying and complete.

When we trust Him and not ourselves or others then our minds will not whirl around and around before we can fall asleep at night. Saying to Him, "Thank You, Lord, for everything you have done for me this day" brings us joy, peace, and contentment.

> The Lord is my rock, my fortress and my deliverer; my God is my rock,
> in whom I take refuge, my shield and the horn of my salvation.
> He is my stronghold, my refuge and my savior.
>
> 2 SAMUEL 22:2–3

SEPTEMBER 4

> *But I trust in your unfailing love;*
> *my heart rejoices in your salvation.*
> *I will sing the LORD's praise,*
> *for he has been good to me.*
> PSALM 13:5–6

Unfortunately, we don't always trust our Heavenly Father's love for us. His love is unfailing—meaning it is always dependable and trustworthy. Perhaps our problem with accepting His love promise is because sometimes we don't even love ourselves. When we don't, it is beyond our comprehension how God can love us. If we're honest with ourselves, we can uncover all kinds of faults within us, whether real or imaginary.

Jesus tells us through His disciple and tax collector Matthew: *"Love the Lord your God with all your heart and with all your soul and with all your mind."* Jesus says, *"This is His first and greatest commandment."* He follows with *"Love your neighbor as yourself,"* letting us know that *"all the Law and the Prophets hang on these two commandments"* (Matthew 22:37–40).

If we do not love ourselves then we cannot love our neighbor as ourselves. To love ourselves is Jesus' second command, given after admonishing us to love God with our whole heart and soul and mind. Jesus reprimands us when we fall into the sin of self-condemnation. The evil forces of this world gloat when they entice us to find fault with ourselves, allowing us to fall into the sin of self-condemnation, with our believing we are unworthy of God's love for us.

Anytime we commit this sin, let us hastily confess it to our Heavenly Father, and then our hearts will break forth with singing praises to Him and rejoicing in God's salvation and His everlasting love for us.

Love your neighbor as yourself.
MATTHEW 22:39

SEPTEMBER 5

I will say of the LORD,
"He is my refuge and my fortress,
my God, in whom I trust."
PSALM 91:2

We often look back on our past times with deep appreciation and gratitude for having been blessed with faithful parents, siblings, grandparents, aunts, and uncles, and even longtime friends, whom we believed would always be there for us. As our lives move on, however, many of these loved ones no longer surround us on a daily basis. Some have been called home to be with God while others, or even we ourselves, have moved to different locations. Sometimes we long to seek shelter in their loving arms, even though we know this is no longer possible.

We have all moved on from what was and no longer is, but praise God we have our Mighty Fortress who is always with us and in us, for He remains *the same yesterday, today, and forever* (Hebrews 13:8). He *is* our *refuge and* our *fortress*. We praise Him that He is trustworthy, knowing in the depths of our beings that He is forever with us.

God is our refuge and strength, an ever-present help in trouble.
PSALM 46:1

SEPTEMBER 6

We wait in hope for the LORD;
he is our help and our shield.
In him our hearts rejoice
for we trust in his holy name.
PSALM 33:20–21

Waiting does not come easily for modern man. Few of us enjoy doing it. We want what we want, and we want it immediately. We can either fume and fuss and complain while waiting, or we can do it God's way—in hope. This means we are confident and optimistic, anticipating God's glorious wonders that in His time and in His way will fall at our feet, filling our hearts with gratitude and praise.

Waiting means trusting our Heavenly Father because He knows us through and through. We cannot know what is best for us in any circumstance. Only God is able to do this. We can never depend on our own wisdom, for if or when we do we fall into the sin of pride, which is abhorrent to God.

God *is our help and shield*—in Him *we trust*. Even if we never see the outcomes of that for which we've waited and hoped, we can rejoice because *we trust in His holy name*. In His time, God makes all things beautiful (Ecclesiastes 3:11).

Wait for the LORD; be strong and take heart and wait for the LORD.
PSALM 27:14

SEPTEMBER 7

What good is it for someone
to gain the whole world,
yet forfeit their soul?
MARK 8:36

Jesus asked a crowd of people surrounding Him this question, which He also asks us today. If we ignore following Him with all of our heart, soul, spirit, and mind, focusing on what the world has to offer us instead of what He freely gives us, what have we accomplished? Absolutely nothing! We will have lost our souls.

Earthly wealth, prominence, fame, importance, medals, brilliant minds with supposedly splendid problem solutions, etc., mean absolutely nothing without God's Holy Spirit in us directing us and leading us on His paths for us. When we accept Jesus as our Lord and Savior we are saved to live for Him and to serve Him. We become children of God, and as such our focus no longer is on ourselves or our ways but on God and His ways for us.

Anything we accumulate in life is never ours to do with as we please. We came into the world with nothing, and we leave the world with nothing but what the Holy Spirit enables us to accomplish while walking with Him.

It's perfectly alright to gain fame and fortune, but it means nothing without the Holy Spirit dwelling in us, directing our paths, and causing us to do what God placed us on earth to do— love Him, live for Him, and serve Him with everything He places in our lives. Without Him we can do nothing.

I can do all this through him who gives me strength.
PHILIPPIANS 4:13

SEPTEMBER 8

*Having loved his own
who were in the world,
he loved them to the end.*
JOHN 13:1

In the devotional book *Springs in the Valley* by Mrs. Charles E. Cowman, we are told a story by Sadhu Sundar Singh. He passed a crowd of people who were putting out a jungle fire at the foot of the Himalayas when he saw several men gazing at a tree that was on fire. When he asked the men what they were looking at, they pointed skyward to a nest of baby birds at the top of the tree and the mother bird wildly flapping her wings trying to protect her young but unable to do so.

He said he thought the mother bird would fly away from the hot flames, but she didn't. "She flew down, spread her wings over her young ones, and in minutes was burned to ashes with them" (p. 272).

Jesus did the same for us. He gave up His life, was crucified, died, and was buried, and arose from His grave so that we could be saved from the deadly fire of our sins and become His children forever. We will live with Him in the heavenly realms when He calls us home to be with Him.

God is love.
1 JOHN 4:16

SEPTEMBER 9

But grow in the grace
and knowledge
of our Lord and Savior
Jesus Christ.
2 PETER 3:18

How do we get to know someone to whom we've been introduced? There are many ways, but the best way is to communicate on a regular basis with them and discover many facets about them, which bonds us together. When we are introduced to Jesus Christ and come to the place of accepting His work on His cross for us bringing us into a relationship with Him, God admonishes us through Peter to *grow in the grace and knowledge of our Lord and Savior Jesus Christ.*

Our Heavenly Father had bestowed His grace, His unmerited favor, on each and every one of His children. We are to grow in His unmerited favor, something we learn to treasure as we fellowship with Him and follow in His footsteps. The more we fellowship together, the more knowledge we gain about Him. This enables us to live the kind of life He has called us to live minute by minute and day by day, through the good times and the bad times as well.

This growth process is called sanctification—meaning as we mature in Him, live in Him, and achieve through Him, the more we nurture that which He predestined us in Christ to become. As we do so, we will travel with Him down many excruciating, agonizing, unbearable, and painful highways, but He is continually with us and in us. We are never alone throughout our journey together as we are learning we can trust Him more and more each and every step of the way.

To him be glory both now and forever! Amen.
2 PETER 3:18

SEPTEMBER 10

But I trust in your unfailing love;
my heart rejoices in your salvation.
PSALM 13:5

We all ask God the same question King David did: *"How long, LORD? Will you forget me forever?"* (Psalm 13:1). We're not told what David was experiencing when he pled thus with the Lord. However, we do know David asked God how long four times in a mere two verses of Scripture. David assumed God not only hid His face from him, causing David to wrestle with thoughts of sorrow in his heart, but also God didn't respond to his petition when he asked why his enemy was triumphing over him. How many times do we say these same words of David, also pleading with God to *look* on us and *answer* by putting His *light* in our *eyes* so that we will not *sleep in death* (v. 3)?

Let us never give up or give in to any situation God allows into our lives. Instead, let us shout with David as he finally proclaimed: *"But I trust in your unfailing love: my heart rejoices in your salvation."* As we do so we can rejoice as did David, singing to our Heavenly Father and praising His name, thanking Him for being so good to us.

But those who hope in the LORD will renew their strength.
They will soar on wings like eagles; they will run, and not grow weary,
they will walk and not be faint.
ISAIAH 40:31

SEPTEMBER 11

The Lord is my light and my salvation—
whom shall I fear?
The Lord is the stronghold of my life—
of whom shall I be afraid?
Psalm 27:1

It is quite easy to fall into a pit of darkness, with fear engulfing us, threatening to take us under and not allowing us to return to normalcy. But our Lord God is always with us. We are never alone. We have nothing to fear—absolutely nothing! All we have to do is reach out for God's outstretched hand and grasp it firmly as His light surrounds us, enabling us to see He is mighty to save—He is our *stronghold*. He never leaves us and He will never forsake us. Praise God from whom all blessings flow!

Wait for the Lord; be strong and take heart and wait for the Lord.
PSALM 27:14

SEPTEMBER 12

No discipline seems pleasant at the time, but painful.
Later on, however, it produces
a harvest of righteousness and peace
for those who have been trained by it.
Hebrews 12:11

Experience has taught us that no one seems to enjoy, much less like, *discipline*. However, whether young or old, everyone will encounter it, and when we do usually it will not be pleasant. Depending on how discipline is conducted, it troubles our souls because we know we've fallen short of what is expected of us. It plants a seed in us that *later produces* and develops a vast *harvest of righteousness and peace* in our hearts that we never could have experienced without it.

Let us raise our hands in thanksgiving to our Heavenly Father for training us through His discipline.

Endure hardship as discipline; God is treating you as his children.
HEBREWS 12:7

SEPTEMBER 13

You have made known to me
the paths of life;
you will fill me with joy
in your presence.
ACTS 2:28

Life is filled with all kinds of twists and turns and pathways leading in every direction. Sometimes we don't know which way to go when approaching life's crossroads. Should we keep going straight ahead or turn right or left or turn around and go back? It results in a guessing game for us when we depend on ourselves to make up our minds.

It is only when we know that we know that our Heavenly Father has made His paths of life known to us to follow throughout our lifetimes that we stop when several roadways intersect and patiently wait for God's directions. In His presence He fills our hearts with joy, even though we understand His choice will not be a pleasant one but one filled with all kinds of troubles.

It is only when we get to the end of a particular roadway, with another one beneath our feet, that we are able to raise our hands in praise to our Lord for growing us into what we are becoming. We are to dedicate our lives to God's highways, going His way and not ours.

We live by faith, not by sight.
2 CORINTHIANS 5:7

SEPTEMBER 14

But who are you, a human being,
to talk back to God?
Shall what is formed
say to the one who formed it,
"Why did you make me like this?"
ROMANS 9:20

Only when we take to heart God's ways in any and all situations can we joyfully and eagerly submit to God's plan for us—not insisting on our own plans for ourselves. Our Heavenly Father's ways are not our ways, nor are His plans our plans (Isaiah 55:8). Yet far too often we rebel against God—we talk back to Him, disliking the road on which He has placed us.

No one wants to hear words about putting our affairs in order because we have only days or months to live, or be laid off from work, or have a home repossessed, or lose anything we believe is precious. However, we are free to voice the same question Jesus did while hanging on His cross: *"My God, my God, why have you forsaken me?"* (Matthew 27:46). Our Lord God was with Jesus every step of His way while He was being crucified, but God did not respond to Jesus' *why* question. More than likely, God will not respond to our *why* questions either.

Far better for us to pray the words Jesus spoke while in the Garden of Gethsemane: *"Father, if you are willing take this cup from me; yet not my will, but yours be done"* (Luke 22:42). Whatever comes into our lives is not there by accident. There are no coincidences for God's children.

Jesus said, *"The one who sent me is with me; he has not left me alone, for I always do what pleases him"* (John 8:29), and *"If you hold to my teaching, you are really my disciples. Then you will know the truth, and the truth will set you free"* (John 8:31–32).

SEPTEMBER 15

Praise be to the Lord,
to God our Savior,
who daily bears our burdens.
PSALM 68:19

Our Lord God cannot bear our burdens if we don't take them to Him in prayer. It is only as we listen to Him and obey Him when He tells us to cast all our anxieties and burdens on Him (1 Peter 5:7) that He hears our words of woe and rescues us.

And as we do so, let us remember that in God's time His relief will come—not in our time. In His time, God makes all things beautiful (Ecclesiastes 3:11).

Wait for the Lord; be strong and take heart and wait for the Lord.
PSALM 27:14

SEPTEMBER 16

Consider him who endured
such opposition from sinners,
so that you will not
grow weary and lose heart.
HEBREWS 12:3

Far too many of us are impatient. We find waiting wearisome. It causes us to fret and worry, turning this way and that as we strive to accomplish what we want to complete. Usually, it takes a long time for us to learn to sit and be still in God's presence and wait for Him to lead us in the direction in which He wants us to go.

If we don't carefully pay attention to what surrounds everything going on in us and around us and patiently wait for our Lord to act, then we will grow weary and lose heart, groaning and tossing our hands into the air in disgust and finding fault with everything.

Our Heavenly Father never grows *tired or weary* (Isaiah 40:28), even as He endures opposition from sinful men. *He gives strength to the weary and increases the power of the weak* (v. 29). And He tells us: *Those who hope in the LORD will renew their strength. They will soar on wings like eagles; they will run and not grow weary, they will walk and not be faint* (v. 31). It's far better to soar with eagles than mumble and complain and become impatient.

> **But if we hope for what we do not yet have, we wait for it patiently.**
> ROMANS 8:25

SEPTEMBER 17

> *You are the light of the world.*
> *A town built on a hill*
> *cannot be hidden.*
> MATTHEW 5:14

God's Holy Spirit in us shines brightly. It guides us every step of the way, every moment of the night and day. His light is to shine through us for others to see. As a *city on a hill cannot be hidden*, so too is God's light in us. It is only when we ignore it or put it aside that it cannot be seen by anyone but ourselves, and many times not even ourselves.

Let us take God's brilliant light in us seriously—never concealing it, but placing it on a hill so that others can see God's light in us, thereby allowing His light to shine through us for all the world see.

> **Let your light shine before others, that they may see your good deeds**
> **and glorify your Father in heaven.**
> MATTHEW 5:16

SEPTEMBER 18

Though he brings grief,
he will show compassion,
so great is his unfailing love.
LAMENTATIONS 3:32

When teaching anything to our children, we know it often brings unhappiness, even heartaches and sorrows, their way. They grumble and complain and ask why they have to sit in the corner; or why they can't go outside and play; or why they can't go over to their friend's house, talk on the telephone, or are not allowed to do what they want to do. They even toss mean looks our way and grit their teeth. They are not happy with us.

So why do we discipline our children to teach them something they need to learn? We do it because we unfailingly love them. We want them each to grow into a responsible, gracious, loving, and kind person.

Our Heavenly Father does the same for us. In order to grow us into what He created us in Christ to become, He allows us to experience many trials and tribulations. No matter what sorrow, grief, burdens, or misfortunes we face, He forever loves us and is compassionate with us. As His children we react to His teachings in many of the ways our children react to ours. We want nothing to do with it—that is until we get to the other side of it and realize we could never be what we are becoming in Christ had our Father not disciplined us, teaching us His ways are not our ways nor are His thoughts our thoughts (Isaiah 55:8).

Trust in the LORD forever, for the LORD, the LORD himself, is the Rock eternal.
ISAIAH 26:4

SEPTEMBER 19

Gladness and joy will overtake them,
and sorrow and sighing will flee away.
ISAIAH 35:10

As God's children we have been redeemed—bought through the shed blood of Jesus Christ. We are God's sheep. He is our shepherd. He strengthens our *feeble hands* and steadies *our knees that give way.* He constantly tells us not to be afraid, rather to *be strong*, knowing He will return one day (Isaiah 35:3–4) and take us home to be with Him in His special pasture created especially for us.

Then *the blind and the deaf* will see and hear. Those who are *lame will leap like a deer and the mute* will *shout for joy. And a highway will be there; it will be called the Way of Holiness. Only the redeemed will walk* on it entering His house, *singing* with *everlasting joy* (v. 5–10). We *will dwell in the house of the* LORD *forever* (Psalm 23:6).

As for God, his way is perfect: the word of the LORD is flawless; he shields all who take refuge in him.
PSALM 18:30

SEPTEMBER 20

The Sovereign LORD has given me
a well-instructed tongue,
to know the word
that sustains the weary.
He wakens me morning by morning,
wakens my ear to listen
like one being instructed.

ISAIAH 50:4

It is only when we awaken each morning turning a listening ear to God and paying strict attention to what He is saying, that we comprehend His plans for our day. When listen to Him, He shows us the way to go.

Who would want to miss out on having *a well-instructed tongue*, one able to sustain the *weary*? Who would want to miss hearing His words of comfort and encouragement? Who would want to miss His healing hands upon their weary souls? Who would want to struggle with having enough time and energy to do what they believed needed to be done and end their day dreading the approach of the next one?

It is only as we awaken and choose first to sit in God's presence and listen to Him that we can end our day with joy and thanksgiving. Even though the day might become difficult, we began it listening to our Lord, paying attention to His sweet words of love and encouragement, and knowing He is with us every step of the way.

But seek first his kingdom and his righteousness,
and all these things will be given to you as well.
MATTHEW 6:33

SEPTEMBER 21

But one thing I do:
Forgetting what is behind
and straining toward what is ahead.
PHILIPPIANS 3:13

The apostle Paul wanted the church at Philippi to understand all that he had written to them about pressing on and taking hold of what Jesus Christ had taken hold of for him. He didn't *consider* himself *yet to have taken hold of it* (Philippians 3:12–13). The same is true for each and every one of us today. No one lives a perfect life—one without sin. We have *all sinned and fall short of the glory of God* (Romans 3:23). But we can do what Paul did, even when experience has taught us it is not an easy thing to do.

What is that? Forget the past. Walk away from it. We can never change it. We can never experience the fullness of God's presence in our present moments if we allow ourselves to focus on our past lives. Of all people, Paul knew this. He also knew that to walk away from his past he must focus on *straining toward what is ahead.* Paul pressed *on toward the goal to win the prize for which God has called* him *heavenward in Christ Jesus"* (Philippians 3:13–14).

As we mature in Christ, it becomes easier for us to do the same. Paul even told the Philippians, and us as well, that *if on some point you think differently, that too God will make clear to you.* Forgetting the past and letting it go means living up *to what we have already attained* (v. 15–16).

Show me your ways, LORD, teach me your paths.
Guide me in your truth and teach me, for you are God my Savior;
and my hope is in you all day long.
PSALM 25:4–5

SEPTEMBER 22

So do not fear,
for I am with you;
do not be dismayed,
for I am your God.
I will strengthen you
and help you:
I will uphold you
with my righteous right hand.
ISAIAH 41:10

Regardless of what age we are or how strong we believe we are, from time to time all of us become fearful. We also succumb to multiple feelings of discouragement, allowing ourselves to become disheartened. God knows beforehand that these feelings and thoughts frequently enter our minds. This is why He assures us we are never alone—His help is always available.

In other words, anyone or any situation can come along and push our buttons of fearfulness and dismay, but that's all they can do. It is we ourselves who allow these buttons to have their way in our lives. It is only when we trust our Heavenly Father—knowing it is His strength in us that upholds us, not our strength and thankfully reaching out for His outstretched holy hand, knowing He is with us and will never leave us and is always whispering in our ears His words of strength and hope—that we move forward. We are never alone. He will always strengthen us and help us by upholding us with His *righteous right hand.*

For I am the Lord your God who takes hold of your right hand and
says to you, Do not fear; I will help you.
ISAIAH 41:13

SEPTEMBER 23

They will have no fear of bad news;
their hearts are steadfast,
trusting in the LORD.
PSALM 112:7

What happens when the telephone rings in the middle of the night? We frightfully awaken, terror gripping our hearts. Certainly this is not good news, we believe as we struggle to take another breath. We fear hearing shocking news because no one calls at this hour of the night just to chat. Regardless of when it occurs, bad news comes our way. From time to time, it happens to all of us.

Our Heavenly Father tells us not to be afraid when something of this nature occurs. This is why it's so important for us to remain firm in our faith in the Lord, knowing He is with us and will always uphold us. Yes, we might scream and yell and fall to our stunned knees, not being able to comprehend what we've been told; nevertheless, God enables us to carry on. Since we are not all the same, we will respond in diverse ways.

God admonishes us to hold fast, trusting Him to see us through whatever comes our way. It will take time and probably a lot of it to get back on track, but we know in our hearts that our Lord never puts more on us than we can bear.

Trust in the LORD with all your heart and lean not on your own understanding.
PROVERBS 3:5

SEPTEMBER 24

The Lord is good,
a refuge in times of trouble.
He cares for those who trust in him.

Nahum 1:7

God is so good. There is nothing more comforting than knowing He cares for those who trust in him. Regardless of what comes along and threatens to take us under, God is there. He is our sanctuary, our protector, the One whom we can trust to rescue us. He hides us in the shelter of His wings. He is our safe haven.

As for me, I will always have hope; I will praise you more and more.

PSALM 71:14

SEPTEMBER 25

Instead, you ought to say,
"If it is the Lord's will,
we will live and do this or that."
JAMES 4:15

Since we never know what will happen tomorrow, why do we spend countless hours being anxious about it, worrying about what to do with it or what will happen when it gets here? In the fourth chapter of James, written by Jesus' half-brother, God asks us a question: *"What is your life?"* He then answers it: *"You are a mist that appears for a little while and then vanishes"* (v. 14).

God tells us that, instead of spending useless hours fretting about the future, we need to tell ourselves: *"If it is the Lord's will, we will live and do this or that."* That's the end of it! Our Lord God always responds when we petition His will for our lives. At such times, all we need to do is go to our Heavenly Father in prayer and request His help in whatever it is we're fretting and fuming and agonizing over.

Therefore do not worry about tomorrow, for tomorrow will worry about itself.
Each day has enough trouble of its own.
MATTHEW 6:34

SEPTEMBER 26

Come to me,
all you who are weary and burdened,
and I will give you rest.
MATTHEW 11:28

During our lifetimes we have received innumerable invitations. Some have been accepted, some have been refused, and some have been ignored. There is one outstanding invitation, however, that we must never put aside. It is from Jesus Christ, and it is His promise to us.

Whenever we are weary and burdened, all we have to do is seek His face. We know when we do that, whatever is taking us down. He will bring us back up resting in His everlasting arms. There is no better place to be at the present moment than in His presence, reveling in His glorious riches planted deeply within our hearts.

Let us all call out to Him right now, resting in His assurance that He is forever in us, with us, and for us. He *will never leave* us *nor forsake* us (Deuteronomy 31:6). We are never alone.

> Take my yoke upon you and learn from me, for I am gentle and humble in heart,
> and you will find rest for your souls.
> MATTHEW 12:29

SEPTEMBER 27

Fight the good fight of the faith.
Take hold of the eternal life
to which you were called
when you made your good confession
in the presence of many witnesses.
1 TIMOTHY 6:12

The only way we can be prepared to live the life our Heavenly Father has called us to live is to grasp what we were given the moment we accepted Jesus Christ as our Lord and Savior. When God's eternal life takes hold of our hearts, we become His children and members of His team—meaning we must flee from those who teach false doctrines and who do not agree with our Heavenly Father's instructions. Our assignment is to *agree to the sound instruction of our Lord Jesus Christ and to godly teaching.* We have to turn our backs on our opposing team's *controversies and quarrels that result in envy, strife, malicious talk, evil suspicions and constant friction between men of corrupt mind*—those *who have been robbed of the truth and who think that godliness is a means to financial gain* or anything that might get them to where they want to go (1 Timothy 6:3–5).

As God's children we are to *flee from all this, and pursue righteousness, godliness, faith, love, endurance, and gentleness* (v. 11). As a member of God's team we will experience multiple good fights in order to win against the opposing team of the evil one. As such we must continually allow God to train us to be excellent players on His team.

> To him be honor and might forever. Amen.
> 1 TIMOTHY 6:16

SEPTEMBER 28

In order to keep me from becoming conceited,
I was given a thorn in my flesh,
a messenger of Satan, to torment me.
2 CORINTHIANS 12:7

The apostle Paul received *surpassingly great revelations* from God as he walked with Him (2 Corinthians 12:7). His mission was to spread the gospel of Jesus Christ, which he did. In the process of so doing, *a messenger of Satan* was permitted by God to torment Paul through what he called *a thorn in* his *flesh.* We are not told what Paul's *thorn* was, but Paul assures us it was there for a godly reason—*to keep* him *from becoming conceited.*

Do you not think our Heavenly Father also allows us to carry "*a thorn in* our *flesh*" as we testify for Him, carrying out our God-given mission for Him? Everyone has weak spots—perhaps pride, arrogance, self-importance, feelings of superiority, and such. The more we grow in Christ and the more we learn about Him and from Him, the tendency for us to become conceited and boastful will rear its ugly head.

Just as Paul did not elaborate on his thorn, we don't either. Our job is the same as was Paul's—put on God's weapons of warfare and *fight the good fight* (1 Timothy 6:12), praising and thanking our Heavenly Father for everything He either sends or allows in our lives to grow us in Christ, enabling His light to shine through us.

My grace is sufficient for you; for my power is made perfect in weakness.
2 CORINTHIANS 12:9

SEPTEMBER 29

For where your treasure is,
there your heart will be also.
MATTHEW 6:21

Throughout our lifetimes, we collect many treasures. Depending on where we are in life, they vary from simple ones to extraordinarily great ones. Nothing more than a mere marble can become a gem of magnificence for a young child, while a teenager may highly treasure graduating at the top of the class. Young parents raising their children can value that above anything else. Reaching middle age can bring about holding tightly to retirement plans, making sure enough has been accumulated to travel or rest or accomplish things our working life did not allow us to do.

Unfortunately, too often it takes time and many difficult circumstances for us to comprehend our greatest treasure, which is our maturing relationship with our Heavenly Father. It has always resided in our hearts since the day we became His children. He's walked with us every nanosecond of our journey with Him, enabling us to *do all things through Jesus Christ who strengthens* us (Philippians 4:13 NKJV).

He loves us, He leads us, He guides us, and He directs our steps. There is no greater treasure on the face of the earth or in the heavens above than becoming a beloved child of the King, giving our lives to Him to do with it as He chooses—His will for us, not our will for ourselves.

Then he said to them all:
"Whoever wants to be my disciple
must deny themselves
and take up their cross daily
and follow me."
LUKE 9:23

SEPTEMBER 30

I know that my Redeemer lives,
and that in the end he will stand on the earth.
JOB 19:25

We can shout with Job of the Old Testament his exact words: *"I know that my Redeemer lives, and that in the end he will stand on the earth."* Jesus Christ paid the penalty for our sins. It is through His death and resurrection that we have been set free from our sins. God the Father, God the Son, and God the Holy Spirit—the Trinity—enable us to live the kind of life we are called to live.

No matter what comes into our lives or departs from our lives, we have the everlasting hope that, in God's time, Jesus will return and stand again upon the earth. There will be no more sin, no more tears, no more pain, no more sorrow, and no more grief. We will be in the image of our Savior, Jesus Christ, with nothing but joy and peace infiltrating our hearts, souls, and beings.

Come, Lord Jesus.

My ears had heard of you but now my eyes have seen you.

JOB 42:5

OCTOBER

OCTOBER 1

And surely I am with you always,
to the very end of the age.
MATTHEW 28:20

Everyone experiences times of feeling lonely, believing no one cares for them. No matter which direction we look, no one is there. We feel completely alone—isolated. Loneliness clings to us, waiting to take us down regardless of how hard we are struggling for our next step, much less our next breath.

Even though no one is standing beside us, holding our hand, encouraging us to keep on keeping on, we are never alone. All we have to do is cry out to Jesus and ask for His help. He takes us in His ever-loving arms and whispers His sweet words of encouragement while pointing to His weapons of warfare resting at our feet.

"The evil one is after you, My child," He says. "Pick up my weapons and use them."

"Yes, Lord," we reply. "Will You help me do it?"

Smiling, He whispers, *"Never will I leave you; never will I forsake you"* (Hebrews 13:5).

The Lord is close to the brokenhearted and saves those who are crushed in spirit.
PSALM 34:18

OCTOBER 2

*My son, do not make light
of the Lord's discipline,
and do not lose heart
when he rebukes you,
because the Lord disciplines
the one he loves,
and chastens everyone
he accepts as his son*
HEBREWS 12:5–6

Because we belong to our Heavenly Father, He will discipline us. We are His children. Regardless of age, no one looks forward to being reprimanded because this means we've strayed off course and displeased our Father and disobeyed Him. We may want to make light of what we've done or said, but our Father does not make light of it. Just as we discipline our children out of love for them, so too does our Heavenly Father discipline His children. Just as we train our children to grow into godly men and women, so too does our Heavenly Father train us to grow into what He created us in Christ to become.

Our children have a tendency to lose heart when we rebuke them. As children of God, we also lean in that direction. As our children learn to accept our correction, so too must we learn to accept God's correction of us. Just as we allow our children to experience many painful situations to help them grow into maturity, our Heavenly Father does likewise for us. Whatever comes into our lives is there for a godly reason.

Let us never make light of God's correction or lose heart when He rebukes us. Nothing ever comes into our lives that He does not allow or send. *God is love* (1 John 4:16).

I will put my trust in him.
HEBREWS 2:13

OCTOBER 3

Righteousness guards the man of integrity,
but wickedness overthrows the sinner.
PROVERBS 13:6

hoices are ever before us, schooling us in one of two directions: one of integrity or one of wickedness. We are free to go either way. Even though God has a plan for our lives, He gives us freedom to choose. We can go our way or we can go God's way. The righteousness of God guards our integrity—our honesty and uprightness. It helps us stay on the right path. Wickedness, however, is the aim of the evil one—to lead us into temptation and create in us a spirit of meanness and unscrupulousness. Its aim is to do us in.

Righteousness or wickedness. What is our choice today?

Choose for yourselves this day whom you will serve . . .
But as for me and my household, we will serve the LORD.
JOSHUA 24:15

OCTOBER 4

And my God will meet
all your needs
according to
the riches of his glory
in Christ Jesus.
PHILIPPIANS 4:19

e never have a need that our Heavenly Father does not meet. Never! He never leaves us nor abandons us. We are never alone. Never! Thankfully, He does not grant us all our wants. It is we who confuse the two words: need and want. We want this, that, or the other. This doesn't mean we need this, that, or the other. It simply means we wish to have it.

We don't want adversity, hardships, or harsh conditions to come our way. Yet if or when they do, it is because we need them in our lives for God to mature us into the person He created us in Christ to become. Absolutely nothing enters our lives that God does not allow to be there. If it is there, its purpose is to open our eyes to what God is doing in our lives.

Instead of saying, "I don't want this," why not say, "I need this to grow in Christ."

Instead of saying, "I want what I want when I want it," why not say, "Thank You, Lord, for meeting all my needs."

Needs or wants. Which is it?

> And the peace of God, which transcends all understanding,
> will guard your hearts and your minds in Christ Jesus.
> To our God and Father be glory for ever and ever. Amen.
> PHILIPPIANS 4:7, 20

OCTOBER 5

Let us then approach
God's throne of grace
with confidence,
so that we may receive mercy
and find grace to help us
in our time of need.
HEBREWS 4:16

Let us not resist God's promptings as He urges us toward His throne of grace. We know we can be confident that He will sweetly welcome us there. He already knows why we come to Him. He delights in our seeking His way, trusting Him to direct our steps. His mercy and grace is forever available to help us. It delights Him not only to hear our words of need but also our words of thanksgiving as we let Him know how much we appreciate the hope He places in our hearts—that which enables us to keep on keeping on and never give up.

How blessed we are to be children of the King.

> Come to me, all you who are weary and burdened, and I will give you rest. Take my yoke upon you
> and learn from me, for I am gentle and humble in heart, and you will find rest for your souls.
> MATTHEW 11:28-29

OCTOBER 6

I will refresh the weary
and satisfy the faint.
JEREMIAH 31:25

Our batteries can run low and need to be recharged. No matter how exhausted we are, God is always there to revive us and restore our souls. Sometimes we act as if every ounce of energy has been drained from our spirits to the point of our believing we can never be revived. Nothing could be further from the truth.

Our Lord God is aware of everything that comes into our lives. As our Heavenly Parent, He picks us up in His ever-loving arms and sings His love song to us. All we have to do is *be still and know that* He is *God*, the One who *will never leave* us *nor forsake* us (Deuteronomy 31:6).

Be still, and know that I am God . . .
The LORD Almighty is with us.
PSALM 46:10–11

OCTOBER 7

But as for me,
I watch in hope
for the LORD,
I wait for God my Savior;
my God will hear me.
MICAH 7:7

Regardless of what others do or suggest we do, our goal is to watch in hope for the Lord. This means having the courage to stand firm, believing it is faith that gives us the confidence needed to wait on God. In His time and in His way, our Lord always responds. Our responsibility is to hope, trust, and wait, even if it means a lifetime of so doing. God always hears us. As we watch and wait, clinging to hope, we grow ever more into what God created us in Christ to become.

We have this hope as an anchor for the soul, firm and secure.
HEBREWS 6:19

OCTOBER 8

We live by faith,
not by sight.
2 CORINTHIANS 5:7

The statement "seeing is believing" is not accurate. We cannot always believe what our eyes tell us. Faith is a different matter altogether. It reaches far deeper than sight could ever go—into the depths of our souls and beings.

For us to live by faith means we trust God's Word. He loves us so deeply that He allowed His only Son to be sacrificed for our sins. We are never alone, for God places His Holy Spirit in us to lead, guide, and direct our paths. We can rely on God, being confident that He is who says He is: the great I AM, *Immanuel—God with us*, in us, and for us (Matthew 1:23). Nothing can ever separate us from Him. We have the assurance He *will never leave* us *nor forsake* us (Deuteronomy 31:6).

Let us arise each day trusting in Him and thanking Him for all He has done for us, is now doing for us, and will continue to do for us until He returns again or we meet Him in heaven, where we will live with Him forever.

Now faith is confidence in what we hope for and assurance about what we do not see.
And without faith it is impossible to please God.
HEBREWS 11:1, 6

OCTOBER 9

Fear of man
will prove to be a snare,
*but whoever trusts in the L*ORD
is kept safe.
PROVERBS 29:25

Many of us are people pleasers. What others think about us seems more important than what we think about ourselves. We dress to please others. We wholeheartedly seek to agree with them. We strive to present ourselves in a way that gains their approval. We allow their noose to be worn around our necks.

Let us arise, children of God. Our trust in Him alone is what keeps us safe and secure. If we are right with our Lord, it doesn't matter if others judge us or how they do so. What is important is that we faithfully keep on God's track and His alone, striving to please Him in all that we do or say. It is God our Father whom we seek to please—putting Him foremost in our hearts and minds—not others or even ourselves.

But seek first his kingdom and his righteousness,
and all these things will be given to you as well.
MATTHEW 6:33

OCTOBER 10

He saw the disciples straining at the oars,
because the wind was against them.
MARK 6:48

After Jesus fed five thousand people with nothing more than five loaves of bread and two fish, and twelve basketfuls of broken pieces were left over, His disciples did not understand the miracle *about the loaves* (Mark 6:38–44, 52).

After Jesus dismissed the crowd, He *made his disciples get into a boat and go ahead of him to Bethsaida.* Then *He went up on a mountainside to pray* (v. 45–46). By the time night arrived, a strong wind came along and the disciples strained at their oars as they tried to make headway. Knowing what was happening, Jesus *went out to them, walking on the lake.* The disciples were stunned, believing it was His *ghost.* Frightened, they *cried out* (v. 48–49).

Immediately He spoke to them and said, "Take courage! It is I. Don't be afraid." As soon as He climbed into the boat, the wind died down (v. 50–51). Imagine! These men had just witnessed Jesus feeding a humongous crowd with such little food, even having some left over, and then saw Him doing the impossible feat of walking on water. Did it not occur to them that if Jesus could feed so many with so little then He could easily walk on water and help them?

Do we not do the same today—witness Jesus' miracles time and again, yet succumb to struggling with life's oars as fierce winds threaten to take us under, not even realizing God knows and is already with us? Our Lord God always walks to us in our times of need, even on water, climbing into our boats and calming our storms.

Nothing is impossible with God. He knows everything about us—where we are, what is happening to us, and our need for Him to intervene and help us. Let us never harden our hearts. Our Lord God never leaves us nor forsakes us. He is always with us.

> Trust in him at all times, you people; pour out your hearts to him, for God is our refuge.
> PSALM 62:8

OCTOBER 11

We were under great pressure,
far beyond our ability to endure,
so that we despaired of life itself.
2 CORINTHIANS 1:8

Have you ever experienced pressure in your life so great that you believed you could not endure it, fearful it might take you under? Many of us have. What do we do when something of this nature comes into our lives? The apostle Paul spent many *sleepless nights* due to *hunger, beatings,* and *imprisonments*; yet he also experienced *patience and kindness in the Holy Spirit and in sincere love.* He continued on *in the power of God* while being *beaten, yet not killed.* Even through his sorrow, he rejoiced through the love of Christ in him (2 Corinthians 6:5–10).

Through all kinds of pressures Paul made it his *goal to please* God, whether he continued to live or if he died (2 Corinthians 5:9). He clung to living *by faith* and not by what was happening in his life (v. 7). He knew that God was with him and in him. God admonishes us through Paul not to *lose heart* even if *outwardly we are wasting away, yet inwardly we are being renewed day by day* (2 Corinthians 4:16).

Paul understood he had God's *treasure in* a jar of *clay* for a purpose: *to show that this all-surpassing power is from God and not* of his doing. Even though he was *hard pressed on every side,* he wasn't *crushed* or bewildered or *in despair* or feeling *abandoned* (2 Corinthians 4:7–9). Regardless of life's pressures, Paul looked *to the Lord and His strength* and *always* sought *His face* (Psalm 105:4).

We always carry around in our body the death of Jesus,
so that the life of Jesus may also be revealed in our body.
2 CORINTHIANS 4:10

OCTOBER 12

When you make a vow to God,
do not delay to fulfill it.
ECCLESIASTES 5:4

At times every one of us has made a vow to God that we either delayed to fulfill or did not fulfill at all. This is one of the reasons we need to be careful what spills from our tongues. No one is guiltless when it comes to careless speaking. Thoughtless words damage others' hearts as well as our own, while grieving the Holy Spirit.

Rather than saying, "I'll never do that again, Lord," let us say, "Through the power of Christ in me, Lord, I'll never to do that again." Since we know that we can do all things through Christ, we have God's strength in us to do it. If, however, we disobey God, *He is faithful and just* to *forgive us . . . and cleanse us of all unrighteousness* (NKJV). Let us never hesitate to go before God's holy throne and plead for His forgiveness for our sins.

If we confess our sins, he is faithful and just and
will forgive us our sins and purify us from all unrighteousness.
1 JOHN 1:9

OCTOBER 13

Do not love the world
or anything in the world.
1 JOHN 2:15

What powerful words of God this verse expresses through His beloved disciple, John. It's so simple and easy to love the world and everything connected to it, isn't it? Yes, but God tells us not to do it. Why do you suppose God tells us this? To keep us close to Him and from the sins of the world embedded so deeply in us? Exactly.

Just as all kinds of food were available to Adam and Eve while in the Garden, God instructed them not to eat from one particular tree in the center of Eden. He told them if they did they would surely die, meaning sin and spiritual death would enter the world. Eve had no need for the fruit on that particular tree, but she craved it anyway. The more she looked at it, the more she wanted it. It appealed to her sense of desiring the one thing God had forbidden her to have.

We also live in a beautiful world—not one as glorious as Adam and Eve's but without doubt also exceedingly tempting. God forbids much of what we see: innumerable and enticing people, places, and things that capture our attention—like power, fame, fortune, glory, fancy cars and houses, outstanding clothing and jobs, and on and on. Focusing on these things results in our falling in love with the world and not focusing on our love for God, who blesses us and enables us to live for Him. Our love belongs to God—not the world. It is God whom we serve—not the things of the world. It is He with whom we will live forever in His heavenly realms—not on our sinful planet.

Our earthly life is limited to a number of years, but with God in heaven our life continues forever. Let us not eat from the particular forbidden tree of the love of the world that takes our eyes away from our precious Lord and Savior and His Holy Spirit, who was planted in our hearts the moment we came to Him and promised to live our lives for Him and not for ourselves. Let us not submit to the temptations of the world. Instead, let us turn to God, trusting Him to deliver us from our love of the world, thereby loving and living in the world for Him.

The world and its desires pass away, but whoever does the will of God lives forever.
1 JOHN 2:17

OCTOBER 14

I have learned the secret
of being content
in any and every situation,
whether well fed or hungry,
whether living in plenty
or in want.

PHILIPPIANS 4:12

There is a secret to being content regardless of what comes into our lives; however, it takes time to grasp the meaning of the secret as it seeps into our ears. It comes slowly. It seems at first like a faint whisper that urges us to submit ourselves to trusting our Heavenly Father more and more as He directs every step we take along the paths He lays before us. As time moves on, we discover learning the true meaning of His secret is not always pleasant. In fact, it can be unbearable—seemingly bound and determined to take us under, leaving us gasping for our next breath or heartbeat, with no desire to hear His secret at all.

The more terrifying our steps, the more intense His whisper grows, enabling us to joyfully clutch His outstretched Hand and trust Him while carefully absorbing His secret words: *We live by faith, not by sight* (2 Corinthians 5:7), and *I can do all this through him who gives me strength* (Philippians 4:13).

Though he slay me, yet will I hope in him.

JOB 13:15

OCTOBER 15

There is no one holy like the LORD;
there is no one besides you;
there is no Rock like our God.

1 SAMUEL 2:2

Hannah was barren, unable to have children. Her husband, Elkanah, deeply loved her. His other wife, Peninnah, gave him many sons and daughters. Year after year, Peninnah kept provoking Hannah in order to irritate her. Apparently, Peninnah provoked Hannah so severely that Hannah wept bitterly while in the house of the Lord. Praying silently to the Lord, she asked Him to *look on* her *misery and remember* her *and not forget* her and her need and *give* her *a son.* If He did so, she would *give him to Lord all the days of his life* (1 Samuel 1:1–11).

Eli, the high priest, saw her lips moving with no words coming from her mouth and assumed she was drunk. He reprimanded her. Hannah told Eli she wasn't drunk but was petitioning the Lord to give her a child. Eli responded saying, *"Go in peace, and may the God of Israel grant you what you have asked of him"* (v. 12–17).

The Lord did bless Hannah and answered her prayer. After Hannah gave birth to Samuel, she kept him with her until he was weaned. She then honored her oath and took him to the temple and gave him to the Lord under Eli's care (v. 20–28).

To gain the desire of her heart, Hannah had to give up the desire of her heart. She returned to the Lord what He had given her. After doing so, she fell to her knees in prayer and declared her heart rejoiced in God, for through Him her horn was lifted high enabling her to boast over her enemies while delighting in God's deliverance (1 Samuel 2:1). No earthly person could do for her what the Lord had done for her.

The same is true for us today. No one can do for us what our Lord can and will do when we ask Him. He is holy. There is no one like Him. We have no *rock like our God* (1 Samuel 2:2), who gave His Son, Jesus Christ, for us—to cleanse us of all our unrighteousness, declaring us *joint heirs with Christ* (Romans 8:17 NKJV).

Sing praises to God, sing praises; sing praises to our King, sing praises.

PSALM 47:6

Praise the LORD, O my soul. I will praise the LORD all my life; I will sing praise to my God as long as I live.

PSALM 146:1–2

OCTOBER 16

Praise be to the God and Father
of our Lord Jesus Christ,
the Father of compassion
and the God of all comfort,
who comforts us in all our troubles,
so that we can comfort those in any trouble
with the comfort we ourselves
receive from God.
2 CORINTHIANS 1:3–4

Let us raise our voices to our Heavenly Father, as did the apostle Paul, and praise Him for His kindheartedness. He is always at our side comforting us, regardless of our circumstances. As God relieves us and replenishes us, He lets us know the troubles we have endured for His sake were there for His purposes—one is to grow us more into that which He created us in Christ to become, and the other is to enable us to comfort others during their plights. The best way to understand what others are experiencing is to have walked a path similar to the one they now travel. We know that just as God took us in His arms during our dilemmas and relieved us and helped us, our mission is to do likewise for others.

Submit yourselves, then, to God. . . .
Come near to God and he will come near to you.
JAMES 4:7–8

OCTOBER 17

Be alert and of sober mind.
Your enemy the devil
prowls around like a roaring lion
looking for someone to devour.

I PETER 5:8

D o we not know, do we not understand the necessity for being self-controlled and alert? Peter, the disciple of Christ, understood this quite well. Yet he betrayed Jesus, denying three times that he ever knew Him, even after Jesus had warned him that he would do so. Jesus told Peter, *"Simon, Simon, Satan has asked to sift all of you as wheat"* (Luke 22:31).

Peter quickly *replied, "Lord, I am ready to go with you to prison and to death"* (v. 33).

Jesus answered, "I tell you, Peter, before the rooster crows today, you will deny three times that you know me" (v. 34).

Far too often we do likewise, forgetting our *enemy the devil* constantly *prowls around like a roaring lion, seeking to devour* us (1 Peter 5:8). Let us notice, however, Jesus told Peter that *Satan* had *asked to sift* him *as wheat.*

Remember in the Old Testament when holy *angels came to present themselves before the* LORD, *Satan also came with them. The* LORD *said to Satan, "Where have you come from?"* (Job 1:6–7). Of course, God already knew why Satan was there, because he is constantly *roaming throughout the earth* looking for a chance to snatch anyone out of God's hands. Take note in this instance, however, that Satan did not ask God's permission to tempt Job, but God asked Satan if he had noticed Job, saying, *"There is no one on earth like him; he is blameless and upright, a man who fears God and shuns evil"* (v. 8).

Smirking, Satan replied that, of course, Job was blameless and upright, fearing God and shunning evil, because God had given him everything. But would he still do this if God took everything away from him? Then God gave Satan permission to take everything away from Job except his life (v. 9–12).

It is inconsequential whether God is asked by Satan to tempt us or God simply allows Satan to tempt us. Either way, God is on our side, alerting us to be self-controlled and prepared. We are Christian soldiers. He equips each and every one of us for spiritual warfare. All we have to do is put on His armor and fight God's *good fight.*

Fight the good fight of the faith. Take hold of the eternal life to which you were called
when you made your good confession in the presence of many witnesses.

1 TIMOTHY 6:12

OCTOBER 18

In peace I will lie down and sleep,
for you alone, LORD,
make me dwell in safety.
PSALM 4:8

Far too many of us struggle with being able to fall asleep when we go to bed at night. We lie there struggling to keep our minds off our troubles and concerns, allowing ourselves to become increasingly anxious about the happenings of our day and our fears of what may come tomorrow.

At such times we should do what King David did, for apparently he too frequently had trouble falling asleep. Let us make the same commitment David made—*In peace I will lie down and sleep.* Then let us assure ourselves that, like David, we trust our Heavenly Father to keep us safe from everything—our worries, concerns, fears, insecurities, troubles, and all evil—that we allow to disarm us, even if it is ourselves. It is God alone who makes us *dwell in safety.*

Know that the LORD has set apart his faithful servant for himself;
the LORD hears when I call to him.
PSALM 4:3

OCTOBER 19

Do not let your hearts be troubled
and do not be afraid.
JOHN 14:27

The world we live in today overflows with wickedness. Whether we turn to the right or the left, we see evil everywhere—even in some of God's children who have somehow taken a detour from His Word. If we're completely honest with ourselves, it terrifies us and makes us wonder what will become of our children and grandchildren, who are surrounded on every side by such malevolence.

Cause us to know, O Lord, that your *Advocate*, your *Holy Spirit* whom You sent to live in us when we took Jesus into our lives, will *teach* us how to live for You and *remind* us to stay continually connected to You. Help us to remember Jesus; words: *"Peace I leave with you; my peace I give you. I do not give to you as the world gives."* And then, Lord, let us heed Your words as you commanded us, saying, *"Do not let your hearts be troubled and do not be afraid"* (John 14:26–27). Help us remember we always have a choice—to submit to You or not submit to You. Lord, as Your children, we pray we will not allow ourselves to turn from Your holy presence and Your Word.

Never will I leave you; never will I forsake you.
Jesus Christ is the same yesterday and today and forever.
HEBREWS 13:5, 8

OCTOBER 20

My dear brothers and sisters,
take note of this:
Everyone should be
quick to listen,
slow to speak
and slow to become angry.
JAMES 1:19

Reading these words of God can cause us to hang our heads in shame, for all of us are guilty of not intently listening to our Heavenly Father and His Spirit in us or to the words of His Son, Jesus Christ. We also need to be quick to listen to others as they speak to us. One of the greatest gifts we can give to those in distress is not necessarily speaking to them but listening to them. Let us do so, even if it means covering our mouths in order to keep silent. The time will come for us to speak, and it will come in God's time, not ours.

Perhaps if we heeded these words of God and held them tightly in our hearts, and at the same time numbed our tongues, we would not enter the pathways that lead to anger. So let us *be quick to listen, slow to speak, and slow to become angry.*

I can do all this through him who gives me strength.
PHILIPPIANS 4:13

OCTOBER 21

I am the good shepherd.
JOHN 10:14

The Lord is our Shepherd. We never want for anything. He provides all our needs (Psalm 23:1). *The good shepherd lays down his life for the sheep* (John 10:11). He not only loves us, but He owns us. Once we belong to Him, we are forever in His hands. No one can snatch us away.

Others may come along and assure us they can solve our problems and take care of us, but they will quickly flee when suffering rears its ugly head. They are nothing more than *a hired hand* (v. 12). It is the Lord God who never abandons us. We are never alone. We know His voice when He calls out to us. We are to follow Him wherever He leads us (v. 3–4).

Our Shepherd stands at His gate and invites everyone to come in. He continually looks around for those who are not His sheep and calls them to listen to His voice and come join the rest of His flock.

Come to me, all you who are weary and burdened, and I will give you rest.
MATTHEW 11:28

OCTOBER 22

Since you cannot do
this very little thing,
why do you worry about the rest?
LUKE 12:26

Experience has taught us that in and of ourselves we can do nothing, but through Christ we can do all things. Why then do we fret and worry about everything, knowing ahead of time it's not only fruitless to do so but a waste of time as well? Could it be because we allow the sin of pride to indwell us, permitting ourselves to believe we are capable enough to take care of anything that comes our way?

For whatever reasons we give ourselves, we all have a tendency to believe we can control everything that comes into our lives or the lives of our loved ones. It is not possible for us to do so. God's Holy Spirit in us, placed there when we accepted Jesus as our Lord and Savior, is He on whom we are to depend. When we take our heavy burdens and cast them at the feet of God as He instructs us to, through Christ we can do anything.

Cast your cares on the LORD and he will sustain you;
he will never let the righteous be shaken.
PSALM 55:22

OCTOBER 23

I am the true vine,
and my Father
is the gardener.
JOHN 15:1

When we accept Jesus Christ as our Lord and Savior, our Heavenly Father takes us and connects us to His true vine in His garden. It is our Gardener's job to prune us as well as to remove our branches that bear no fruit. This means clipping our wings from time to time so that we can grow into what He created us in Christ to become. It also means cutting us to the core so that we can grow taller and produce more lovely fruit and flowers that will bless both us and others.

It is only after our Gardener has approached us with His shears and we allow their sharpness to bring terrifying pain to our souls or His sword that cuts us down so low we wonder if we'll ever survive, that we experience magnificent joy and peace as we see what His pruning produces in our lives.

What a stupendous Gardner we have! Hallelujah! Praise His name!

Blessed are all who take refuge in him.
PSALM 2:12

OCTOBER 24

My steps have held to your paths;
my feet have not stumbled.
PSALM 17:5

Our Heavenly Father places a variety of paths beneath our feet in our journey with Him. Some bring joy, and some are filled with deep sadness, profound misery, and grief. As David of the Old Testament fled for his life from King Saul, who sought to kill him, David sang a song beginning with the words: *"I love you, LORD, my strength."* He proclaimed *the Lord* was his *Rock*, his *Fortress*, his *Deliverer*, and the One *in whom* he could *take refuge* ((Psalm 18:1–2).

How it must have calmed his spirit to sing aloud: *"He reached down from on high and took hold of me; he drew me out of deep waters"* (v. 16). David knew beyond a shadow of doubt that with God's *help* on his side he would be able to *advance against a troop* and even *scale a wall* if needed (v. 29).

He proclaimed God's *way* was *perfect* and His *Word* was *flawless*, and God was his *shield* as he took *refuge in Him* (v. 30). God gave David the *strength* (v. 32), making the impossible not only possible and doable but also perfect.

Regardless of what road the Lord places beneath our feet, His pathway is there for a purpose. Let us raise our hands in thanksgiving, praising our Lord God for loving us so deeply that He sent His Son into the world to die for our sins.

Therefore I will praise you, Lord, among the nations;
I will sing the praises of your name.
PSALM 18:49

OCTOBER 25

God made him
who had no sin
to be sin for us,
so that in him
we might become
the righteousness of God.
2 CORINTHIANS 5:21

Once we accept Jesus Christ as our Lord and Savior, we become blameless before God. He adopts us into His holy family as His children. We belong to Him forever. No sin we ever commit is held against us when we confess them to our Heavenly Father. This is the most glorious gift ever given, but it did not come without great cost. God's Son, Jesus Christ, willingly sacrificed himself so that we who believe in Him could live forever in God's house. Jesus tells us: *"My Father's house has many rooms; if that were not so, would I have told you that I am going there to prepare a place for you?"* (John 14:2).

Most of us have lived in a number of houses in various places during our earthly life, but when we arrive in heaven we will live forever in God's house. Imagine! Our saved loved ones will be in the same house with us. We will be reunited with them!

> For God so loved the world that he gave his one and only Son,
> that whoever believes in him shall not perish but have eternal life.
> JOHN 3:16

OCTOBER 26

> *So I say,*
> *walk by the Spirit,*
> *and you will not*
> *gratify the desires*
> *of the flesh.*
> GALATIANS 5:16

God admonishes us through the apostle Paul to live according to the Holy Spirit's pathway for us, meaning He is always leading, guiding, and directing our behavior and our ways. It is up to us to decide whether to follow the Spirit's leadership or not. God always gives us free choice—we can go His way or we can go our way.

Since we live by the Spirit, let us keep in step with the Spirit (Galatians 5:25). We all have a sinful nature that is in conflict with God's Spirit in us. Our Heavenly Father wants His children to bear much fruit—*love, joy, peace, forbearance, kindness, goodness, faithfulness, gentleness, and self-control* (v. 22). We can't do this without God's help, but we can do all things through Jesus who enables us to do it.

> And God will meet all your needs according to the riches of his glory in Christ Jesus.
> PHILIPPIANS 4:19

OCTOBER 27

*Have mercy on me, L*ORD*,*
for I am faint;
*heal me, L*ORD*,*
for my bones are in agony.
My soul is in deep anguish.
*How long, L*ORD*, how long?*
PSALM 6:2–3

From time to time we all feel weak. It's a given as we walk life's paths. Sometimes we are so weary we feel like throwing our arms skyward and proclaiming with David, *"How long, L*ORD*, how long?"* Our grief and sorrow clutch us by our throats and threaten to annihilate us. We convince ourselves we will never come out of the darkness that seems to penetrate into the depths of our souls. And then it happens.

A brilliants light shines in the distance as if our Heavenly Father is signaling us with a secret message: *Be still, and know that I am God; I will be exalted among the nations, I will be exalted in the earth* (Psalm 46:10). We hear His quiet voice encouraging us to trust Him and be patient with His plans for us. He is forever with us and *will never leave* us *nor forsake* us (Deuteronomy 31:6).

His outstretched hand clasps our own and lifts us up out of our pit of despair, for we know we are *confident of this:* we *will see the goodness of the L*ORD *in the land of the living.* All that is required of us is to *wait for the L*ORD*; be strong and take heart and wait for the L*ORD (Psalm 27:13–14).

Be dressed ready for service and keep your lamps burning.
LUKE 12:35

OCTOBER 28

Therefore my heart is glad
and my tongue rejoices;
my body also will rest in hope.
ACTS 2:26

No matter what crosses our paths or regardless of what comes our way, along with the disciple Peter, who three times denied knowing Jesus, we can shout the gladness of our hearts and sing to the hills our hope in the One who set us free from our sins.

We live in hope because we know that our Lord God will never abandon us or forsake us. He is forever with us. God strengthens us to do all things through His Son, Jesus Christ, and because of this we can say with King David, *"You have made known to me the paths of life; you will fill me with joy in your presence"* (Acts 2:28). Hallelujah and amen.

OCTOBER 29

Therefore do not be foolish,
but understand what the Lord's will is.
EPHESIANS 5:17

What is God's will for His children? The apostle Paul explains it to us, succinctly telling us to be *filled with the Spirit* and speak to each other *with psalms, hymns, and songs from the Spirit,* and then *to sing and make music from* our *heart to the Lord.* He also reminds us to give *thanks to God the Father for everything, in the name of our Lord Jesus Christ.* Then he instructs us to *submit to one another out of reverence for Christ* (Ephesians 5:18–21). We cannot do these things unless we are filled with God's Spirit.

Therefore, let us not be foolish—rather, let us be wise in Christ. As we obey this command, it is not a difficult thing to fall to our knees and thank our Lord God for all the things He allows to come into our lives, regardless of how draining, sorrowful, or agonizing they are.

If God is for us, who can be against us?
ROMANS 8:31

OCTOBER 30

There is no wisdom,
no insight, no plan
that can succeed
against the LORD.
PROVERBS 21:30

Nothing that ever enters our lives or comes into our minds is able to abolish what our Lord God has planted within us to accomplish His will for us, which is to grow us into that which He created us in Christ to become. He is forever on our side. Regardless of what comes our way and threatens to destroy us, let us take up His shield of faith. Let us praise His name and thank Him for who He is and what He has done, is doing, and will continue to do for us until we see His glorious face at the gates of heaven inviting us to come in.

Great is the LORD and most of worthy praise; his greatness no one can fathom.
PSALM 145:3

OCTOBER 31

I said, "Oh, that I had the wings of a dove!
I would fly away and be at rest."
PSALM 55:6

Nothing seems to hurt more, causing deep pain to the depths of our beings, than the betrayal of a friend—someone with whom we've shared many pleasant memories. But this is what apparently happened to King David, who confessed his anguish because he was overcome with feelings of *fear and trembling* as darkness engulfed him. It brought not only suffering his way, but intense anger as well (Psalm 55:3–5).

David wanted to run away, shouting, *"I would flee far away and stay in the desert; I would hurry to my place of shelter, far from the tempest and storm"* (v. 7–8). David was so consumed with anger he wished *death* to *take* his *enemies by surprise* and *let them go down alive to the realm of the dead* (v. 15).

Do his words not remind us of times when we also wanted to run away—far from whatever storm dumped us into the depths of despair—no matter what it was that hurt us so deeply? Not all of us have been betrayed by a friend, but all of us have entered times of profound discouragement in our lives and wanted to do nothing but escape.

We have cried out to our Lord, the One who always *saves* us, talking with Him about our distress and knowing, as did David, that our Heavenly Father always *hears* our *voice* (v. 16–17). And then like David, hopefully, we cast our troubles on Him, for we know no one cares for us like our Savior does. He will always sustain us and deliver us. Then we will not run away from God; instead, we will run to Him.

> Surely your goodness and love will follow me all the days of my life,
> and I will dwell in the house of the Lord forever.
> PSALM 23:6

> But as for me, I trust in you.
> PSALM 55:23

November

NOVEMBER 1

Be strong and courageous.
DEUTERONOMY 31:7

Before Moses died, he commanded Joshua to *be strong and courageous* because God had selected Joshua to follow in Moses' footsteps and lead His people into the Promised Land. Our Lord God also speaks these same words to us today. Regardless of what comes into our lives, we must *be strong and courageous*. God has an ultimate mission for all of our lives.

In so doing, our pathways will not always be easy. In fact, they will be filled with much pain and sorrow. These events come into our lives so that we can gain godly wisdom and understanding and trust our Heavenly Father because we know He loves us with His *everlasting love* (Jeremiah 31:3) and *will never leave* us *or forsake* us (Deuteronomy 31:6). God not only is with us always, but His Holy Spirit lives in us!

Let us joyfully take up the banner of our Lord Jesus Christ, singing praises to His name as we march as God's soldiers into His heavenly realms for us—our Promised Land.

The LORD himself goes before you and will be with you;
he will never leave you nor forsake you. Do not be afraid; do not be discouraged.
DEUTERONOMY 31:8

NOVEMBER 2

*Let them sacrifice thank offerings
and tell of his works with songs of joy.*
PSALM 107:22

As parents, we love to hear thankful words from our children. We bask in them with our hearts overflowing with joy. Even though our children have grumbled and complained and pointed fingers of accusation our way far too many times, we know they love us. Yet we cannot hear their grateful words that tickle our ears often enough. The same is true for our Heavenly Father. He does far more for each of His children than any earthly parents could ever do for their children.

God knows us inside and out. He accomplishes miracles in our lives. He works on our behalf. Nothing is impossible for Him. All we have to do is *ask*, *seek*, and *knock* (Matthew 7:7). He is always there and ready to answer.

So join me today, my brothers and sisters in Christ, as we deeply praise our glorious Heavenly Father with basketfuls of breathtaking thankful and joyful words overflowing our hearts for all He has done, is doing, and will continue to do in our lives.

> **Let the one who is wise heed these things and ponder the loving deeds of the Lord.**
> PSALM 107:43

> **Rejoice in the Lord always. I will say again: Rejoice!**
> PHILIPPIANS 4:4

NOVEMBER 3

Sing and make music
from your heart
to the Lord,
always giving thanks
to God the Father
for everything,
in the name of
our Lord Jesus Christ.
EPHESIANS 5:19–20

It is not easy to *sing and make music* in our hearts when our hearts are broken, but through Christ in us it is doable because *with God all things are possible* (Matthew 19:26). Even though we know nothing enters our lives that God does not allow, our Heavenly Father assures us He will work everything out for our good—that is as we trust Him and follow His will for our lives. He calls us *according to His purpose* for us (Romans 8:28), not our purpose for ourselves.

The key to accomplishing this is to always thank God for everything, regardless of how painful and upsetting it is. All we have to do is fall to our knees and ask our Heavenly Father to help us fight and endure what He has allowed into our lives. We thank Him as we walk through

His valleys of suffering because He loves us so much He never gives up on us. He continues to grow us into what we could never become without His work in us.

Through Jesus, therefore, let us continually offer to God a sacrifice of praise—
the fruit of lips that openly profess his name.
HEBREWS 13:15

NOVEMBER 4

Whatever you do,
work at it with all your heart,
as working for the Lord,
not for human masters.
COLOSSIANS 3:23

Regardless of what comes our way, it is there because our Heavenly Father either directly sends it or allows it into our lives. Whatever is in front of us is there for His purpose. As we meditate on this, letting it soak into our hearts and minds, we slowly comprehend God's ultimate intention for us and understand we are to *work at it with all* our hearts, souls, and beings. Our Heavenly Father has laid His pathway beneath our feet for us to study, learn, and grow as we thank and trust Him every step of the way.

It is only when we grasp that we are continually working for the Lord God and not for ourselves or for anything or anyone else that we can take great joy, gaining peace in any and all situations that come our way.

For it is God who works in you to will
and to act in order to fulfill his good purpose.
PHILIPPIANS 2:13

NOVEMBER 5

*I press on
toward the goal
to win the prize
for which God
has called me heavenward
in Christ Jesus.*
PHILIPPIANS 3:14

No matter what game or contest comes along, most of us want to win. We can be very competitive in so doing, sometimes even dishonest. Our Heavenly Father's objective is for us to *press on toward* His *goal* for us. It is not a game or even a contest because we've already won by growing into what He created us in Christ to become—His image.

During the process, however, even though we experienced much joy and peace, we also fall into the depths of despair, pain, misery, and agony. This is why He urges us to *press* onward, especially when we toss our hands skyward and scream at the top of our lungs, begging and pleading with Him to take our suffering away.

It is only when we see our Heavenly Father face-to-face in heaven, when His prize soaks into the innermost part of our beings, that we grasp the wonder of it all—Christ in us! Our old sin nature no longer exists!

Let everything that has breath praise the LORD. Praise the LORD.
PSALM 150:6

NOVEMBER 6

And do not grumble.
1 CORINTHIANS 10:10

Everyone grumbles. We whine and complain, feeling sorry for ourselves. We want what we don't have, and if we get it we don't want that either. Moaning and groaning surrounded humanity after sin entered the world when Eve succumbed to the devil's temptation to eat from the Tree of the Knowledge of Good and Evil in the Garden of Eden.

Even if we manage to squelch our words, our minds spew forth gripes and nitpickings—often hypercritical of many things and events that cross our paths. Our Lord God commands us through the apostle Paul to quit grumbling, and yet we continue to do it. Why? Could it be because we don't recognize it as sin—thinking it's nothing more than silly words or thoughts?

When we continue to engage in a conduct God has forbidden us to do, it is sin. No matter what the sin, God enables us to conquer it through the strength of Jesus Christ in us. All we have to do is request His help. It is doable. Nothing is impossible with God.

Yes, it will take time to get grumbling out of our systems, but in God's time it will happen. We can overcome sin by requesting His help and waiting on the Lord—another command He has given us and one that we also struggle to accomplish—Wait!

Do everything without grumbling or arguing,
so that you may become blameless and pure, "children of God without fault in a warped
and crooked generation." Then you will shine among them like stars in the sky.
PHILIPPIANS 2:14–15

NOVEMBER 7

For God loves a cheerful giver.
2 CORINTHIANS 9:7

The last meal my husband and I shared together was in a restaurant. I did not like the taste of the food on my plate. I did not complain about it, but, knowing me as he did and without saying a word, he took my plate away and replaced it with his own. This is the sort of man he was—a sweet and cheerful giver. It mattered little what crossed his path or when it occurred, he was willing to give whatever he could to help someone else.

In my daughter's eulogy at his funeral service three days later, she related the story of her dad telling a customer who could not pay for his prescribed medications not to worry about it but pay him when he could. This is the kind of man who walked beside me for almost fifty-one years of my life—*a cheerful giver* indeed, one who now lives in the presence of the One *who loves a cheerful giver.*

Each of you should give what you have decided in your heart to give,
not reluctantly or under compulsion, for God loves a cheerful giver.
2 CORINTHIANS 9:7

Whoever sows generously will also reap generously.
2 CORINTHIANS 9:6

NOVEMBER 8

For everyone who asks receives;
the one who seeks finds;
and to the one who knocks,
the door will be opened.
MATTHEW 7:8

Apparently, many today do not heed the words Jesus taught during His Sermon on the Mount regarding asking, seeking, and knocking. Jesus made it very plain that all we need to do to receive something is simply ask for it. Jesus clearly teaches that *everyone who asks* will receive as they seek Him while knocking on His door.

"Well, I've done that too many times already," some might say, "and it got me nowhere!"

Really? How many times have our children asked for this or that and we made them wait, seemingly ignoring their request? Probably innumerable times. But in the interval we said something like, "Not now. I have to think about it."

Unfortunately, in our impatience, it irritates us when our Heavenly Parent doesn't respond immediately. Do our children give up when we don't respond to their requests? No! They keep on seeking that for which they asked, knowing the doors to our hearts are open to them and when or if the time comes for us to grant what they seek then we will do so. Perhaps, in the meantime, our children begin to comprehend that what they want is not good for them or not what they need at the present time. Yet knowing we love them and want the very best for their lives, they wait—though probably like us, impatiently.

Our Heavenly Father does even more for us. He enables us to grow while we wait. We come to understand that He absolutely heard our request and, instead of giving us that for which we pleaded, He gives us something far better, something we need but may not have been aware of—something far more superior than what we requested. Ask, seek, and knock!

Wait for the Lord; be strong and take heart and wait for the Lord.
PSALM 27:14

NOVEMBER 9

You have made your way
around this hill country
long enough;
now turn north.

DEUTERONOMY 2:3

As God's people wandered in the desert heading toward the Promised Land, God gave Moses a command that we must heed today—move on! We spend far too much time and wasted energy nitpicking about the paths our Heavenly Father places beneath our feet. Instead of joyfully accepting and learning from what He either allows or sends into our lives, we do what the Israelites did—pout and complain and find fault with everything, refusing to move on to where He is leading us.

Regardless of what comes our way, we must grab hold of His shield of faith and hold our heads high, knowing that our Lord God is with us and *will never leave* us *nor forsake* us (Deuteronomy 31:6).

Such confidence we have through Christ before God.

2 CORINTHIANS 3:4

NOVEMBER 10

He has blocked my way
so I cannot pass;
he has shrouded
my paths in darkness.
JOB 19:8

From time to time all of us have felt as if our Lord God *has blocked* the *way* in which we hoped to proceed. We believe we can actually feel His presence standing between us and what we want to do or where we want to go, preventing us from moving forward. Somehow we convince ourselves the sun has suddenly vanished from the sky and nothing but *darkness* surrounds us. We don't like it, even though we suspect what we're up to is a giant no-no to our Father, and we close our ears to what we know He is saying to us and wants for us.

Nevertheless, we insist on moving forward because we have convinced ourselves that our plan is better than God's way. What nonsense! Yet, if we're honest with ourselves, all of us have done something like this at times—just like our children have done to us.

Suddenly our eyes open as we envision ourselves as a rebellious child, one determined to throw a fit if necessary to get what we want and when and how we want it. We realize as a child we must trust our Father to know best.

Then will the eyes of the blind be opened . . .
And a highway will be there; it will be called the Way of Holiness;
it will be for those who walk on that Way.
ISAIAH 35:5, 8

NOVEMBER 11

Therefore as God's chosen people,
holy and dearly loved,
clothe yourselves with
compassion, kindness, humility,
gentleness and patience.
COLOSSIANS 3:12

Because we have been sanctified through the shed blood of our Lord Jesus Christ, our Heavenly Father tells us we are His *chosen people, holy and dearly loved*, and as such He commands us to be compassionate and kind people, humble and not proud, with a spirit of *gentleness and patience* imbedded in our innermost beings. We cannot do this in and of ourselves; but through the strength of Christ in us we can not only do it but excel at it as well. We must also *forgive* others as our Heavenly Father has forgiven us (Colossians 3:12–13).

God's love in us binds us together in His perfect unity of *compassion, kindness, humility gentleness, and patience* so that we are able to *bear with each other* (v. 13) and become what He has called us to become.

So then, just as you received Christ Jesus as Lord, continue to live your lives in him, rooted and built up in him, strengthened in the faith as you were taught, and overflowing with thankfulness.
COLOSSIANS 2:6–7

NOVEMBER 12

Whoever believes in me,
as the Scripture has said,
rivers of living water
will flow from within him.
JOHN 7:38

John, one of Jesus' twelve disciples, recorded in his Gospel these words of Jesus spoken on the last day of the Jewish Feast of Tabernacles—words that incited extreme anger among the Pharisees. After being told what Jesus said, *the chief priests and the Pharisees sent temple guards to arrest* Jesus (John 7:32). Jesus invited those present to *come to* Him if they were *thirsty* (v. 37) and needed a life-giving blessing, assuring them that *whoever believes* in Him would have *rivers of living water flow from within them.*

This is what lives inside us: *rivers of living water*—God's Holy Spirit, whom our Heavenly Father sends to us the moment we take Jesus Christ as our Lord and Savior. It is His Spirit in us who enables us to become what God created us in Christ to be. The Holy Spirit guides and directs our paths. Our mission is to follow Him wherever He leads and obey all He instructs us to say and do. If or when we turn a deaf ear to Him, it grieves and quenches His Spirit in us.

How blessed we are to have His *rivers of living water* flowing in us.

Through Jesus, therefore, let us continually offer to God a sacrifice of praise—
the fruit of lips that openly profess his name.
HEBREWS 13:15

NOVEMBER 13

I have told you these things,
so that in me
you may have peace.
In this world
you will have trouble.
JOHN 16:33

Before being betrayed and arrested, Jesus told his disciples that the time had come when they would *be scattered, each to* his *own home.* Jesus let them know they would leave Him all *alone*—but He wasn't going to be *alone* because God was with Him (John 16:32). These words are His same words for us today—in Him we *have peace.* He also lets us know that as long as our residence is on earth, we will have troubles; yes all kinds of predicaments and difficulties that are clouded with pain, sorrow, and despair. But we are never alone for our Heavenly Father is continually with us. He has told us, *"Never will I leave you; never will I forsake you"* (Hebrews 13:5).

Let us take heart, brothers and sisters in Christ! Jesus has *overcome the world* (John 16:33).

The Lord is my helper; I will not be afraid. What can mere mortals do to me?
Jesus Christ is the same yesterday and today and forever.
HEBREWS 13:6–8

NOVEMBER 14

*Humble yourselves
before the Lord,
and he will lift you up.*
JAMES 4:10

We know that *God opposes the proud but shows favor to the humble* (James 4:6). Why then do we so frequently take matters into our own hands, convinced we are quite able to handle everything by ourselves? Nothing could be further from the truth. We can do nothing in and of ourselves; but with Christ in us we can do all things.

All that God requires of us is to *submit* ourselves to Him and to *resist the devil*. When we do, Satan flees from us (James 4:7). The closer we are to God, the closer He is to us. It is not He who takes a step away from us, but we who take a step away from Him.

So let us get off our high horse and deflate the giant balloon of arrogance we blew up in our head and confess our sin of pride to our Heavenly Father so that our hearts become purified—with us giving glory to God for His work in us.

The pride of your heart has deceived you.
OBADIAH 1:3

NOVEMBER 15

Fix your thoughts on Jesus.
HEBREWS 3:1

In the world in which we live today, one with television, smart phones, and countless electronic thingamajigs with all kinds of abilities to seemingly master the universe, we fix our thoughts on those things instead of fixing our *thoughts on Jesus*. He is the master of the universe. We should not allow those things that surround us and entice us to concentrate on them to take our minds off what our Lord God tells us to keep our minds focused on.

Nothing and no one can do for us what Jesus did and continues to do. He not only died for our sins so that we can live through Him, but He also makes it possible for us to live eternally in the heavenly realms with the Trinity—the Father, the Son and the Holy Spirit.

It is only as we *fix* our *thoughts on Jesus* that we gain victory over Satan, who roams to and fro seeking those whom he can destroy. We are God's Christian soldiers called to battle, fighting the good fight that He empowers us to win.

I can do all this through him who gives me strength.
PHILIPPIANS 4:13

NOVEMBER 16

Now faith is confidence
in what we hope for
and assurance about
what we do not see.
HEBREWS 11:1

Through the writer of the book of Hebrews, our Heavenly Father tells us what faith is. *Faith is* what we can be confident of, what we can rely on—believing our Lord God knows us to the core of our beings and loves us with His everlasting love and constantly works on our behalf. Faith means trusting God, regardless of what happens or threatens to take place. Faith believes God *will never leave* us *nor forsake* us (Deuteronomy 31:6).

We can always be sure for *what we hope* because in God's time His work in us produces needed courage to forsake that which is not His will for our lives. By relying on Him we gain confidence that He is with us every step we take.

We will then finally grasp that what we *do not see* is everlastingly assured—*Christ in* us, our *hope of glory* (Colossians 1:27), as we grow in the image of Jesus Christ.

Being confident of this, that he who began a good work in you will
carry it on to completion until the day of Christ Jesus.
PHILIPPIANS 1:6

NOVEMBER 17

When the cloud remained.
Numbers 9:19

As Moses journeyed with God's people to His Promised Land, a pillar of cloud by day and a pillar of fire by night hovered above the tabernacle. *Whenever the cloud lifted above the tent, the Israelites set out; wherever the cloud settled, the Israelites encamped. At the Lord's command the Israelites set out, and at his command they remained in camp* (Numbers 9:17–18).

God's Holy Spirit in us does the same. We are on a journey with our Heavenly Father, headed for our Promised Land with Him in His heavenly realms. On our journey of becoming the image of Jesus Christ, we travel many roads—some extremely delightful and some enormously painful. Regardless of what our paths contain, we must hold fast to them until the Holy Spirit tells us to move on.

Like the Israelites, we too are impatient people—wanting to get to our destination without lingering along the way, especially when difficulties arise. We grumble and complain as did they, but it gets us nowhere other than sinking into a pit of despair. So when the Holy Spirit's cloud hovers over us, let us take courage and wait on the Lord. In His time, God makes *everything beautiful* (Ecclesiastes 3:11).

> At the Lord's command they encamped, and at the Lord's command they set out.
> They obeyed the Lord's order, in accordance with his command through Moses.
> NUMBERS 9:23

NOVEMBER 18

When Jacob awoke from his sleep, he thought,
"Surely the LORD is in this place,
and I was not aware of it."
GENESIS 28:16

Every human being has a God-given mission. Our Heavenly Father wants all people everywhere to be introduced to His Son, Jesus Christ, and accept Him as their Lord and Savior. Many of us immediately take His Hand, with joy bursting forth from our hearts. Some take more time to entrust their hands into His. Others want nothing to do with Him, instead preferring to go their own way.

Nothing is more glorious than to embark on our journey of finding Him in our lives—the One who leads, guides, and directs every step of our way. He was there all along, but we were not aware of it.

Let us heed His final words to His disciples, *"Therefore go and make disciples of all nations, baptizing them in the name of the Father and of the Son and of the Holy Spirit, and teaching them to obey everything I have commanded you. And surely I am with you always, to the very end of the age"* (Matthew 28:19–20).

He was afraid and said, "How awesome is this place!
This is none other than the house of God; this is the gate of heaven."
GENESIS 28:17

NOVEMBER 19

Let us then approach
the throne of grace
with confidence,
so that we may receive mercy
and find grace to help us
in our time of need.
HEBREWS 4:16

Regardless of what we say or what we do, we can always approach God's throne of grace, where His unmerited favor continually resides. God is always with us and for us, no matter what. However, when we sin, the peace of God in us is tainted until we approach His throne and confess our sin, asking forgiveness for it. *If we confess our sins, he is faithful and just and will forgive us our sins and purify us from all unrighteousness* (1 John 1:9).

Our Heavenly Father is a totally merciful Father, unlike our earthly dad. Our earthly dad can do just so much for us, but with God in us we can do all things through His mighty power. Without Him we can do nothing—nothing at all. God's forgiveness and mercy always surround us. All we have to do is ask and we will receive.

Through God's unmerited favor toward us, we can always find His help in our time of need, regardless of what it is.

Ask and it will be given to you; seek and you will find;
knock and the door will be opened to you.
For everyone who asks receives; the one who seeks finds;
and to the one who knocks, the door will be opened.
LUKE 11:9–10

NOVEMBER 20

As for God,
his way is perfect:
the LORD's word
is flawless.
PSALM 18:30

Have you ever been traveling down an unknown road, one that seems as if it might be going the wrong way? All of us have. The magnificence of hanging on to God's path beneath our feet—not turning and seeking a better way—is the assurance of knowing not only His is the best way to go but it's the only way to get to where we're going. If we take a detour and stray from God's road, it takes us much longer to get to God's destination for us.

God's *way is perfect*. It is *flawless*. Let us not detour, but keep trusting Him to lead and guide us every step of His way.

He makes my feet like the feet of a deer; he causes me to stand on the heights.
PSALM 18:33

NOVEMBER 21

Shout for joy, you heavens;
rejoice, you earth;
burst into song,
you mountains!
ISAIAH 49:13

Several times during our fifty years together, my husband wanted to replace my engagement and wedding rings with newer and more expensive ones. I refused his sweet offer, much preferring to keep to my original rings.

A year before his death, a group of teenagers were driving around downtown, where we owned several buildings. They decided throw some bricks through the windows of our buildings, causing quite a bit of damage. Of course, the kids were charged with misconduct and ordered to pay restitution, which took almost five years after my husband's death for them to accomplish.

Several weeks ago, the center diamond in my wedding ring became loose and fell out. I searched and searched, but I could not find it. So I took my ring to a jeweler and selected another diamond to replace the lost one. I paid for it with the repayment check for the damaged windows from years ago—the check that arrived the same week I lost the diamond. There was eighty-four dollars left over—more than enough to celebrate our approaching wedding anniversary!

My husband may not have gotten the opportunity to buy the new rings he wanted to give me, but he got his wish. My replenished ring now looks brand-new, and I think of it as his present to me, not only for our wedding anniversary, but his Christmas gift to me as well.

Great are the works of the Lord; they are pondered by all who delight in them.
PSALM 111:2

NOVEMBER 22

Even youths grow tired and weary,
and young men stumble and fall.
ISAIAH 40:30

It's encouraging to know that the older generations are not the only ones who *grow tired and weary*, with a tendency to *stumble and fall* down. Every now and then, even young people feel depleted and weak and wonder if they can even take their next breath or next step.

Regardless of our age, our Lord God admonishes us through his prophet Isaiah to remember: *The Lord is the everlasting God, the Creator of the ends of the earth. He will not grow tired or weary, and his understanding no one can fathom* (Isaiah 40:28).

If we want to *soar on wings like eagles, run and not grow weary, walk and not be faint,* our Lord God *will renew* our *strength* as we hope in Him, trusting Him to do all He promises (v. 31).

The grass withers and the flowers fall, but the word of our God endures forever.
ISAIAH 40:8

NOVEMBER 23

I consider everything a loss
because of the surpassing worth
of knowing Christ Jesus my Lord,
for whose sake I have lost all things.
PHILIPPIANS 3:8

What would it mean to us if we lost everything we deem important—especially our family and friends? Could we go on? Would we go on? We need to ask ourselves these questions. The apostle Paul lost everything He knew and practiced in order to gain the privilege of knowing Christ Jesus as His Lord and Savior, following Him wherever He led, and obeying what He told him to do.

Regardless of what we hold dear to our hearts—whether a person, a place, or a thing—as a follower of Jesus Christ we must relinquish it if this is His will for our lives. Our Heavenly Father never takes anything away from us without, in His time, instilling His peace that passes all understanding in our beings.

It is not easy to let the past go and continue onward, but through the strength of Christ in us it is doable. *And if on some point you think differently, that too God will make clear to you* (Philippians 3:15). Our assignment is to *live up to what we have already attained* (v. 16).

Therefore, my brothers and sisters, you whom I love and long for,
my joy and crown, stand firm in the Lord in this way, dear friends!
PHILIPPIANS 4:1

NOVEMBER 24

In your unfailing love
you will lead the people
you have redeemed.
In your strength
you will guide them
to your holy dwelling.
EXODUS 15:13

God had a mission for Moses to accomplish—lead His people to the Promised Land. The people watched God's miracle of allowing them to safely pass through the Red Sea on dry ground and then observed the drowning of the Egyptians who pursued them (Exodus 14:29–30). Afterwards Moses and his sister, Miriam, led the people in singing praises to the Lord (Exodus 15:1, 20).

In God's unfailing love for His redeemed people He guided them to His holy dwelling in the Promised Land. He does likewise for us today—putting us on the right track to our Promised Land of growing into the likeness of His Son, Jesus Christ. Just as they grumbled and complained as they traveled with God, so do we today as we travel with Him. Let us hush and do what Miriam did—dance and sing praises to our Lord God, the one who saved and redeemed us.

Sing to the LORD, for he is highly exalted.
Both horse and rider he has hurled into the sea.
EXODUS 15:21

NOVEMBER 25

Come to me,
all you who are weary and burdened,
and I will give you rest.
MATTHEW 11:28

We have a standing invitation from our Heavenly Father. Anytime—no matter when or where we might be—when we feel absolutely exhausted and drained, weighed down and saddled with troubles by the dozens, He joyfully welcomes us to come to Him and seek His guidance and His rest. He freely gives this to us. All we have to do is come and ask for His help. In His time, God makes *everything beautiful* (Ecclesiastes 3:11).

Be still before the LORD and wait patiently for him.
PSALM 37:7

NOVEMBER 26

We who have fled
to take hold of the hope
set before us
may be greatly encouraged.
We have this hope
as an anchor for the soul,
firm and secure.
HEBREWS 6:18–19

When sailing through life's storms, we know that *hope* is our *anchor*. Hope is confident expectation that our Lord God not only is with us but is there for us as well. Let us never hesitate to flee to Him and grab hold of His outstretched Hand, for it is firm and secure. It is like a breath of fresh air, assuring us that in the strength of Christ in us we can do all things.

Never give up! Never lose courage! Hold onto the *anchor of hope.*

For in this hope we were saved. But hope that is seen is no hope at all.
Who hopes for what they already have? But if we hope for what
we do not yet have, we wait for it patiently.

ROMANS 8:24–25

NOVEMBER 27

How precious to me
are your thoughts, God!
How vast is the sum of them!
Were I to count them,
they would outnumber
the grains of sand.

PSALM 139:17–18

King David, a man after God's own heart, said that the Lord God had searched him and knew him as no human possibly could. He even proclaimed, *"Before a word is on my tongue you, LORD, know it completely"* (Psalm 139:4). God knows everything about us.

Jesus said, *"Even the very hairs on your head are all numbered"* (Matthew 10:30). Jesus also tells us: *"Whoever finds their life will lose it, and whoever loses their life for my sake will find it"* (v. 39), and *"What I tell you in the dark, speak in the daylight; what is whispered in your ear, proclaim from the roofs"* (v. 27).

Yes, how precious to us are God's thoughts and the words He whispers into our ears—so numerous they outnumber the grains of sand. We are fully known by Him!

As the heavens are higher than the earth,
so are my ways higher than your ways and my thoughts than your thoughts.

ISAIAH 55:9

You hem me in behind and before; you have laid your hand upon me.
Such knowledge is too wonderful for me, too lofty for me to attain.

PSALM 139:5–6

NOVEMBER 28

My help comes from the LORD,
the Maker of heaven and earth.
PSALM 121:2

Our Lord God is one who never lets our *foot slip* and who never slumbers or sleeps (Psalm 121:3). He continually keeps us from harm. Even when danger and troubles enter our lives, they are there because God allows them to be there. He *will never leave* us *nor forsake* us (Deuteronomy 31:6). He is always with us.

No matter how troubled or fearful we are, our Lord God continually watches over us. Let us say with the psalmist: *"I will lift up my eyes to the mountains—where does my help come from? My help comes from the LORD, the Maker of heaven and earth"* (Psalm 121:1–2).

NOVEMBER 29

As I was with Moses,
so I will be with you;
I will never leave you
nor forsake you.
JOSHUA 1:5

After Moses died, the Lord passed on the leadership of His people to Joshua, Moses' aide. God told Joshua: *"No one will be able to stand against you all the days of your life. As I was with Moses, so I will be with you; I will never leave you nor forsake you"* (Joshua 1:5). And just as God commanded Joshua to *be strong and very courageous* and not be terrified or discouraged, He directs us to do likewise. God let Joshua know that He would be *with* him *wherever* he went (v. 9).

The same is true for us today. His Holy Spirit in us *will never leave* us *nor forsake* us. He is leading us to our Promised Land—growing us and enabling us to become more and more like the image of His Son, Jesus Christ. During this process, we will experience countless trials and sufferings, but we are never alone. Nothing enters our lives that our Heavenly Father does not send or allow, and these things come to grow us into what He created us in Christ to become.

During our difficulties all that is required of us is to trust our Heavenly Father, take His outstretched Hand, and follow Him wherever He leads us.

Precious in the sight of the LORD is the death of his faithful servants.
PSALM 116:15

NOVEMBER 30

"Though the mountains be shaken
and the hills be removed,
yet my unfailing love for you
will not be shaken
nor my covenant of peace be removed,"
says the LORD,
who has compassion on you.
ISAIAH 54:10

After the death of a dearly loved one, we mourn and grieve our loss. It feels as if a giant earthquake has hit us, ripping the very ground from beneath our feet. We've fallen and believe we can never get up again. Even though our Lord tells us to *seek* Him *while He may be found* (Isaiah 55:6) and to *come* to Him to quench our thirst (v. 1), in our heart of hearts we convince ourselves we will never feel His peace in us again.

And even though our Lord tells us that His *thoughts are not* our thoughts and His *ways* are not our ways because His *thoughts* and *ways are higher* than ours (Isaiah 55:8–9), sometimes we choose to turn from Him, allowing ourselves to sink into the depths of despair and believing we will never see daylight again.

We feel lost and alone, but we are not lost and alone. God is with us every step of the way. He is loving, patient, and kind, and even overlooks our efforts to push Him away, for He continually works in us to bring us into what He created us in Christ to become. Our Father loves us through and through.

Joyfully, the time arises when we are able to see the earth budding and flourishing once again. *The mountains and the hills will burst into song, and all the trees of the field will clap their hands.* There are no more thorn bushes, for they are replaced with junipers; no more *briers* beneath our feet. Once again we are able to *go out in joy* with God leading us *forth* in His *peace* (Isaiah 55:12–13). We feel at home again, rejoicing in our Heavenly Father's lovely garden of heavenly peace.

And the peace of God, which transcends all understanding,
will guard your hearts and your minds in Christ Jesus.
I have learned the secret of being content in any and every situation . . .
I can do all this through him who give me strength.
PHILIPPIANS 4:7, 12–13

December

DECEMBER 1

Devote yourselves to prayer,
being watchful and thankful.
COLOSSIANS 4:2

Prayer is conversing with our Heavenly Father, and includes requesting His help in any and all situations and uplifting others to Him. As we do so we must dedicate ourselves to what He has called us to do—be watchful and thankful while we wait on His response.

Our Heavenly Father works in His time, not ours. Sometimes He responds quickly. Other times He waits, and sometimes He does not seem to reply at all, but He always answers. Perhaps He is waiting for us to be on the lookout, to wake up to what He is accomplishing in us, for when we do our hearts respond in deep gratitude and thankfulness for His love and faithfulness.

It is when our children awaken to our responses to their requests—thanking us not for what they asked but for giving them what is best for them—that they turn around and run toward us with outstretched arms, thanking and hugging us for loving them so and keeping them safe from what is not good for them to have. So let us run to our Heavenly Father and do likewise.

Thanks be to God.
2 CORINTHIANS 8:16

DECEMBER 2

Why, my soul, are you downcast?
Why so disturbed within me?
PSALM 42:5

From time to time all of us have asked ourselves this question, one that seems to have over-whelmed mankind since the beginning. Everyone experiences sadness, loneliness, disappointment, and discouragement; and far too often we can't seem to place our finger its cause.

It matters not what brings us distress. What matters is what we do about it. We can join the psalmist saying, *"Deep calls to deep in the roar of your waterfalls; all your waves and breakers have swept over me"* (Psalm 42:7), but this does not answer our questions. We can even join the psalmist in comparing a *deer* that pants for *streams of water* with our becoming breathless for God, exclaiming how thirsty our souls are and asking where we *can go and meet* with Him (v. 1–2). We may even join the psalmist proclaiming how life used to be when we shouted with joy and thanksgiving, but we no longer feel this way (v. 4). We might even convince ourselves God has forgotten us and is not interested in relieving our sadness.

Not true, dear ones. God is not only with us, but, unlike the psalmist of old, His Holy Spirit lives in us. Let us take our questions to His heavenly throne, not allow them to ferment in our worldly minds. God has the answers we need.

Put your hope in God, for I will yet praise him, my Savior and my God.
PSALM 42:11

DECEMBER 3

But the fruit of the Spirit
is love, joy, peace, forbearance,
kindness, goodness, faithfulness,
gentleness and self-control.
GALATIANS 5:22–23

When we yield to God's Spirit in us, seeking to do His will and obey what we are instructed to do or say, we are able to bear much fruit—fruit that we could never produce on our own. Every fruit that springs forth from us begins with love, for God has instructed us to love Him, love ourselves, and love our neighbors as ourselves. When we do, joy spirals forth from within God's peace that accompanies it.

It takes time for fruit to ripen, bringing shouts of joy to those who take a bite. Patience waits for us to let joy in when it knocks on our doors and wants us to welcome kindness and goodness, which stand on the other side of joy. As they come along and penetrate our hearts, minds, and souls with their aromas, we grow into more faithful ambassadors of God. As we do so, we become gentler and more self-controlled than we ever imagined we could be.

How thankful and grateful we are to God's Holy Spirit who dwells in us, leading us to God's destination—the road on which we are to travel until we meet Him at the end.

God is love.
1 JOHN 4:8

DECEMBER 4

In the same way,
let your light shine before others,
that they may see your good deeds
and glorify your Father in heaven.
MATTHEW 5:16

In His Sermon on the Mount, Jesus taught His disciples and the crowds who assembled, as well as us today, many principles. Among these are His teachings about light, letting us know we *are the light of the world*. He then expounds on these words by comparing our light to being *a town on a hill* that *cannot be hidden* (Matthew 5:14). He elaborates further by letting us know that it's useless to *light a lamp and put it under a bowl* because it is only when we put our light on a stand to shine that those around us will be enlightened by it (v. 15).

This is what He requires we do with the light He gave us when He adopted us into His family. As we live for Christ, others will see Him through the way in which we live. When we do not guard our thoughts, our tongues, our desires, and our actions, or if we refuse to follow the leading of the Holy Spirit in us and go where He directs us to go and speak what He commands us to say, then our light no longer sits on a hill. It is hidden from view. No one can see it—sometimes not even ourselves.

God's command is: *"**Let** your light shine before others."* Our Heavenly Father always gives us a choice, so He frequently tells us to *let*, which means allow.

Everyone who hears these words of mine and puts them into practice is like
a wise man who built his house on the rock.
MATTHEW 7:24

DECEMBER 5

Against all hope,
Abraham in hope believed.
ROMANS 4:18

Many times we utter the words, "I hope so!" But when we say them, what then? Do we just stop there or do we do as Abraham did, who *in hope believed*? Abraham and his wife were without children because Sarah was barren. When he was one *hundred years old*, Abraham *faced the fact that his body was a good as dead and that Sarah's womb was also dead* (Romans 4:19). Nevertheless, Abraham's faith did not weaken. He believed what God promised him—that he would become the father of many nations.

Abraham didn't waver through unbelief. *In hope*, he *believed*. He never weakened in his faith. Yes, he sinned and made mistakes, as we all do, but He was a good and wise man also—He trusted God to do what He said He would do. Later, after Abraham experienced and rejoiced in the miracle of gaining Isaac as his son, God called Abraham to take his son—the one he loved so much—*to a region of Moriah* and *sacrifice him there* (Genesis 22:2). Abraham got up early the next day and left to do what God had instructed him to do. Three days later Abraham *looked up and saw the place in the distance* (v. 4).

He told his servants to stay with the donkey while he and Isaac walked on, saying they would worship together and then return. Abraham *carried the fire and the knife* and placed *the wood for the burnt offering on Isaac*. Understanding they needed a sacrifice offering, Isaac asked his father: *"The fire and the wood are here . . . but where is the lamb for the burnt offering?"* (v. 5–7).

Abraham told his son that *God* would *provide the lamb for the burnt offering. When they reached the place God had told him about, Abraham built an altar*, put the *wood on it*, and *bound Isaac and laid* the boy *on top of the wood* (v. 8–9).

This is when *the angel of the LORD called out to him from heaven*: *"Do not lay a hand on the boy."* The angel told Abraham that God now knew he feared Him *because* he *withheld* nothing *from* Him—not even his *only son* (v. 11–12).

As *Abraham looked up* he spied *a ram in a thicket*. Immediately *he went over and took the ram and sacrificed it as a burnt offering instead of his son. Abraham called that place The LORD Will Provide. The angel of the LORD called* out again, informing Abraham of God's words: *"I swear by myself, declares the LORD, that because you have done this and have not withheld your son, your only son, I will surely bless you and make your descendants as numerous as the stars in the sky and as the sand on the seashore."* God also let him know that *all nations on earth will be blessed, because you have obeyed me* (v. 13–18).

Abraham in hope believed. God will provide when He puts us in the exact place He wants us to be, the place called *The LORD Will Provide.*

Give praise to the LORD, proclaim his name; make known among the nations what he has done.

PSALM 105:1

DECEMBER 6

Blessed is the one
who perseveres under trial.

JAMES 1:12

No matter what kind of situations enter our lives, our Heavenly Father urges us through the writings of James, a leader in the early Jerusalem church, to hang in—to keep on keeping on. We are never to give up on what God has either allowed or directly sent into our lives. Whatever is there is for His purpose: to grow us into what He has created us in Christ to become.

No, it will not be easy to accomplish, but it is doable since God is with us, in us, and *will never leave* us *nor forsake* us (Deuteronomy 31:6). We can do all things through Christ who strengthens us (Philippians 4:13).

Yes, God knows we will cry many tears, fighting loneliness and desperation, perhaps even anger, wondering where He is in the mess in which we find ourselves as we whisper to Him, "I can't go on, Lord! I can't."

Yes, we can and we do; and when we do we discover a newer "us," one who understands why God either sent or allowed such misery into our lives. Then we finally comprehend we are becoming more than we ever dreamed we could become before such wretchedness dogged our heels.

Praise be to the LORD forever! Amen and Amen.

PSALM 89:52

DECEMBER 7

Sing and make music
from your heart
to the Lord,
always giving thanks
to God the Father
for everything,
in the name of
our Lord Jesus Christ.
EPHESIANS 5:20

It is only when we continually thank our Heavenly Father for everything that is happening in our lives that we gloriously delight in singing and making music in our hearts for God's peace within us. In fact, it may even surprise us how much we enjoy smiling and laughing and grasping God's peace overflowing in our hearts as we look heavenward, praising Him and thanking Him for loving us so majestically and walking along beside us, no matter what happens in our lives or threatens to take us under.

Thank You, Lord, in the name of Jesus Christ. Amen.

I will give thanks to you, Lord, with all my heart;
I will tell of all your wonderful deeds. I will be glad and rejoice in you;
I will sing the praises of your name, O Most High.
PSALM 9:1–2

DECEMBER 8

In your anger do not sin:
Do not let the sun go down
while you are still angry.
EPHESIANS 4:26

Anger is an emotion. It alerts us that something has gone awry in our lives. It is not sinful to be angry. What is sinful is the way we respond to it. We can allow our mouths to erupt in all kinds of verbal rubbish or we can keep our mouths shut as we silently petition help from our Heavenly Father. If we are so outraged that we can't accomplish this, then we must politely excuse ourselves, letting the one to whom we are speaking know we must take a moment by ourselves but we will soon return.

Even if the person protests, we leave. Then let us seek a quiet place and talk to the Lord, telling Him exactly what is in our hearts and on our minds. Of course, God already knows, but this allows us to talk it out with Him, ridding ourselves of the bitterness and resentment that appears to have taken us captive. As we remind ourselves that we can do all things through Christ, then we can reconnect with the one with whom we were angry.

When we do connect, our first mission is to apologize for our outburst if there was one, ask for forgiveness, and leave the rest in God's hands. If the other person refuses to accept our presence or our apology, then we can leave with a smile on our face and with God's peace in our hearts, praising our Father that we did *not give the devil a foothold* (Ephesians 4:27) while he tempted us to sin.

I will give thanks to the LORD because of his righteousness;
I will sing the praises of the name of the LORD Most High.
PSALM 7:17

DECEMBER 9

She is clothed with strength and dignity;
she can laugh at the days to come.
PROVERBS 31:25

Among the many characteristics of *a wife of noble character* in the epilogue of King Lemuel's sayings in Proverbs 31, we are told she is a woman of *strength and dignity*—she respects herself and uses her resources to *speak wisdom* with *faithful instruction on her tongue* while watching *over the affairs of her household.* Not only do her children grow into adulthood calling her *blessed,* but so does her *husband*—praising her for who she is (v. 10, 25–28).

Nothing is mentioned about her *charm* or *beauty* as both are considered *deceptive* and *fleeting* compared to what is of greater value (v. 30). What is most important is she praises the Lord and *opens her arms to the poor and extends her hands to the needy* (v. 20). She is *noble,* surpassing all those around her. She is a woman *worth far more than rubies* (v. 10). It is *her works* that *bring her praise.*

Honor her for all that her hands have done,
and let her works bring her praise at the city gate.
PROVERBS 31:31

DECEMBER 10

I sought the LORD,
and he answered me;
he delivered me from all my fears.
PSALM 34:4

At times the person we're calling does not answer the phone, apparently not at home, so we leave a message to let them know we called. If we really need to talk with the one we called, it can leave us feeling desperate, so wanting to hear the other's voice and get feedback on whatever might be bothering us.

Thankfully, this is not so with our Heavenly Father. He is always home. He always answers His phone. He is forever with us, around us, and in us. Whatever we fear, whatever disturbs us, or when we feel lonely, eager to hear His comforting words, He is there. He is our Good Shepherd, who faithfully cares for us—His sheep.

> **Now, our God, we give you thanks, and praise your glorious name.**
> 1 CHRONICLES 29:13

DECEMBER 11

> *I am the LORD,*
> *the God of all mankind.*
> *Is anything too hard for me?*
> JEREMIAH 32:27

Trust, faith, hope—powerful words—yet when searching for peace far too often we ignore them. Nothing is too hard for God! Nothing! Why then do we grasp for His peace that passes all understanding in faithless ways? Our Lord God is the God of all mankind! All that is required of us is to search for Him with all of our hearts, souls, and beings, trusting He will never abandon us. He gives us His wonderful shield of faith to help us in our times of need. He also instructs us on using His other weapons of warfare.

As Christian soldiers we are at war with God's enemy—Satan. Nothing pleases the evil one more than when a child of God tosses all hope of peace in a slimy pit along with God's shield of faith—not trusting God to do what He says He will do. One of the goals of God's Holy Spirit in us is that we live in His peace that *transcends all understanding* (Philippians 4:7). There is only one way to do this: trust Him, believe Him, and hope in Him, for nothing is impossible for God!

> **Jesus looked at them and said, "With man this is impossible,**
> **but with God all things are possible."**
> MATTHEW 19:26

DECEMBER 12

May your unfailing love
be my comfort.
PSALM 119:76

Regardless of what comes along in life, no matter how agonizing or painful it is, our Heavenly Father is always there to comfort us. His love is unfailing. Always! Our love for our children can in no way be compared to God's love for His children. Our means of helping our children are totally unlike God's means of doing so for His children. Nothing is impossible for our Heavenly Father, whereas much is not only impossible for us but unmanageable as well.

We are like little lambs in that we have a tendency to stray, getting ourselves off-track and seeking our way back to our Shepherd's sheepfold. Our Shepherd's unfailing love always awaits our return and comforts and soothes our fearful hearts.

Our Heavenly Father tells us: *"Can a mother forget the baby at her breast and have no compassion on the child she has borne? Though she may forget, I will not forget you! See, I have engraved you on the palms of my hands; your walls are ever before me"* (Isaiah 49:15–16).

DECEMBER 13

Then Mary took
about a pint of pure nard,
an expensive perfume;
she poured it on Jesus' feet
and wiped his feet with her hair.
JOHN 12:3

The apostle John tells us that *six days before the Passover, Jesus arrived at Bethany, where Lazarus lived, whom Jesus had raised from the dead. A dinner was given in Jesus' honor,* and, of course, *Martha served* (John 12:1–2). As Mary knelt at Jesus' feet, anointing them with *pure nard, an extremely expensive* imported *perfume,* Jesus' disciple *Judas Iscariot objected.* He wanted to know why such a costly perfume as Mary used was not *sold and the money given to the poor* (v. 3–5).

Judas was the keeper of the disciples' money bag, and Jesus knew Judas was a thief, stealing money for his own personal use. Jesus said nothing at this time other than, *"Leave her alone"* (v. 7), letting them all know Mary's actions were intended beforehand, using the perfume to anoint Him for *the day of* His *burial. "You will always have the poor among you, but you will not always have me,"* Jesus said (v. 6–8).

The next day a *great crowd heard that Jesus was on His way to Jerusalem.* Once there, Jesus told the crowd, *"The hour has come for the Son of Man to be glorified . . . Whoever serves me must follow me; and where I am, my servant also will be. My Father will honor the one who serves me"* (v. 12, 23, 26).

At the dinner prepared to honor Jesus, Mary wanted to serve Him and honor Him with all her heart. She gave Jesus what she valued most. May we do likewise for the Son of God—honor Him, faithfully serve Him, and sit at His feet worshiping Him. Let us fill our earthly travels with the fragrance of our good works done in the name of Jesus Christ. Let us freely give our all to the One who gave His all for us—the One who died for our sins.

> Whoever wants to be my disciple must deny themselves and
> take up their cross and follow me.
> For whoever wants to save their life will lose it,
> but whoever loses their life for me will find it.
> MATTHEW 16:24–25

DECEMBER 14

*Who of you by worrying
can add a single hour to your life?
Since you cannot do this very little thing,
why do you worry about the rest?*
LUKE 12:25–26

Many of us begin our day worrying and end it the same way. Somehow we believe that the more we worry the better off we'll be when what we are worrying about either happens or doesn't happen. Regardless of how a day goes, worrying doesn't help at all; it only hurts the one who engages in it.

Jesus asks us a pivotal question: *"Can worry add a single hour to your life?"* Absolutely not! Then why do we do it? Worry does nothing but take us out of the Lord's presence—the exact place we need to be, where we can request His help and thank Him ahead of time for it.

As God said through King Solomon in Proverbs 3:5–6: *Trust in the LORD with all your heart and lean not on your own understanding; in all your ways submit to him, and he will make your paths straight.*

Blessed are those who find wisdom, those who gain understanding.
PROVERBS 3:13

DECEMBER 15

Your word is a lamp to my feet,
a light on my path.
PSALM 119:105

To hear God's words is crucial. They enable us to walk in His light and guide us along the paths He places beneath our feet. To keep from stumbling and falling or injuring ourselves, we must keep His words in our hearts. His light surrounds us as we spend time reading the Bible and memorizing many of its verses. When we do so, we can clearly see the direction in which He is leading us. Not only this, but our tongues are so coated with His love that others can see Him in a way they have never been able to see Him before. His light shines in us and through us to them.

How sweet are your words to my taste, sweeter than honey to my mouth!
I gain understanding from your precepts; therefore I hate every wrong path.
PSALM 119:103–104

DECEMBER 16

For the word of God
is living and active.
Sharper than
any double-edged sword,
it penetrates even to
dividing soul and spirit,
joints and marrow;
it judges the thoughts and attitudes
of the heart.
HEBREWS 4:12

Not only does God's Word light our paths, making it possible for us to see through our dark days and troubling times, but His Word is alive, urging us on to godly action. Human words can be like a double-edged sword also, but they cannot penetrate into our *soul and spirit, joints and marrow* as does God's Word. In fact, human words can kill our spirits, causing us to want to toss in the towel for the multiple problems that infiltrate our souls and drag us downward.

Human words may judge the attitudes of our hearts through our actions, but they can never judge our thoughts unless we verbalize them. God, and God alone, knows our thoughts. His words can heal us as we listen to them and put into action what He has spoken to us.

How grateful we are that God's Word is living and *active*—as we read it or hear its gentle whispers fill our ears from God himself, or immerse ourselves in His Word, or by someone He appoints to speak for Him.

Nothing in all creation is hidden from God's sight.
Everything is uncovered and laid bare before the eyes of him to whom we must give account.
HEBREWS 4:13

DECEMBER 17

Let the peace of Christ
rule in your hearts,
since as members of one body
you were called to peace.
And be thankful.
COLOSSIANS 3:15

Have you ever been the recipient of a gloriously wrapped gift but never opened it? Instead, you place it on a shelf somewhere in the house, from time to time glancing its way and perhaps wondering what's inside it.

Peace is a gift from God. It is something He freely gives to all His children. However, if we don't accept it, it cannot do for us what God intended it to do. So God Almighty tells us to *let* His *peace rule in* our *hearts. Let*—one word, yet how valuable and vital that one word is. Our Heavenly Father always gives us a choice: to go His way or to continue on in our way.

His gift of *the peace of Christ* can either *rule in* our *hearts* or not rule in our hearts. The decision is ours. Let's open His gift of peace and allow it to *rule in* our *hearts* as we raise our hands in praise and thanksgiving to Him for gifting us so magnificently.

And whatever you do, whether in word or deed,
do it all in the name of the Lord Jesus,
giving thanks to God the Father through him.
COLOSSIANS 3:17

DECEMBER 18

For the LORD is good
and his love endures forever;
his faithfulness continues
through all generations.

PSALM 100:5

Have you ever noticed how human love wanes, sometimes bouncing from full intensity to perhaps moderation or even vanishing? Although human love can be intense and constant, nevertheless it can be very fickle. It often depends on what is going on around it—what is happening at the moment and how it is viewed by those involved with it.

Godly love is vastly different. It never bounces back and forth. Not only is God's love good, but His *love endures forever*, regardless of what we think or do or say. Our Heavenly Father is our forever God, the One who sticks with us through thick or thin. His *faithfulness* is so pure that His *love* never ends—it *endures forever*. We can always count on it.

The one who calls you is faithful, and he will do it.
1THESSALONIANS 5:24

DECEMBER 19

I will go before you
and will level the mountains . . .
I will give you hidden treasures,
riches stored in secret places.

ISAIAH 45:2–3

While growing up in Atlanta, Georgia, my childhood friend and I loved to hop into her parents' car and travel with them to explore the Blue Ridge Mountains. We were thoroughly impressed by their spectacular and awesome beauty. We longed to climb every one of them, but, of course, that was impossible. However, as I was growing up, it never occurred to me what the prophet Isaiah meant when he wrote God's words, *"I will go before you and level the mountains."*

Not until later when I experienced climbing life's excruciating mountains of agony, stress, and troubles did I discover God's *hidden treasures stored* for me on such pilgrimages. He not only blessed me by leveling my distressing mountains, but also taught me valuable lessons while doing so. I now know that had I really tried to climb one of the Blue Ridge Mountains, my believed victory in so doing would have been meaningless compared to taking God's hand and faithfully trusting Him to lead me through the valleys of life's anguishes.

Give thanks to the Lord, for he is good; his love endures forever.
PSALM 118:29

DECEMBER 20

Give thanks to the Lord,
for he is good;
his love endures forever.
PSALM 118:1

Our Heavenly Father's *love* is endless—it *endures forever!* No matter how we look, what we say, or what we do, God loves us forever. He never gives up on us. He never leaves us or rejects us, no matter how gruesome the task of picking up the pieces of our broken lives and putting them back together again. He is always there for us. We are never alone!

Were we truly aware of what forever means and what God's love is like, we would spend countless minutes and hours of every day raising our hands in praise to our Heavenly Father for watching over us, taking care of us, and enabling us to grow into what He created us in Christ to become. Our main priority of every day would be to glorify Him by spending time with Him in His Word, putting Him first in our lives, and leaving everything up to Him, while joyfully accepting any path He places beneath our feet—willingly taking His hand and following Him wherever He leads!

You will keep in perfect peace those whose minds are steadfast, because they trust in you.
Trust in the Lord forever, for the Lord, the Lord himself, is the Rock eternal.
ISAIAH 26:3–4

DECEMBER 21

My heart, O God, is steadfast;
I will sing and make music
with all my soul.
PSALM 108:1

It isn't until we confess to our Lord God that we are unwavering, dedicated, and committed to Him, not turning to the right or to the left but continuing onward under any and all circumstances, that we can *sing and make music* to Him *with all* of our souls.

The more challenging our paths, the more sorrows we bear, the more we fight His good battles, and the more we mature in our Christian faith, the more we know without a shadow of doubt that the musical notes springing from our lips touch our Heavenly Father's heart. As His Christian soldiers we joyfully march to war, carrying the cross of Jesus with us every nanosecond of time.

The LORD will guide you always;
he will satisfy your needs in a sun-scorched land and will strengthen your frame.
You will be like a well-watered garden, like a spring whose waters never fail.
ISAIAH 58:11

DECEMBER 22

*All those gathered here
will know that
it is not by sword or spear
that the LORD saves;
for the battle is the LORD's,
and he will give all of you
into our hands.*

1 SAMUEL 17:47

Young shepherd boy David had a heart after God. David's father, Jesse, sent him with food for his brothers, who were in the Israelite army fighting the Philistines. David spoke to some soldiers, asking, *"What will be done for the man who kills this Philistine and removes this disgrace from Israel?"* David's oldest brother, Eliab, reprimanded him for speaking to a group of men standing near the battlefield (1 Samuel 17:26, 28).

Ignoring Eliab's rebuke, David asked the same question of another man. Their conversation was overheard and reported to King Saul, who straightway sent for David. When David met with Saul, the youth volunteered to go and fight the giant, Goliath. *Saul replied, "You are not able to go out against this Philistine and fight him; you are only a young man, and he has been a warrior from his youth"* (v. 29–33).

Immediately, David informed the king that if he could kill *a lion or a bear* that came after his sheep, certainly he could slay *this uncircumcised Philistine* who had *defied the armies of the living God.* King Saul then gave David permission to fight Goliath, but he told David to put on the king's *tunic* and *coat of armor* and *a bronze helmet* before going into battle. After walking around in Saul's armor, David quickly let the king know he couldn't go into battle dressed that way. After taking off the armor, David *took his staff in his hand, chose five smooth stones from the stream, put them in the pouch of his shepherd's bag and, with his sling in his hand, approached the Philistine* (v. 34–40).

Goliath ridiculed David asking, *"Am I a dog, that you come at me with sticks?"* The giant then cursed David and told him he would end up dead, with the birds and beast devouring him (v. 43–44).

If young David could respond saying, *"You come against me with sword and spear and javelin, but I come against you in the name of the LORD Almighty, the God of the armies of Israel, whom you have defied"* (v. 45), then why do we not say likewise to God's enemy who plagues us? David further let Goliath know that God was going to hand him over to him because he was going to *strike* him *down* and *cut off* his *head* (v. 46). What then, prevents us from responding to God's enemy in the same way?

> All those gathered here will know that it is not by sword or spear that the Lord saves;
> for the battle is the Lord's, and he will give all of you into our hands.
>
> 1 SAMUEL 17:47

DECEMBER 23

> *Therefore, holy brothers and sisters,*
> *who share in the heavenly calling,*
> *fix your thoughts on Jesus,*
> *whom we acknowledge as*
> *our apostle and high priest.*
>
> HEBREWS 3:1

Perhaps the reason we so often fall short of that which our Heavenly Father calls us to do is because we allow ourselves to become consumed by what God has given us to do. Somehow, we believe that we are not wise enough, experienced enough, or skillful enough to successfully accomplish His projects. So instead of getting on with them, we waste much time worrying about them and many times do not even do them.

It is only when we *fix* our *thoughts on Jesus,* who gave His life for us, that we are more than able through His work in us to do anything He calls us to do. Anything!

> But seek first his kingdom and his righteousness,
> and all these things will be given to you as well.
> Therefore do not worry about tomorrow, for tomorrow will worry about itself.
> Each day has enough trouble of its own.
>
> MATTHEW 6:33–34

DECEMBER 24

When they looked up, they saw no one except Jesus.
MATTHEW 17:8

Astounding events come and go in our lives. Occasionally we recognize them for what they are, but much of the time we are like *Peter, James, and John* when they were *led* by *Jesus up a high mountain by themselves* (Matthew 17:1) to see what it was God wanted them to experience. In God's time and in His exact place as we follow His leading, we feel as if Jesus is also being *transfigured before* us, with *His face* shining *like the sun, and His clothes* becoming *white as the light* (v. 2). It is as if we cannot only feel His presence in us and with us but can also reach out and touch His holy hand.

Of course, like Peter, we want to stay on our mountaintop experiences with Him, not return to what we call normalcy. We desperately want to hear God say to us the same words He spoke to His three disciples: *"This is my Son, whom I love; with him I am well pleased. Listen to him!"* (v. 5).

When we grasp what our Heavenly Father has spoken to us, comprehending it completely and praising and thanking Him for what He is teaching us, we return to normalcy, no longer in such an exquisite place. Yet it is forever with us because we listened to God and kept His words close to our hearts as they little by little transformed us into what He created us in Christ to become.

Yes, my soul, find rest in God; my hope comes from him.
Truly he is my rock and my salvation; he is my fortress, I will not be shaken.
PSALM 62:5–6

DECEMBER 25

The virgin will conceive
and give birth to a son,
and they will call him Immanuel
(which means "God with us").
MATTHEW 1:23

The day Mary, the mother of Jesus Christ, gave birth to Him is the day *Immanuel* came to dwell among us in the flesh. He remains constantly with every one of God's children. Let us never forget or take lightly what our Lord God did for us, is doing for us, and will continue doing until God calls us home or Jesus returns again to take us home with Him, where we will live forever in His presence.

Come, Lord Jesus, come! Let us pause right now, raise our hands heavenward, and praise and thank the Trinity—God the Father, God the Holy Spirit, and Jesus Christ, God's Son—*Immanuel.* Today we celebrate the *birth* of *"God with us,"* who came to save those who are lost.

I will extol the LORD at all times; his praise will always be on my lips.
PSALM 34:1

DECEMBER 26

Whoever finds their life will lose it,
and whoever loses their life for my sake will find it.
MATTHEW 10:39

What does Jesus mean when He tells us if we find our life we will lose it, and if we lose our live for His sake we will find it? Is He not informing us that we are born two times—our initial birth and our spiritual birth? When we accept Jesus Christ as our Lord and Savior, we are born anew. We discover God's ultimate goal for us is to grow into the image of His Son, Jesus Christ. We are no longer who we were at our physical birth, but now we are growing into a new creature in Christ with a specific mission from our Heavenly

Father. In order to accomplish it, our holy God will either send or allow difficult circumstances into our lives to mature us in Christ.

It is not until we meet Him in heaven that His mission for us is completed. We are then in the image of His Son—His ultimate goal for each and every one of His children. Nothing in life is more precious than becoming like Jesus Christ!

But thanks be to God! He gives us the victory through our Lord Jesus Christ.
1 CORINTHIANS 15:57

DECEMBER 27

I will instruct you and teach you
in the way you should go;
I will counsel you
with my loving eye on you.
PSALM 32:8

The Holy Spirit penetrates every fiber of our being when we surrender our lives to Jesus Christ and accept Him as our Lord and Savior. He instructs us and teaches us not only what to say or to do but also which path to take among the multitude of choices before us. We are not to imitate *the horse or mule, which have no understanding* whatsoever (Psalm 32:9). Instead, we must pay strict attention to God's continuous instructions to us along our pathways.

God is our *hiding place,* the One who *will protect* us *from trouble and surround* us *with songs of deliverance* (v. 7). He not only counsels us but continually watches over us.

For we trust in his holy name.
May your unfailing love be with us, LORD, even as we put our hope in you.
PSALM 33:21–22

DECEMBER 28

Yes, my soul, find rest in God;
my hope comes from him.
Truly his my rock
and my salvation;
he is my fortress,
I will not be shaken.
PSALM 62:5–6

When we are tired and weary, we often seek needed rest in the wrong places and in wrong ways. Many turn to alcohol, drugs, food, parties, shopping, and the like—things that do not satisfy our souls. What we have sought is nothing but a quick fix. God alone is the only thing, the only One who can calm our minds and spirits. Our *hope* rests in Him—in no one and in nothing else.

He alone is our *Rock*—a Stone that cannot be crushed. It is He who rescues us, picking us up out of the miry clay that has sucked us into its deep, dark, *slimy pit.* It is He who gives us a firm place on which to stand. The Lord God is our Stronghold, the One who puts *a new song in* our mouths—*a hymn of praise to God,* a melody that others will not only hear but will see our Lord God in (Psalm 40:2–3).

Our Heavenly Father is our Helper—our Deliverer. In Him and through Him we *will not be shaken.*

I waited patiently for the LORD; he turned to me and heard my cry.
PSALM 40:1

DECEMBER 29

Therefore, there is now
no condemnation
for those who are
in Christ Jesus.
ROMANS 8:1

It doesn't matter what others say about us or think about us. As long as we are right with God, another's disapproval of us is meaningless—so why do we hang on to it? We must let it go and, as we do so, meditate on the countless cruel and heartless words people spoke about Jesus Christ. Nothing hindered Jesus from carrying out the mission God sent Him to earth to complete.

Others' criticism and disapproval of us need not cause us deep pain, for it can only do so if we focus on it and allow it to have its way with us. Let us continually keep our eyes trained on Jesus and trust God's Holy Spirit in us, who enables us to do what He has called us to do. Let us remember that God has told us multiple times that nothing will hinder us because He is our Strength. He is continually reminds us to never give up.

Not that I have already obtained all this, or have already arrived at my goal,
but I press on to take hold of that for which Christ Jesus took hold of me. Brothers and sisters,
I do not consider myself yet to have taken hold of it. But one thing I do:
Forgetting what is behind and straining toward what is ahead.
I press on toward the goal to win the prize for which
God has called me heavenward in Christ Jesus.
PHILIPPIANS 3:12–14

DECEMBER 30

*"I am the Alpha
and the Omega,"
says the Lord God,
"who is, and who was,
and who is to come,
the Almighty."*
REVELATION 1:8

On this date, December 30, 1955, my now-deceased husband and I stood before our Heavenly Father, committing ourselves to each other in holy matrimony. On this day, December 30, 2006, I buried the one who stood at my side for almost fifty-one years. He is now in the presence of our Heavenly Father. Richard no longer stands by my side, but, hallelujah and amen, he is now with our eternal God. As I remain behind I am not alone, for my Heavenly Father is with me. I will meet them both when I reach heaven and rejoice to see my Heavenly *Father's house* of *many rooms* (John 14:2)—with Richard occupying one of them—the place God prepared for each of us to dwell when He calls us home to be with Him in the heavenly realms.

Whether I meet Jesus in the air when He returns or if He calls me home beforehand, I know the way to the place where *the Alpha and the Omega* resides, the One *who is, and who was, and who is to come, the Almighty.*

Jesus answered, "I am the way and the truth and the life.
No one comes to the Father except through me."
JOHN 14:6

DECEMBER 31

To him who is able to keep you from stumbling
and to present you before his glorious presence
without fault and with great joy—
to the only God our Savior
be glory, majesty, power and authority,
through Jesus Christ our Lord,
before all ages, now and forevermore! Amen.
JUDE 24–25

This is my prayer for every reader of *Listen to the Silence*. The words God placed in my heart and hands encourage all of us to faithfully continue on the road He has put beneath our feet, as we take His outstretched hand and closely follow Him wherever He leads.

When I first sat down to pen these words given to me by our Heavenly Father, I never knew the tremendous blessings that would enter my heart, soul, and spirit as I walked with God by my side and intently listened to His sweet whisperings throughout our journey together.

My prayer for each and every reader is that God's glorious peace and joy will saturate your souls as you daily walk with Him and listen to His fragrant, soft words of love and wisdom, allowing them to sink deeply into your hearts.

Let us all raise our hands in thanksgiving and praise to our Almighty God, loving, trusting, and following the One from whom all blessings flow!

Hallelujah and Amen!

When Jesus spoke again to the people, he said,
"I am the light of the world. Whoever follows me will never walk in darkness,
but will have the light of life."
JOHN 8:12

Also available by Betty McCutchan

In His Time, God Makes All Things Beautiful
a 366-day devotional

13-digit ISBN: 9781935265863
10-digit ISBN: 1935265865